Acclaim for Sounds of Silence

"For Nan, the messages from Karl have cleared her doubts about the reality of the spirit world, and for many others it has reaffirmed the beauty and love that exists there."

– Nisha Ghosh, *The Times of India*, Pune

"Intense and moving, *Sounds of Silence* is an unusual story of love, life and death."

– Hemal Ashar, *Sunday Mid-Day*

"One of the most honest and touching books I have read in my life. I consider it an important publication of the present times, right here in India, which recounts the theory of life after death. It is written so simply and yet from the heart."

– Meher Castelino, *The Sunday Free Press*

"Hope is the underlying theme in the book and with complete candour Nan tells of her experiences."

– Sujata Assomull, *The Indian Express*

"Ever since *Sounds of Silence* appeared in 1996, it has led a charmed life. The book received favourable reviews even in the mainstream press. It was quoted, talked about, passed from hand to hand. By now it has acquired the status of a spiritual gem, one that has helped many take their first faltering steps on the path. That Nan and her book have given hope and succour to thousands at the depths of their despair is indubitable."

– Suma Varughese, *Life Positive* Magazine

"*Sounds of Silence* is a beautiful, moving record of a mother's interaction with her young son after he died as a result of an accident. The book is simply written, endearing in its humour and its refusal to preach. It is a story of God-realisation, of Hope, of peace and of strength, meant especially for people disillusioned by life and God as Nan herself once was."

– Ashvina Vakil, *Society* Magazine

"*Sounds of Silence* is a story of a love that never dies. The book speaks of what all of us are curious about – the paranormal. But Nan does more, she bares her soul and writes about a love that began with her son but culminated with the writing of *Sounds of Silence*."

– *Citadel* Magazine, Pune

"There have been so many miracles that have occurred since I read *Sounds of Silence,* all the ways Meher Baba and Karl revealed themselves to me through Nan, and guided me forward. And I know that this experience of having connected with that realm and contributing in my own little way through audio-visual medium, has reshaped my own calling!"

– R. A. Mahiema, Series Producer, Reality TV, UK

"The book expresses events and thoughts in a simple manner and is a valuable contribution in this area of experience. Everything is laid out without apology, softening of the truth or attempt to pretend. The book is completely absorbing and difficult to put down. It is a splendid book and a classic contribution to spiritual literature."

– Don Stevens, close friend and Editor of Meher Baba's books

"This book is a strong guide to all and for all towards the Truth. It is not only well written and beautifully designed, but it points to God's unfathomable ways and the uniqueness of each soul's journey to the source."

– Eruch, Voice of Baba – Interpreter of His gestures

SOUNDS OF SILENCE

A BRIDGE ACROSS TWO WORLDS

Nan Umrigar

YogiImpressions®

YogiImpressions®
SOUNDS OF SILENCE
Yogi Impressions LLP
1711, Centre 1, World Trade Centre,
Cuffe Parade, Mumbai 400 005, India.
Website: www.yogiimpressions.com

First published in India in 1996 by
Huma Enterprises

Revised Edition: March 2006
Nineteenth reprint: October 2025
ISBN 978-81-88479-35-1

Printed at: Manipal Technologies Limited

He is the One who in
the dress of dream
Clothed us to make us
naked Truth supreme
The One that all men seek
and few men find
For He lives in the realm
beyond the mind.

– Francis Brabazon

Contents

Acknowledgements ..... *ix*
Preface ..... *xiii*

Karl 1
His Dream 8
The Race 13
The Silence 17
The Writing 21
The Message 28
Jimmy 32
Patrick 36
The Awakening 42
Lights Through The Mist 47
Precious Moments 54
1987 60
My Family 65
The Net Widens 75
Nicol 81
Pilloo 90

Africa 95

Stanstead Hall 99

Is Baba God? 106

"The Thief of Hearts" 119

The Messenger 126

The Dhuni 136

The Ocean of Love 141

Meher Baba Centre – London 150

To Look Within 154

Some Lessons to Learn 162

Meher Baba's Cricket Team 168

The Bouncers 177

Faith 183

Baba's Gift 191

Baba's Love 196

Karl 203

Appendix

A. Prayers Dictated by Meher Baba 208
B. Meher Baba's Universal Message 211
C. The Perfect Masters 213
D. Messages from Karl 216
E. Information for Pilgrims to Meherabad... 229
F. Centres of Information about Meher Baba 231
G. Glossary 232
H. Source Notes 236
I. Recommended Reading 238

Acknowledgements

I cannot believe that I have actually written this book. Why I put it all down on paper I really don't know, but I feel that I was propelled by a force outside of myself to do so, a force that somehow made me note down chronologically all that has taken place. "That's all you are really doing," I convinced myself. But as the days flew by, an exciting avenue presented itself. Thoughts and words catapulted into chapters and suddenly – it became a whole book. Strange events mingled with beautiful stories of people who arrived at my doorstep in the most inexplicable ways and remained forever to be my good friends.

I could never have undertaken the task of writing this book without the help and encouragement of one of them in particular, Amie Rabadi. I now know that she was brought to me to fulfil a definite purpose. My deepest thanks go to her for her help, guidance and support, which has been really invaluable. She has kept herself unobtrusively in the background, working tirelessly, correcting chapters and helping me find the right words and sentences. Together, we worked at projecting my thoughts accurately; and there were times when it was her deep feelings that made me re-evaluate these thoughts and put them into perspective. Every other week or so, we held writing sessions, where I read out what I had originally written. More often than not, she silently shook her head in mock despair, but we discussed, questioned, rewrote, joked, had dinner and then I began all over again.

Being rather a private person, I would have preferred to confine my experiences to the limited circle of my family and close friends. But so much has taken place and I know in my heart that a lot more still has to come for that is what life is all about. Sadness and misfortune come to everyone and strange circumstances cause stranger things to take place. So, to all those who have shared their experiences with me for the last fifteen years, but have not been included in this book, I hold out my hand in gratitude. I would like them to know that each one of them has been responsible in some way of contributing to my spiritual awakening and therefore to this book. Some by a word or smile, some by the strength of their faith, and some even by their reservations in believing. A few names have been changed to safeguard privacy, but most have given me permission to use their names. To both these categories, I extend my deepest thanks.

I am indebted to many friends, but among those I can name, I would especially like to thank Mrs. Bhavnagri and her spirit sons, Vispi and Ratu, for opening the door of a new world for me. Mrs. Rishi who opened the door wider and was instrumental in revealing the name of someone who was hiding behind, waiting to be discovered; Mr. Pilloo Kapadia who described to me the beauty of an unknown world, and Ivy Northage, because she eventually clarified it all for me.

I pay special tribute to George Chapman whose healing powers help so many. I have to make a mention of Roy Stemmen, who gave me much encouragement in the early stages, and more so at the time when I was undecided about publishing the manuscript.

There was a critical phase in my life when I needed much help and support. At this stage, Amie and I were joined by Freny Peddar, who listened patiently and whose light-hearted approach helped us get through the most difficult later chapters. It just so happened that I was fortunate to be able to use Freny's talent for the enormous task of designing and setting the pages of the book. I thank her not only for her efforts, but also for her faith and love.

A special thank you goes to Kamal Mulla, Shyla Boga and Chandralekha Moitra for their editorial advice and contacts in the literary world; to Rabindra Hazari for his legal advice, and to Sarosh Dastur for his patience and help with all the problems we faced whilst working with the computer. Sarosh came along when we needed him the most.

I wish to thank all persons and organisations mentioned in the source notes for giving me permission to use information and to reprint excerpts from various material.

Most of all, my sincere thanks to the Avatar Meher Baba Trust, Bal Natu and Bhau Kalchuri for all the information, help and encouragement that they have given me; and to Ward Parks for putting it all together and helping me with the necessary permissions.

I am deeply indebted to Hilla Talwar and the Kotwal family, whose love for God was instrumental in showing me the way.

I also thank Phiroze and Phiroza Mehta for being my friends, and who without question believed in the truth of my experience.

I have to especially thank my husband for his strong arguments, for and against, which always gave me food for much thought and which prevented me from getting carried away by my own emotions. It was, at times, his critical approach that made me delve deeper to find the answers.

I have to mention my beloved family who have shared happy times with me and who have stood by me through all the difficult ones.

Last of all, my son Karl, without whom this book would never have been written – he has made me write it.

Preface

Young Karl Umrigar had only one passion in life – horses and racing. At the age of eighteen, his childhood fantasy came true —he raced to fame. The world was at his feet for he had won every major race of the season, but tragedy struck. Karl died of an accident on the racetrack.

However, this is not a story of his rise to fame or of his tragic end, it is a faithful account of what happened six years later – of Karl's determination to show his mother the way out of grief, to happiness.

I am his mother.

The years that followed his death were dark ones for me, but in 1984 something happened which was to change my life forever. It was the day I embarked on my journey into the realms of mysticism and automatic writing. 'Sounds' filtered in from the 'silence', and I began to converse with an energy-force which I eventually believed to be my son. I was exhilarated but at the same time could not help questioning this phenomenon. Was this fantasy, imagination, or just plain wishful thinking on my part? Was there really a higher energy, a higher consciousness – angels, guides, guardians and a God?

It did not take Karl long to guide me to a place quite alien to my way of being or belief, and to the *Samadhi* of a man known as Meher Baba and believed to be the '*Avatar* of the Age'. The life of a Spiritual Master held no interest for me, but the manner and tenacity with which my "spirit son" led me to Him, intrigued me. To understand what was happening, I sought out and began meeting 'mediums' here in India, and abroad, asking questions to which they seemed to have no answers. "In the ambit of spiritualism," Coral Polge said, "there has never been a recorded experience such as yours." In the effort to explain some of it to those who arrived at my doorstep, to find answers to the connection between Karl and Meher Baba and therefore, between Meher Baba and me, I had to repeat my story over and over again.

To Amie Rabadi, the first who rang my doorbell, Karl's communication was unquestionable. As time went by, not only did she depend on her own instinct and detailed study of Meher Baba, she also came forward to encourage and support me when, in spite of all my insecurities, I decided it was time to share my experience with the outside world. She then began to direct and selflessly involve herself with the writing, publishing, and distribution of the book. "This book will have a far-reaching effect on many," she said, "and above all it will be of the heart, for that is the seat that belongs to Meher Baba, whose love graces us all. As for our children, they too belong in our hearts and therefore to Baba – and that is enough for me." I must admit at this point that while my stubborn focus of attention was Karl and his stories, it was Amie who steered me throughout and towards the conclusion of the book, where not only had I to acknowledge that my love for Meher Baba was absolute, but that He was and is God to me.

Sounds of Silence was published in December 1996 – and the first copies went out into the world. In spite of reassurances from friends and family, I was nervous about its reception. Would anyone listen? Would they believe? But I really needn't have worried so much. The book took on a life of its own and touched the hearts of many people. Its appeal seemed to lie in the fact that it was not only a true story of a young boy who had been well-known in India, but it was also about the love of a mother and son – about a love that never dies. It was something new, something different. The book reached out to thousands of people and interest seemed to rise by the day. Reviews and write-ups appeared in local newspapers and international magazines. Ladies' Clubs and the Rotary Club organised meetings and seminars to discuss its contents. Could all this really happen? Could it be true? Slowly but surely, the interest crept from social gatherings into homes, where people began discussing the incredible incidents that had taken place, sharing the beautiful messages that came through Karl from the spirit world, and marvelling at the help that some of them had received from his Master, Meher Baba. It progressed into people wanting to know more about the Master.

So it has gone on. The response has been overwhelming – the reactions spontaneous and heart-warming. "I am not afraid of death any more," or "...I keep it by my bedside for it makes me feel loved and protected" or "Whenever I am in trouble, I just open a page and I get my answers," were some of the comments I received from people who read the book. Through its pages, Karl, in his own inimitable way, has encouraged people to make their own connections with the *Avatar* and to look at life from a new perspective. With Baba's help, many hearts have been healed. Those who were bereaved came to know that their loved ones are not lost forever. Broken relationships have been cemented and new ones formed. People have been shown how to let go of pain and suffering, and find inner peace. Many lives have undergone a change for the better.

It has now been nine years since *Sounds of Silence* was first published. Yet the interest in the book appears to keep on growing. The time has now come for it to still go further – to reach out to a world that has evolved to a new awareness – a world that is in search of peace, happiness, and a spiritual love that is timeless.

Nan Umrigar
Jan 2006

Notes:

1. *Till such time as the Author is convinced of the Godhood of Meher Baba, all references by her pertaining to Meher Baba are made in small letters e.g.* 'his' *instead of* 'His'.
2. *The quotes and messages from Karl, which you will come across in this book, have been reproduced faithfully without any alteration or editing on the Author's part.*

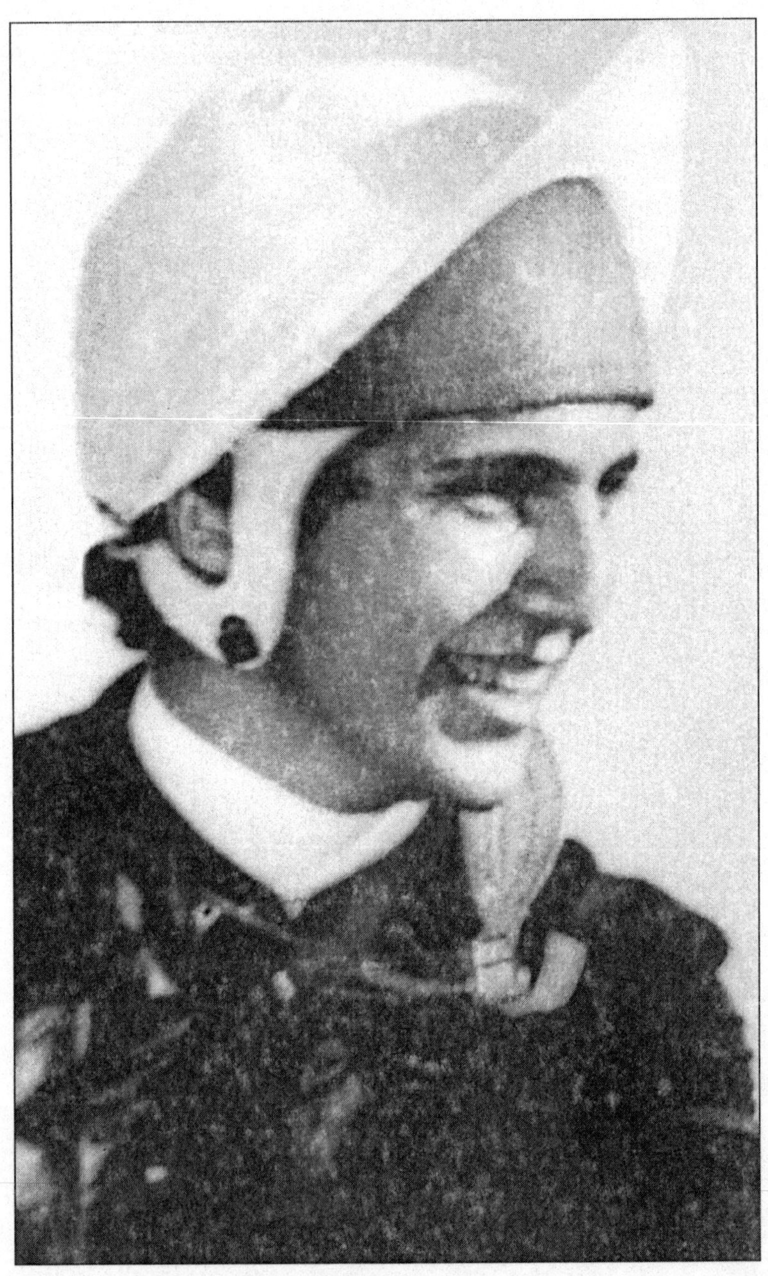

Karl

CHAPTER 1

Karl

"Wake up, Ma, it's morning." My eyes flew open with the excitement in Karl's whisper. I responded quickly, "OK son, I'm up!" But before I could focus on anything, or swing my legs to the floor, he was gone.

As I splashed my face with water, I heard the impatient rattle of tea cups. Minutes later, with the towel still wiping the sleep out of my eyes, I returned to the bedroom and caught glimpses of him putting on his breeches and sweater and frantically pulling on his boots in between gulps of hot tea. Snatching cap and whip in hand, he raced out of the door calling, "Come on Mum, I'll be late for work." Caught up by his urgency, I threw binoculars, stop-watch, pen and book into my bag and dashed out behind him.

It was still dark as we drove into the racecourse – into a time and place that was always special to me. I walked over soft tan and dewy grass, savouring all the sounds of a beautiful morning. I could hear the muted call of birds as they fluttered in the trees and the thud of huge red almonds as they fell onto the damp earth below. The snort of horses could be heard as they champed on their bits, straining at the reins as they were being led around the trainer's ring, waiting to be exercised. Shadowy figures criss-crossed my path as I made my way to my usual seat in the stands. I settled in and watched the golden glow of the sun creep slowly through the mist. Adjusting my binoculars, I looked out for Karl and caught his graceful figure cantering along with the others. Leaning back in my chair, I thought proudly of what the day promised to hold for him.

It was Sunday, April 15, 1979 – the last day of the Bombay racing season.

Karl had just broken the Indian record of fifty-four winners in a single season. By the end of the day, he only had to notch a few more wins to keep ahead of his arch rival who was four behind in the winner's tally. He would then receive the Championship Trophy and fulfil the dream that he had cherished for as long as I could remember.

I thought of our bags, packed and ready for Karl's first trip abroad, where he was to match his skills with the best in his profession. What did the future hold for him, I wondered?

My mind drifted pleasurably as it swung way back to the day Karl was born – October 4, 1960. He was a premature baby weighing four pounds and four ounces. I remember the moment when my doctor drew our attention to his frightening body weight and warned us to prepare for any eventuality. Saddened with helplessness, I lay crying softly, praying for his survival.

The first time I set eyes on his puckered little face and thin and scrawny body, my heart went out to him. I longed so desperately to reach out and hug him closely, but could not touch him because of the numerous tubes that the doctors had inserted into almost every vein in his fragile body.

As the days went by, I sat next to him, talking quietly, hoping and praying that little Karl would sense my love and my need to enjoy a lifetime with him. These moments would often be interrupted by a nurse who wheeled in bottle after bottle of blood that was to be transfused into him. I worried endlessly. The only way to feed him was through a pipette, which regulated drops of milk into a digestive system that had not fully developed. How was he ever going to survive?

Every evening Karl would turn blue and have the medical staff and family running anxiously to his bedside to turn on the oxygen cylinder. The crisis would be averted and somehow, he would get through another day.

Thus he battled on with a mysterious single-mindedness of his own, a trait that was to follow him throughout the life he had determined was worth fighting for.

Karl grew into a spirited child who never lacked courage. He was tiny and skinny, but had a strong will to win. He directed his energies at trying desperately to keep up with his handsome elder brother, Neville, who was well on his way to becoming a brilliant athlete. In his final year of school, Neville received seven colours for excelling in almost every sport and was given the honour to lead the march-past and carry the school flag.

Little Karl, therefore, had a hard time keeping up with this excellence and gravitated more towards boxing, which he used with a great deal of proficiency. Sometimes, his frustration broke through, resulting in a major hand-to-hand between the two boys. His small but strong little hands would attack Neville with unimaginable fury; his head, covered with thick dark hair, would lower as he bent his wiry torso and charged like a bull into the ring, unmindful of the consequences. Woe betide anyone who laughed – for then, all hell would break loose!

In spite of the rivalry, the brothers shared a relationship that was special. Neville always played the role of protector and defender, while Karl retained the spirit of an attacker and fighter. I always knew that he would remain headstrong and stubborn, but I also knew of another side to his nature – soft, loving and sensitive to the needs of his family. Without being prompted, he would hasten to help his old grandparents negotiate a difficult step or get them comfortably seated in their chairs. He took a special delight in smaller children, holding them on his lap and playing with them for hours. His baby sister, Tina, became the recipient of much of this affection. If ever I was cross or chose to punish him, he would come running headlong to give me a bear hug and the most lovable smile would light up his face. Everything was, of course, forgotten in a matter of seconds.

When he was a child, his favourite resting place was my lap. But even as he grew older, this need continued and he would still burrow his head in my lap and go to sleep.

But the love and passion of his life was horses.

It became increasingly clear to us during Karl's kindergarten years that school to him was merely a playground, where alphabets were made more exciting because he associated them with the names of horses and jockeys. That was the only way he would learn! His heroes were trainers and games were always races out of starting gates.

Being an avid lover of the horse myself, I spent much time at the stables teaching him how to groom, feed and water the animals. A special treat for the day was to double seat with me and canter around the racecourse or in and out of the area surrounding the stables. He knew no fear, and by the age of two, could sit a pony on his own.

I remember the day vividly – a misty morning in the hill station of Matheran where we went regularly on holiday. I was taking Karl with me on the leading rein and as we trotted through the bazaar, the sight of this tiny two-year-old, mounted like a prince on his small pony, arrested the attention of the passers-by. Heads turned and smiles soon turned to applause as Karl rode on, oblivious of the effect that he was having on the crowd. I wondered then, but I know now that he had been born with an affinity and love for horses that was rare and precious. I also knew that this charisma would make crowds set their sights on him and applaud as they did that day.

Every Christmas, when other little children would ask for toys, he would be thrilled to receive a bag full of coins that paid for rides around the bandstand near our house. He would spend every *paisa* of every rupee, till all the money was over, and then he would beg for more. The syces, who hired out the ponies, loved him. They would say, *"Yeh toh jockey bunnay-walla hai,"* (He is sure to become a jockey). It seemed they knew more about his future than we did!

Karl on Fury

By the time Karl was seven years old, he was an excellent horseman who rode bareback, did show jumping and took part with great success in the mounted sports. For all his efforts and achievements, we gifted him with his first pony, aptly named Fury.

But his greatest dream was racing.

Karl would fashion make-believe horses out of pillows, ingeniously hooking belts over them, straddling and beating them with his whip, till the cotton flew out like snowflakes around the room. He would work himself into a frenzy with his own loud running commentary and in this way, he rode many an imaginary winner for himself!

I remember a time when my husband and I left for the movies, leaving Karl with his fantasies. When we returned three hours later, he was still at it, sweat pouring profusely from his body. His voice rose to a fevered pitch, "...and it's Karansingh on Sombrero coming round the bend two lengths ahead of Eric Eldin on Storm... and it's Sombrero from Storm, Sombrero from Storm, Storm from Sombrero as they pass the winning post locked together!" We watched, amazed, as he collapsed into his pillow with outstretched arms and heaving shoulders, quite oblivious of the time and the fact that we had gone and returned. Such was his passion!

Can you wonder then that Karl showed little interest in academics, for he was a dreamer, living in his own private world. He had to be threatened with dire consequences if he did not do his homework – but somehow, he always had a ready excuse. One day, he failed to take his workbook to school. When his teacher scolded him, he blithely replied, "Oh, you know Sir, I took my book to the racecourse to study and, would you believe it, the horse ate it up!" History and geography were subjects that brought out the dumb act in him, but his eyes would light up and sparkle as his over-active brain would give rapid-fire responses to questions on rides and wins, lengths and distances. He probably inherited this expertise from his father Jimmy, whose racing pictures evoked an intense interest in Karl. He loved to be tested with these pictures and none could win an argument with him over the result of any race, for his "racing" mind knew each horse and rider even if we covered the names with our hands. His answers shot out at us without hesitation for he had ridden them all in the privacy of his own room on his make-believe horse – the pillow!

When he was ten, the day dawned on his first gymkhana race. The fact that he had won on Fury made him very happy, but it was not enough. He wanted more, much more. On the following gymkhana race day, he sat outside the weighing-in enclosure and looked expectantly at the owners going in and out. When questioned about this, he replied, "Oh, Ma, I am waiting in case I get a chance ride."

"Come on, off with you," I scolded. "You know your father will never allow it." And with that, I literally dragged him off to join the spectators in the stands.

But on the very next Sunday, Karl was hiding in the same place again. This time, luck was on his side and he soon came hurrying towards me, his face pink with pleasure, pulling along a big burly companion. "Look Ma, he wants me to ride his pony, because he has no jockey. Oh, please, please, just this once let me do it," he begged. I did not have the heart to refuse him, but it was not an easy thing he asked of me. First of all, I had to face his father's wrath and secondly, I had to get him to ride at the declared weight of 45 kg when he was a mere 30 kg. With the help of a friend, I rushed around getting a heavy saddle and a weight bag and somehow, finally, we were ready. But the worst shock was yet to come. When the pony in question came into the paddock, I took one look at it and wanted to run away. It was thin, scrawny and had sores and scabs all over its body. Besides that, it had to be pulled along for it could hardly walk! Karl did not seem to see any of this, nor the thunderous face of one of the officials, his father, who came marching up to us. "What is the meaning of this?" he demanded. But it was too late to change anything and an ecstatic Karl mounted his pony and went off to the starting post.

The bell sounded and they were off. I looked anxiously for Karl, but he was not with the field as they came around the bend and down the straight. He was still nowhere in sight when they passed the winning post! I scanned the tracks with my binoculars and it was much later that I saw a little figure intently urging on the pony, who would not do anything but just amble along. He eventually passed the winning post, quite oblivious of the fact that the others were already entering the saddling enclosure. But did he stop after the post and turn around? No, he just continued to ride! In exasperation, I gave up on him to concentrate on other things; but soon, to my horror, I saw him coming back to clash head on with the horses which were leaving the paddock for the next race! I dashed to get hold of him knowing, that if he had his way, he would have turned and gone with them to take part once more.

But he was so happy! He was not deterred by the fact that his pony was ugly or could not raise a gallop or that he had come last. It was the simple joy of being able to ride. His day was made. He had ridden another race and a part of his dream had come true.

Years went by, but not quickly enough for the boy, for as soon as he turned fifteen, Karl begged his father's permission to apply for a jockey's licence. After much deliberation and discussion with the family, we concluded that we could not deny him something that had become an obsession. And so we agreed, on the one condition that he was to finish his schooling. He was ecstatic. He doggedly appeared for his final exams, knowing in his heart that he was but a hair's breadth away from the fulfilment of his dream.

He waited anxiously for the day.

CHAPTER 2

His Dream

"Memsahib, ... memsahib." The waiter, bearing hot coffee and muffins, announced himself a few times before I became aware of his presence. So preoccupied was I with thoughts of Karl, that I had even forgotten to press the buttons of my stop watch and was oblivious of the morning gallops. I sipped my coffee gratefully and soon drifted back to where I had left off – back to the year 1976.

It was in the month of December that Karl was eventually given permission by the Royal Western India Turf Club to ride work, morning exercises or trial work-outs. This was also a period used to check him out and to see how he could cope. He was overjoyed. He had finally become one of "the boys."

Every morning, Karl would be up on his own, needing no alarm, and by 5.30 a.m. he would cycle to work. I can still see his little figure dressed in a khaki shirt and breeches with whip stuck upright into his waistbelt. With his riding helmet slung over the handlebars, he would pedal off into the distance, waving happily.

I would, of course, follow by car and reach in time to watch him standing in line with all the other apprentice boys and be witness to the joy on his face when some trainer picked him to ride his horses in work. I can still see him slurping tea from the saucer as "the boys" did, crowding the *chaiwalla* (tea vendor), who sat crouched with a stainless-steel can of hot, steaming tea. I can hear his voice through the morning mist shouting "aye-yup," a warning for the slow work horses to move out of his way as he flashed by at break-neck speed. I still remember him riding the last horse when everyone had finished and gone home. Sometimes, he would surreptitiously give the horses two rounds instead of the customary one, just so he could ride some more. He was always the first to come and the last to go.

Karl was finally granted a licence to ride professionally on January 20, 1977. His first mount was called Loyal Dream. It could not have been more symbolic for him, because it had been a dream that he had cherished for all of his young life. He really expected that winning would be easy, for he had great confidence in his own ability. But when he lost that first race, he was, for once, a little crestfallen. The press was not too kind either, for he was "just a gymkhana rider" with expectations of making it into the big time without any formal training whatsoever. But as was his nature, he persisted, undaunted by his first failure. There followed a few times when he came very close to winning and was just the proverbial short-head away. But then, he would grit his teeth and vow to us that he would definitely win the next time.

And so it went on till the day Karl got his first winner – March 5, 1977, only a month and twelve days after he began. He was over the moon!

After that, there was no holding back. Karl went from strength to strength, winning doubles, trebles and quadruples. Then, on April 6, 1977, just seventy-three days after his first mount, he rode five winners in a single day – a rare feat for any apprentice boy and a world record in itself! The crowd went wild and the press was quick to sing his praises. He had started off as a boy without any formal training, "just a gymkhana rider," but now, headlines screamed, "Young Karl Umrigar Magnificent." They acclaimed him to be "A rising track star," "A prodigy," "A genius," "A boy wonder."

The racing public grew to love his smile and enthusiasm as day after day, he continued to beat the well known names in racing. People threw flowers, garlands, kind words and much praise his way when he brought in winner after winner. But throughout all this, Karl's head remained unturned and he continued to be generous with those from humble beginnings. Though he had his earnings, we were careful to give him an allowance which he chose to distribute amongst the many who flocked to him asking, *"Baba, aaj kya khelengay?"* (Baba, what should we play today?). Karl would laugh and always give them the names of two or three horses that he thought were good, mostly, his own.

Jimmy and I took great pride in watching over his progress.

Although I taught him to be a horseman, it was his father, with his extraordinary knowledge of racing, who proved to be the guiding light throughout Karl's exceptional career.

I remember the days filled with cheerful arguments, when, despite apparent handicaps and known form, Karl would throw a challenge at his father, threatening to prove us all wrong by winning on a horse that stood no chance at all. We listened to Karl, but did our betting on our own fancies – more often to our regret, for Karl would point his finger at us from the winner's enclosure to say, "I told you so," showing absolutely no sympathy whatsoever for our dwindling fortunes. We were proud of this unbending quality and his ruthlessly clear independence. Those were happy days when the family participated together with fun and laughter.

"I told you so!"

On August 14, 1977, in just a little over six months, Karl lost his racing allowance. This is a ruling that automatically comes into force after an apprentice jockey rides forty winners and becomes a full jockey. His rise was the fastest in the world at the time, and no one has eclipsed it to this date.

It was Karl's luck to have a wonder horse called Royal Tern, so early in his career. The day he first mounted this animal, he came home animated and said, "Mum, I have a champion in my stable." He diligently went every day to break him in. He took great pains to see that everything went well with his training, and even refused a chance, offered by Tommy Smith, champion trainer for twenty years in Australia, to study and work with him in that country. We stood by this decision because we realised that Karl was a natural and that his own enthusiasm and his father's guidance and expertise were his best teachers.

Royal Tern lived up to all of Karl's expectations. After winning a couple of preliminary races, the pair was all set for the big race of the South India season – The Bangalore Derby. There was many a well meaning friend who advised the Goculdas family, the owners of Royal Tern, not to entrust their wonder horse to such an inexperienced boy, for after all, in their eighty-two-year-long association with racing, the family had had only one classic winner. Karl waited with trepidation – would they replace him? But they remained steadfast in their belief, that despite his tender years, he would be able to withstand the pressure and tension of riding a classic and come out victorious.

It was July 16, 1978, the night before the big race. It poured with rain. My family, who had travelled down to Bangalore to be with Karl, sat huddled together in the dead of night listening to the steady downpour and thunder. With sinking hearts, we worried. Would Royal Tern would be able to handle the soft going for he had never galloped in it before? Would Karl be able to guide him successfully and ward-off the combined effort of four challengers, all belonging to one owner who was making a desperate bid for the coveted crown? We whispered, so that our voices would not awaken the sleeping Karl, but he slept on like a king, blissfully unaware of the storm raging around him, flat on his back with hands behind his head! He was not at all bothered, for he had enough faith in himself and his horse.

Karl rode an immaculate race, oblivious of the other horses, their tactics, the muddy course or torrential rain. He won by two lengths over his rival. His triumphant smile as he passed the winning post was a delight to witness. He was only seventeen-and-a-half years old and the youngest jockey in the world to win a Derby!

The champagne was enjoyed by everyone and many toasts were raised to the courage of this little boy. Somewhere, someone had touched him with a magic wand to make his dream come true. But he left his glass of bubbly with me after just one sip. "You finish it Mum," he said, for it was time for him to go home. He had to be up early the next morning to exercise his horses, a job he was already looking forward to.

Karl on Royal Tern

The year 1978 was a glorious one for Karl. He won many big races, including the Indian 2000 Guineas and the Indian Oakes. Finally, it all culminated in the one race that is every jockey's cherished hope and dream – the Indian Derby.

On February 4, 1979, Karl and Royal Tern, now sure of themselves and each other, comfortably accomplished the ultimate. To the delirious delight of the vast multitude which packed the Mahalakshmi Racecourse that day, the thirty-seventh running of the Indian Derby passed into history – the names of Karl Umrigar and Royal Tern added forever to its scroll of honour.

But was Karl's heart at rest? No. He wanted to ride more horses, more races, more winners and eventually as the season drew to a close, he broke the record of fifty-four wins in a single season. Now with one more day to go, he was on the threshold of receiving the Championship Trophy. All he had to do was to hold on to his lead of four. Words cannot describe how proud of him we were!

"Come on Mum, my work is over. Let's go home." His voice shook me out of my reverie – how long had I been dreaming? The green tracks and the white railings of the racecourse swam back as my eyes slowly came to focus on Karl's smiling sweaty face.

CHAPTER 3

The Race

The day seemed no different from any other as we all sat in my bedroom for our usual round of pre-race discussions and friendly quarrels, with even little sister Tina adding her tuppenny bit. Before the arguments became too heated, Karl retired to take a nap prior to leaving for the races.

The moment had arrived. I went to the lift to see Karl off as usual and as the doors shut, my excitement grew with the anticipation of having the whole family witness his ride to glory. There was never any doubt in our minds that he would definitely win his Championship.

The very first race of the day held a meagre field of three horses. The capacity crowd had hardly settled, when the buzzer was heard, indicating that the runners were off. A few seconds later, there was a gasp from the crowd. "Karl has fallen!" shouted Jimmy. Through my binoculars, I had also seen Karl's horse stumble and go down, dislodging him in the process. I was not unduly disturbed for he had fallen many times before, but, when he did not get up, I began to experience the first stirrings of fear. My eyes stayed riveted to his motionless form till I saw the ambulance speed towards him. Only then did I find my legs and race behind Jimmy to the dispensary. The ambulance crept towards us and as they lifted him out, we rushed to his side. "Are you hurt Karl?" I asked, as his hand reached out to hold mine. "No," he answered, dazed and unsure of himself. "What happened Mum?" he asked, and then he coughed, a peculiar, gurgling kind of cough that frightened me. I unbuttoned his racing colours with feverish fingers and saw on his strong lean chest, the red mark of a horse's hoof. I took one long disbelieving look and felt the blood drain from my face. I heard my own voice panic, "Let's get him to the hospital."

Cold corridors swept by as Karl was rushed into the X-ray department accompanied by a friend, a doctor who happened to be at the races. Being a Sunday afternoon, none of the technicians were on call and the X-ray room was deserted. Precious minutes ticked away before they discovered the extent of the damage. Due to a kick by the horse and the internal bleeding, Karl's lung had collapsed and the first emergency procedure, a tracheotomy, had to be performed. Nobody had the time or foresight to prepare Neville and Tina for what they were about to witness, for they had refused to leave Karl's side. As the knife deftly entered the trachea through a section just at the base of the throat, there was a sudden gush of blood. The children were horrified. Specialists were rushed in and the large doors of the operating theatre were shut firmly in our faces.

We sat huddled outside in the foyer not knowing what the dawn would hold for us. With fear and trembling hearts, we tried to imagine what was happening inside – what would they find? Would they be able to repair the damage? We clasped our hands together and prayed desperately to God to save our beloved Karl. After what seemed an eternity, the doctors reappeared. I searched for hope in their faces, but their eyes told a different story. None of them looked at me before they broke the dreaded news. They felt that Karl would not survive the night.

But he did. The next morning, he opened his brown eyes, held my hand and asked, "Who won, Mum?"

"You did Karl, you did," I assured him through my tears. "You have won the Championship, my son."

And so he had. He had won the Championship Cup he had so longed for and his rival was still one behind him in the winner's tally.

Later that day, complications arose and threw his body into a multitude of problems. Bewildered, we watched helplessly as he was put on blocks of ice and was not allowed to have even a drop of water by mouth. The doctors conferred frantically and decided that the only way to give Karl a chance to survive was to attempt a bypass of the lungs, a relatively new procedure in Bombay.

Time seemed to have been suspended till a decision was reached by the small group of specialists and surgeons in attendance. That night, a rare operation was performed through a major artery. We sat vigil with despairing hearts and minds that were frozen with dread. The hours dragged by. There were no night sounds except for the whisper of those who had come to give us strength and share in our prayers and hope for Karl's recovery.

Karl survived the major operation, but remained in intensive care for many more days and nights, better on some, and worse on others. Throughout all this, the daily papers carried reports of his progress, and families and schools prayed for his recovery. Thousands of people crowded the foyer and grounds of the Breach Candy Hospital, and were reluctant to leave till they got some news of their beloved hero. Rich and poor came to offer their support. We were ready to try anything that could be of help – medicines, prayers, natural herbs – anything. We accepted all their offerings; ash from the tomb of Sai Baba, a Master renowned for His miracles, waters of St. Francis, medals, crosses, anything and everything that might help to save his life.

When energies flagged and spirits were down, my son Neville stood like a rock, confident that nothing could destroy the strength of Karl's will to pull through. On his part, Jimmy was quite certain that the honesty in our lives would account for some sort of justice. Therefore, he thought that nothing bad would ever happen, for he believed that God was in Heaven and *had* to look down upon us with compassion and mercy.

I stood outside the ICU willing Karl to pull through with all my might, my face displaying the ravages of many nights of tension and pain. I just could not accept that so much was happening to my son, the son who had done us all so proud, the son whose integrity and sportsmanship was never in question. I sat with him whenever I was allowed to, reassuring him in between bouts of consciousness that I was near him and that he wasn't alone.

"Mum, I want to go home, I want to go home," he would mouth and I would nod through my stifled sobs and say, "Soon, Karl, soon. I promise I will take you home, my son."

And then, his kidneys failed and a blood clot was discovered in his brain. If that wasn't enough, his left leg was in danger of possible amputation, for gangrene had set in. I screamed in silence hoping that the sound would blot out my mind. "Please, dear God, no more. Please, no more," I pleaded. We hung on. Oh, how we hung on.

After seventeen days of dread and tension, the first glimmer of light peeped through the chink of an open door. The doctor came out actually smiling. The worst was over and Karl was going to survive.

Nothing can describe the reaction from all of us that day as we flew in different directions to give our thanks to God. Jimmy made his way to the Mount Mary Church in Bandra, a church renowned for its miracles and I, to the Parsi Fire Temple. It was the only time I had left Karl's side in seventeen days – only to return to a hell that had broken loose.

"Oh my God, what's happened?" I cried, not daring to know.

"Karl's artery has burst," they said.

I stood staring at the scene in front of me as the doctors worked frantically to save Karl. But, one by one, each moved away with head bowed and I was left with a clear vision of a still, motionless form that had been my son.

"THE KING IS DEAD," said the headlines on the front page of the Indian Express.

Karl was laid to rest on May 3, 1979, amidst the trees and plants of the Towers of Silence... and the silence of a great grief fell upon us.

CHAPTER 4

The Silence

Nothing could have prepared us for the darkness that descended upon us – nothing. We had relied so much on the fact that Karl's honesty and straight-forwardness in a profession where these qualities are hard to come by, had to pay off. Thousands of poor persons had bet their little fivers on Karl and come out winners. Many had earned their daily bread by relying on his ability. We felt betrayed – we gave up God, religion and the belief that if you were good, kind and truthful, nothing could go wrong.

His room remained filled with the fragrance of fresh flowers. Heart-rending letters and poems kept pouring in for days on end. To hide our grief, we went up to Matheran where Karl had learnt most of his riding and which held such happy memories of him. We wanted to be left alone, hoping that the little time away would give us the strength to face life again. But it was a mistake, for everyone and everything reminded us of him. We could not bear to gaze upon the beautiful hills and valleys that he had loved so much. We could not touch the ponies he had so loved, nor speak to the *ghorawallas* or syces with whom he had spent so much time. There was a deep void in our lives that nothing could fill. We came back more miserable than ever, for without Karl, everything was cold and empty.

Home again, we tiptoed around, each searching for corners of escape and private grief – none of us had the strength or ability to sufficiently comfort each other. Life developed into a pattern of an existence so pitiful, that it was hard to even look at each other without reminding ourselves of the tragedy that was Karl.

Jimmy chose to shut out the world. The victories that he had worked so hard towards turned to dust, and those that subsequently came his way were no longer shared in the joyous spirit as in the past. I cried silently in pain and longing for what was to be many long years. I tried my hardest to be the anchor that my family so needed, but I didn't know how. My body would go through the motions, but my mind had screeched to a halt. All I wanted to do was to sleep the sleep of oblivion, never to get up to hear the voices in my head or to face the world again.

We dragged ourselves to the racecourse every day because that was our life, but there was no joy in it any more. To see the same horses that Karl used to ride being ridden by others, to observe familiar jockeys, trainers, owners and the same friends at race meetings, tore at our heart-strings and we returned home in tears.

The children limped around for a long time, their young minds slowly mending, but their hearts – well, that was another story. They went automatically to school and came back to a house that was silent and empty. The void that was Karl could never be filled. There were no more games and no one to argue or fight with any more. They were too shocked and hurt that life could be so, so cruel.

Mary, the faithful *ayah* (maid), who had looked after Karl ever since he was born, would often sit in his room and rock herself in silent misery, as the big tears ran down her dark cheeks. Even Rudy, the little mongrel that Karl had loved so much, would creep under his bed and whimper pitifully.

So it went on for six long and weary years, till one Sunday, on July 29, 1984, the unexpected took place.

My husband and I were sitting in the darkness of our room. The blinds were drawn over windows that usually remained closed, for they overlooked the racecourse and served as a constant reminder of that fateful day. The silence was interrupted by the rustling of newspapers. "Have a look at this," said Jimmy, pointing to an article entitled, "They talk to their dead sons." I looked at him in disbelief, but still picked it up to read. Minutes later, not at all sure of what I had just read, I put the newspaper away.

The next few days would have been easy enough had it not been for the article that nagged at me and came in the way of everything that I did. I had vaguely heard of an experience such as this and of people contacting the departed, but I did not believe that it was possible, for to me, death was the end of everything.

There could not be a way, I thought to myself – there just could not, or else, everyone would want to be able to hold conversations with their loved ones.

I spent many hours thinking and trying to be rational, but those few words in print continued to hover before me. Over the years, I had given up the yearning to have Karl's head lying in my lap, but the agony of losing him still continued. Where could he be? What must he be doing? Who must be looking after him? There was not a day that went by that I did not remember Karl or wish that I could see him, hear his voice, or speak to him – if only just once more. Could anyone understand my longing as a mother?

I finally leafed through the telephone directory to find the one person who possibly might – Mrs. Khorshed Bhavnagri, who wrote the article about her sons.

A week later I found myself nervously ringing Mrs. Bhavnagri's doorbell. A gentle lady ushered me into a room filled with pictures and trophies of her sons, Vispi and Ratu, who had perished together in a car accident. In hushed tones, she related to me how they had "found" their way "back" to their parents through spirit meetings held by a private group of people. These group meetings, that were held every Saturday, had been unknown to her. Somehow, through methods I did not then understand, her sons managed to prove their identities to this group and subsequently to their mother. The boys then requested her to place a pen on paper to enable them to communicate with her. So she began automatic writing.

With a few years of experience behind the "writings," her sons ultimately convinced her to publish an article in the press so that many others could be helped and guided from the spirit world. The boys were determined to "talk" about their "lives after death" and in this way, wanted to reassure all their loved ones left behind on earth.

"You mean you actually speak to them every day?" I asked in disbelief. "Yes, I speak to them and they answer me," she proudly replied.

Mrs. Bhavnagri sounded so confident of her experience and revealed a knowledge of the unknown world that I had no way of disproving. She insisted that there are certain rules to be followed, but in spite of her explanations, I could not figure out the mechanics of automatic writing. Bewildered, I continued to listen till, at last, she framed the one question I had been waiting for.

"Would you like to talk to Karl?" she asked gently. "Yes," I heard myself whisper.

There, I had done it, I thought to myself – there was no turning back. In spite of my reservations and nervousness, I had taken the plunge.

We set up an appointment and I left, my mind still in turmoil. Once home, I sat down and thought about the enormity of what I had done. Was this really possible? Would it really be Karl? Would I actually speak to him?

Too scared to talk to anyone about what I was planning to undertake, but still longing to make contact with Karl, I returned at the appointed time to Mrs. Bhavnagri. This time I was ushered straight into the private room that she used for her daily "talks" with her sons. We sat at a prayer table and her lips began to move silently.

A gentle breeze wafted through the open window as she picked up her pen and poised it over a page. I watched, fascinated, as the first words began to appear.

"Mummy, my dearest Mummy, I love you so much more than you can imagine on earth. On earth I never realised I loved you so much. Please Mummy, forget the past, for now I am very happy. I have worked very hard for these past few years to reach a high level and want to guide you on earth but only few can do so. So do try please."

That was all.

I stared at Karl's message, longing to respond, but I could not speak. Sensing my emotions and seeing that I was close to tears, Mrs. Bhavnagri waited till I had composed myself, and then she asked, "Do you want to say something?" I stared at her blankly, for I did not know what to say or what was expected of me.

"Why don't you try writing, for that is what Karl has asked for," she prompted. I shook my head for I did not know how. Besides, I was not sure if it was the right thing for me to do and whether it would be disturbing Karl and his progress. Used to reactions such as mine, Mrs. Bhavnagri proceeded to give me the necessary confidence and important guidelines just in case I changed my mind.

"May God be with you and give you peace," she concluded.

CHAPTER 5

The Writing

I do not remember how I reached the car, but somewhere in the middle of a crowded bazaar, I found myself braking to a halt. I had just avoided a cow! I sat for a minute in the middle of chaos, surrounded by bicycles, vendors and people. Quickly opening my bag, I stared at the piece of paper. Had this really happened – had my son "talked" to me? With doubts still gnawing at my insides, I drove home with a mind that raced with questions. What if all this was a hoax? How could I be sure? What was I to say to my family? How was I to explain what I had done? Would they be as intrigued as I was? Should I tell them at the risk of their disapproval or should I hold back till I had made up my mind and there was more proof?

In the quiet of the night, I read Karl's message over and over again. I tossed and I turned and I cried. I looked at Jimmy, longing to awaken him so that I could share what had happened to me. I stood at the balcony till it was dawn and watched the early morning light slowly break over the racecourse. So much of Karl was out there I thought, so many memories. Did I want to keep it that way? What if I tried to reach him and failed, I would only have myself to answer to. With the last thought uppermost in my mind, I resolved to "find" Karl by myself.

As soon as everyone was awake, I went through the motions of handling the morning chores, trying hard not to reveal my true feelings. I was so sure that the family would see through my nervousness and guess that something was going on within me, but somehow, I got through the few hours till it was time for Jimmy to leave. Such was my growing excitement, that I almost pushed him out of the door. The moment had arrived.

I locked my bedroom door and with trembling hands, I set up as Mrs. Bhavnagri had instructed. I held the pen over the paper and closed my eyes. "Please Karl, if you are really there, write something – anything," I begged. I waited, unsure of what would happen.

Suddenly, there was a movement. No, it couldn't be! Slowly, very slowly, the pen began to move across the page. I held my breath and watched, fascinated. The initial dot became a faint wavering line. Without warning, it gave way to big sweeping movements. Round the page my hand moved, up and down, and round and round, till just as suddenly, it stopped.

I dashed to the phone, dialled Mrs. Bhavnagri's number and shouted with excitement. "The pen moved, it moved! I can write, I can write!" I don't know what she must have made of my hysteria as I babbled on and on, unable to stop. I can't describe the joy that swept me up into a world that had suddenly changed. Had I really stumbled into contact with my spirit son? Clasping Karl's photograph to my heart, I whirled around the room not willing to let go of a moment of the heady sensation. But the family soon trooped back. I looked at them, yearning to tell them of my new experience, but somehow, I got through the rest of the day holding onto my secret.

With Mrs. Bhavnagri's encouragement, I sat down every single day and watched over the writing. After what seemed an age, the scribble changed to loops. It remained that way for pages and pages, till suddenly the loops began making beautiful patterns. One day the patterned loops changed to letters; e e e e... and o o o... began repeating themselves over and over again, followed by m m m... and w w w... I felt as if I had my life over again with Karl and that somehow he was learning the alphabet once more, but this time from another dimension – and without the horses!

On September 11, more than a month after I had begun, the first word appeared. All the letters I had been writing suddenly joined together and made a full word, *"WHEREVER."* This word ran for many pages until the next word came and that really touched the innermost core of my heart. *"MUM"* he wrote, *"Mum, mum, mum."* Exactly fourteen days later these two words joined together with a third word, and finally read, *"WHEREVER MUM HOME."*

I sat and wept.

Karl's early efforts at communicating

I went back in time to the scene in the hospital room where Karl had held my hand and looked beseechingly into my eyes. "I want to go home," he had said, "Mum, I want to go home." "I will never leave you Karl," I remember saying, "I am right here to help you fight this battle. I promise I will take you home." At that time, I did not know that I would not be able to keep my word, nor did I know that this request would be his last.

Now here it was – dancing on a page right in front of me – *"WHEREVER MUM HOME!"*

The tears flowed as I rocked myself, with my arms tightly wrapped around my chest. A new found life-source began to creep through my body till there remained no doubt in my mind. I was certain. My son Karl had returned home.

The years of emptiness receded as each morning Karl diligently practiced. Each word, no matter how often repeated, brought infinite joy to my soul.

Karl soon spelt out another word, *"MEHER."*

I was puzzled, for there was no one of that name in my family or in my group of close friends. So back I went to Mrs. Bhavnagri with my pages filled with the words, "Meher." Who or what was "Meher?" Mrs. Bhavnagri suggested that I direct my inquiries through another medium, a Mrs. Prabhavati Rishi, whose expertise lay in the handling of the ouija board. I had absolutely no idea of what she was talking about, but having come this far, my inner spirit seemed to have assumed an inexplicable drive. I simply had to find out more about the word – "Meher."

Following directions, I found myself outside an old, decrepit building opposite the Portuguese Church in a locality known as Girgaum. As I climbed the rickety stairs, doubts assailed my mind, "Good Lord, where have I come?" On the landing, a door opened and an old Maharashtrian lady asked me my business. "I wish to contact my son," I said, recalling advice not to give any names. Looking into her diary filled with appointments, she gave me a time for a month later. "Thirty days!" I thought to myself incredulously, "I have to wait thirty days before satisfying my curiosity!" Disappointed, I made my way back home wondering how she could possibly have such a long list of people with queries about the spirit world. Was I the only ignorant one who did not know of the availability of a contact such as this?

On the given date and time, I was back again outside Mrs. Rishi's door. She was already seated at a small three-legged table and invited me to take the chair opposite her. With our hands placed lightly on the table, she uttered a short prayer to her guides for help and protection. Soon, an amazing thing occurred. The table began to tilt slowly towards me. Startled, I sneakily glanced underneath looking for evidence of any external influence, but found none. The medium's eyes were closed and she was deep in concentration with both hands resting lightly on the table. There was no time to think about the phenomenon, for the next thing she did was to ask the spirit person to confirm its presence. "Tap three times," she said loudly. The table responded by tapping out an affirmative! I was incredulous.

Pulling out a rectangular board, she set it on the table and together we placed our hands on a pointer. This was the first time I laid eyes on an ouija board.

"Who are you? Who are you? Please write your name," she asked repeatedly. I could not believe what I saw. The pointer began to move towards the first letter K. The K was followed by an A, an R, and then an L. The board had spelt out his name – *KARL*. I stared, mesmerised, as the letters of our surname followed suit. I could not believe what I was witnessing, as I had not given her any prior information except for the date of Karl's passing into spirit. The first thought that came to my mind was to verify the authenticity of the spirit person who was present. Anxiously I asked if he could remember what had happened to him before he left us. He spelt out, *"I FELL DOWN – BRAIN HAEMORRHAGE."*

Startled by the response, my heart began to race furiously, for it had been a brain haemorrhage that was finally responsible for the loss of Karl's consciousness. He was thus unable to fight for his life any more. This had to be Karl, for another spirit person would never have known. This had to be my son!

Gaining confidence, I began to question him about the writing – "Am I disturbing you Karl?"

"NO MUM," he replied.

"Do you wish me to continue, and will I ever be able to write clearly."

"YES, WITH GOD'S HELP."

"And what are you trying to tell me Karl? Who is Meher?"

"MEHER BABA."

"And who is Meher Baba?" I cried, intrigued.

"HE IS MY GURU," spelt the board.

"What do you want me to do?"

"GO WHEREVER HE IS. GO WHEREVER HE IS," repeated Karl.

The session ended abruptly and I was left stunned!

I thanked Mrs. Rishi for her kind help and went home contemplating everything that my son had spelt out on the board. What was Karl trying to tell me? Had I imagined my "conversation" with him? Could I have influenced the pointer in some way? No, I thought, it could not be, for simply but accurately, he had confirmed the circumstance that had lead to his death. But then followed the extraordinary part. Who was this *guru*, this Meher Baba? What possible connection did he have with Karl? Where was I going to find him? I could not think of a single person who knew of Meher Baba's existence – but no doubt there had to be someone. The problem lay in the next step – I did not know how to proceed.

At eight o'clock the next morning, I sat for my usual writing session with Karl and a new sentence made its appearance. *"MEHER MESSAGE, MEHER MESSAGE,"* he wrote and although it made little or no sense to me, I knew somehow that my son was trying hard to get a message across to me. He had struggled to give me three clues – Meher, *Guru*, and Message. So, all I had to do was to find the *guru* who could give me Karl's all important message.

Easier said than done, for the sentence proceeded no further. I somehow felt that Karl was waiting for me to take some action – almost like a game – a treasure hunt!

It was about this time, and with the greatest of difficulty I might add, that I put aside my fears and considerations and decided to tell the rest of the family about "Karl." The pressure of secrecy had worn me out and besides, I longed to share this with them and gain their support.

I had anticipated angry reactions but nothing similar to what took place the night I eventually broke the news. Disbelief written all over their faces, my son Neville and husband Jimmy were explicit about their feelings. They attacked the impropriety of an act such as mine and as arguments flew across the table, I began to wonder at the wisdom of my disclosure. Instead of being happy with Karl's "return," they were angry with me and felt that he should not have been drawn back to us for our own selfish needs.

They agreed that they knew little or nothing of life after death, but felt strongly that if indeed there was one, Karl should be left alone to get on with his future.

I sat frightened, guilty and hurt. Guilty, because I was the obviously selfish and needy one to whom they referred. Hurt, because they were not even willing to keep an open mind or wait till they were convinced one way or the other. Lastly, I was frightened because I knew I did not have their support. On the other hand, I could not truly blame them for hadn't I taken some time to make up my own mind?

Tina's views were non-controversial and Sabita, my future daughter-in-law, seemed to be the only one who understood and believed more easily in life after death. I just prayed that Karl would be able to give my family enough proof to make them believe the way that I did.

Till then, I resolved to go it alone. Finding "Meher Baba" and the "Message" was to be my next priority – with or without the support of my family!

CHAPTER 6

The Message

It wasn't long before my discreet enquiries paid dividends and I discovered that a Meher Baba had an *ashram* in Ahmednagar. I wrote a simple letter:

> *Dear Sir,*
>
> *I would like an appointment with Meher Baba and if this letter reaches you, could you please direct me as to when and where I should come and how to get there.*
>
> *Thanking you,*
> *Yours faithfully,*
> *Nan Umrigar*

I addressed the envelope to "THE MEHER BABA CENTRE," Ahmednagar, for I had no proper address. I stamped it, posted it and hoped for the best.

Some days later, I was delighted to receive a reply from the Avatar Meher Baba Trust Office. To my utter embarrassment, it said that I could not have an appointment with Meher Baba, as He had "dropped His body" in 1969, but the *Samadhi* or Tomb and the centre were open to visitors. Timings and directions were included. Meher Baba was described as "THE *AVATAR* – THE ANCIENT ONE."

"Dropped His body," "*Avatar!*" What strange words I thought. But this time I did not dare to ask anyone for fear of displaying my ignorance. Maybe Karl would tell me, I said to myself. "Karl, Meher Baba is not even alive, so why should I go there? And for goodness sake, who or what is an *Avatar*?"

Ignoring my questions, he persisted, "*Go wherever He is, see Meher Baba, Meher Baba message, message Meher Baba, go wherever He is.*"

I was just too bewildered and wondered whether I was being wise or just plain stupid. If I were to go, would I be out on a wild goose chase, or would there really be some message waiting for me? One part of me longed to find out and the other kept warning me of giving into an indulgence, a flight of fancy, a whim. I decided to wait and watch.

A few weeks later, it so happened that Sabita, Neville's fiancée, who had so far been my greatest ally, got to know of his intended business trip to Pune. She suggested that we ask him to take me along, since Pune was just a couple of hours away from Ahmednagar. After much begging, Neville grudgingly agreed. "I'll accompany you there and no more," he said, ending any further argument.

Once in Pune, Neville and I hired a cab and drove to Ahmednagar. As we sped along the hot and dusty road, I could not believe that I was actually on my way to an environment totally alien to my way of thinking and being. What was an *ashram*? What did people do there? How did they live, eat, behave and what did they believe? Nervously, I prayed for "the message," hoping that its existence or delivery might increase my confidence in the writing and instil some faith in Jimmy and Neville. I really had no idea what to expect.

My thoughts were interrupted by the sudden appearance of a little board that said "MEHERABAD." We turned into a driveway that led to a simple but beautifully structured building called "Meher Pilgrim Centre." As we stepped out of the car, a lady greeted us with joined hands, a smile and a cheery "Jai Baba." Introducing herself as Dolly Dastur, she proceeded to escort us around.

We walked into the coolness of the Pilgrim Centre and listened to the animated chatter of our guide as she tried to piece together as much of Meher Baba's life as she could. She drew our attention to beautiful stained glass windows and huge paintings of Meher Baba that hung on the walls around and inside the dining hall. On either side were quadrangles with adjacent dormitories that overlooked courtyards filled with cacti and varied greenery. Baba devotees could be seen chatting or reading quietly in corners. In one area of the courtyard there was a cage that housed a noisy parrot, busy cracking nuts and having a go at a *sheesh kebab* of tomatoes and green and red peppers. What a beautiful and peaceful place!

We left the residential area and walked through beautiful gardens towards the older section of the centre. This included a low shed-like structure that used to be called Mandali Hall, a large room that was meant for *darshan* gatherings and talks with Baba's close group of followers called the *mandali*. As we entered, my eyes naturally riveted to the single and only piece of furniture that stood at one end of the large but empty hall.

"This is Baba's special armchair," indicated Dolly, but the rest of her sentence was drowned out by the sound of my own heartbeats; for there, on the wall above the chair, in big bold letters was a plaque bearing the message, "DON'T WORRY – BE HAPPY. MEHER BABA."

I just about heard her say that this was Baba's special message to the world, but it was what my eyes and my heart had been searching for – a special message from my son! I recognised it to be just that and nothing more. Karl wanted us to be happy. I closed my eyes and acknowledged his efforts, "Thank you son, thank you, for I know you have worked hard to convince us of your presence. But why did I have to travel all the way here? Who is this *guru,* this Meher Baba – the man behind the message?"

As soon as we completed the tour of lower Meherabad, as it is called, we were led across the main road and a railway line that ran parallel to it. We climbed a gradual hill, on top of which stood Meher Baba's *Samadhi.*

I had never been to a *Samadhi* before, nor experienced a peace such as the one that surrounded the hilltop that day. There was absolute quiet, disturbed only by the crunch of the gravel under our feet as we walked the last stretch towards the Tomb. Realising that we had little idea of what needed to be done, Dolly directed us to the door of the *Samadhi* and asked us to enter separately and take *darshan* of Baba.

I stepped over the threshold and stood, trying to figure out what to say. For a while, the words did not come. I knelt and placed my head in between the roses and lilies and felt the cool touch of the marble tombstone on my forehead. A great sorrow seemed to well up from somewhere inside of me, and I cried out to this stranger, "Where is my son, my Karl? Is he with you? If so, who are you and what does your message mean?" As I backed out of the room, Karl's words echoed in my mind, *"GO WHEREVER HE IS."*

I had come, but I still had no reason to trust this Meher Baba. Did my son's spirit really reside with him?

I sat on a bench in the quiet of the *Samadhi* area, and slowly felt the tension ease out of my body. Dolly sensed the depth of our sorrow but chose not to question us till she had led us to Mansari, who lived in a little room about twenty-five metres away from the tomb. Mansari, a tiny sari-clad old lady, had come to Baba as a young girl and remained to look after the *Samadhi* area, her home, forever.

"Welcome to Baba," said Mansari, in perfect English, as we walked through her door. We settled ourselves around her and with Dolly's prompting, hesitatingly began sharing Karl's story. She listened very carefully and when it was over, she expressed great surprise at the spirit writing. However, she had no doubt in her mind that it was Baba's love that had led us to Meherabad. "Your Karl must be someone special," she said, "for now he is in Baba's care, and you can be sure that Baba has broken his shackles and set him free."

Though I did not realise the significance of what she had just said, the words nevertheless brought tears to my eyes. Mansari smiled and continued gently, "Don't cry my dear, you will come to know how Baba cares for all those who call out to Him. Your son Karl is your guide to Meher Baba – Jai Baba." I left the hill, greatly moved.

We drove through Ahmednagar town and twenty minutes later, found ourselves entering the blue gates of the Trust office. Seated behind a desk was Mani Irani, Meher Baba's sister. Her smile radiated a warmth and love that words cannot describe. She stood up and welcomed us into a new family, Baba's family. She clapped her hands and people seemed to materialise from nowhere. Beautiful faces from different parts of the world gathered around and listened as we shared our story. Some cried, touched with sadness. Others exclaimed in wonder at the way Baba had brought us to them.

We had entered Ahmednagar that morning as strangers, but this "family" had embraced us with a love and compassion so rare, that we were left with the feeling that we had never really been strangers to them at all. They made us feel very special.

I shall never forget that day. I knew in my heart that I would return, again and again.

CHAPTER 7

Jimmy

Neville and I returned that night to find the family already at dinner. Jimmy's raised eyebrows and facial expression conveyed the scepticism that he so obviously felt. I could imagine the exact words that were racing through his mind. "I told you it would be a waste of time – didn't I?" His supercilious smile faded as Neville enthusiastically related just how beautiful Meherabad was and how kind and loving its people. Neville paused, looked around triumphantly and said, "Mum found the message!" The fact that this came from Neville did little to stop Jimmy from being disdainful, but Tina and Sabita were captivated. They wanted to know just about everything – down to the minutest detail.

Exhausted, but happy, I slept peacefully only to awaken in the middle of the night. I felt a strange sensation, a peculiar tingling that seemed to travel from my fingers up towards the elbow of my right arm. I was not aware of what actually happened till I awoke the next morning clutching a piece of paper in my hand. On the bed, next to me, lay a pen. Intrigued, I opened out the paper and read, *"Meher Baba is very happy, Meher Baba is very happy, Meher Baba is very happy."*

I just sat and stared, for the whole page was filled with just that and I could not remember writing it!

That message marked the beginning of a constant source of chatter from another dimension. From that day on, the pen flew over the pages as legible sentences appeared instead of single words. At first Karl said, *"I do not want to dwell on the pain of the past Mum, let's talk of happy things like flowers and trees and honey and bees."* Then his initial pain and reticence seemed to ease off and he began conversing more easily, until finally one day he said to me, *"Mum I am at peace now."*

Thereafter, I began to ask all the questions that had haunted me ever since Karl died. Did he remember his horses... the last race... did he remember how he had fallen? Did he have much pain when he was in the hospital... what did he feel about his passing? Could he ever know the intense love that we felt for him and the unbearable suffering that we had all gone through... was he happy now? And last of all, the all-important question – HOW AND WHY WAS HE WITH MEHER BABA?

His reply will live with me forever.

"When I first came here Mum, I did not know what had happened. Meher Baba came to take me when I was struggling in pain and unhappiness. He looked after me, He healed my leg and my body that was so badly hurt. He is the kindest and most wonderful friend that a person can ever have – He is my Father in Heaven."

Deeply moved, I wanted to know more.

"And what do you do with Meher Baba?" I asked.

"I am His Right Hand man," he declared, *"I am a maker of His Wishes."*

How absurd, I thought to myself. Karl, Meher Baba's right hand man? What on earth did he mean? Thinking about it, I figured that somewhere in heaven, in a safe and comforting place, Karl resided with Meher Baba. Somehow, this "Father in Heaven" had taken away his pain, and had succeeded in making him well and happy, and even happier working for him.

But I could not imagine Karl – unpredictable, explosive, stubborn, loving little Karl, working for a spiritual Master. In my mind, I could not envisage the connection between the two – how could there ever be one? I pondered on this. And so the days went by.

Each day, my son spoke incessantly of his love and devotion towards this man called Meher Baba. He also continued to shower all his affection on us and especially showed much concern for his father whom he had always loved dearly. Apart from having a racing bond, the two had something special between them. So, despite the separate worlds we lived in, Karl continued to constantly urge me to look after his father and to try to convince him about the communication. "But he does not want to believe in this, Karl," I would state emphatically. Not to be fazed, Karl would patiently send encouraging messages to him, asking him day after day to *"Please, please come to Meherabad."*

I really had no idea how I was going to get him to take the next trip with me, for he remained as sceptical as ever, not only about the communication, but also about life. This annoyed me at times, but somehow, I did not let it get in the way of my writing.

One day, I sat preparing for my writing session with Karl. When I opened my eyes after the prayer, I found Jimmy in the room pretending to be busy. Ignoring him, I put pen to paper and was soon engrossed with Karl. Suddenly, I felt Jimmy sit down next to me. Looking from the corner of my eye, I could see him peeking into the book. This interest was short lived however, for in the next minute I heard a grumble. "This is stupidity," he said and walked away. But the next day, he came back again.

This time, Karl addressed him directly. *"Come to Meherabad Dad, come this once and then if you do not like it, don't come again, but just come this one time."*

After much persuasion from Karl and much nagging from the children, he eventually agreed, "I'll come this once, just once and that's final." I smiled to myself for I knew that Karl had finally won. It had to be!

Karl's excitement grew as each day drew closer and closer to the time we were booked for Meherabad. The thumb of my right hand would suddenly start throbbing and I would know that Karl wanted to "say" something. The pen vibrated in my hand with increasing speed. Everyday, Karl would make new and unusual statements. *"I am always in Meherabad... I live there, I am there... I am Meher Baba's Right Hand man,"* he would repeat.

I cannot deny that I was as excited as Karl, but scared as well. What would happen I wondered? Would Jimmy scoff, turn away and say that I had wasted his time? Or, would he at least keep an open mind and understand that our son was trying desperately to get through to us from another world?

With mixed feelings, I sat down to write before we left for Meherabad. I received an astounding message. *"I am waiting for you Mum. I am going to be there when you come and you will see me for sure, I promise you, and you will know it is me. You will see me clearly for I will show myself to you. Mum, I will be near you. I am a man, a person who is living there by the name of Hamma. Yes, that is right, that's my name. I am not an Indian, I am a foreigner and I am living there just now – I am going to meet you there and say hello to you. Mum, you must not make a scene or cry out. I will come near you and sit down. You want proof of Meher Baba, I am giving it to you. I am fair and good-looking. I will be wearing a red shirt, brown pants, and no shoes on my feet. I am a foreigner between the age of eighteen and twenty five, and my name is HAMMA MAKLANE. I am Baba's Right Hand man."*

To say that I was taken aback is putting it mildly! I read and reread the message and searched every area of my mind for a rational explanation, but failed to get one. I could not keep this from the family, but if I was scared and nervous at the time of the first sharing, this time, I was terrified of their reactions, especially Jimmy's. With fingers crossed, I read Karl's message out to them.

As expected, Jimmy threw a major tantrum. "Enough!" he shouted, "You have taken leave of your senses. This is crazy and I am not coming!" In the midst of this verbal attack, I heard Neville begin to laugh. "This is so like Karl," he said, "he just has to do something sensational." Having thus diffused the situation, Neville continued to talk to his father till he calmed down. Finally, Jimmy grudgingly agreed to take one step at a time and we resumed on course to Meherabad.

CHAPTER 8

Patrick

The flight to Pune was delayed and the journey seemed endless. As the car sped along the dusty road from Pune to Ahmednagar, I had enough time to wonder whether I had gone off the deep end. Would there really be someone waiting for me there? Would Karl really show himself? It was hard to believe. My confidence and trust had been awakened by Meher Baba's previous message – "DON'T WORRY BE HAPPY." But this new message was just too, too much! I was tense as I watched the stern expression of my companion who sat looking straight before him.

The centre was quiet. Its deserted appearance was due to the fact that all the devotees had left for Meherazad, Baba's home. Not wasting a moment, I began looking around surreptitiously for a glimpse of a red shirt, but the only person in sight was Dolly. After a while, a tiny feeling of disappointment arose in me for there was nobody around "waiting for us" as I had dared to hope. I looked at Jimmy and Neville wondering what their thoughts were, but both seemed totally engrossed in the new world which had somehow opened up for them.

We strolled around the familiar Pilgrim Centre and examined the details of the fabulous paintings around the dining hall. We discovered that they had all been painted by a blind artist, Lyn Ott, helped by his wife, both lovers of Meher Baba. At the entrance to the dining room, were three beautiful quotes from Hafiz, a Sufi Master, who was one of Baba's favourite poets. The sun lit up the red and blue hues of the stained glass windows at each end of the dining hall. It is said that they depict a meeting of the East and West, uniting them in Baba's eyes.

When we completed the walk through lower Meherabad,

I heard Dolly say, "*Chalo* (come on), let us go up to the *Samadhi*." And she led the way to the car.

It was an oppressively hot summer's day. The sky was a warm blue, dotted with white, fleecy clouds. The only sound to be heard was the dull drone of flies. Not a leaf stirred – everything was still. We walked towards the Tomb in hushed silence. Then suddenly it happened.

A figure stepped out of the *Samadhi*. My eyes first fell on bare feet, then travelled upwards slowly to discover the colour of brown pants. I continued my gaze upwards, till finally, the blood red of the shirt struck me like a thunderbolt between the brows. I shut my eyes, unable to believe what I had just seen. My body and mind shook uncontrollably, and when I tried to regain some semblance of normality, I found that Neville had clutched my arm in a wild grip. Jimmy's face had turned deathly pale, while his eyes took on the glassy look of total disbelief.

I heard the concern in Dolly's voice, but not her words, as we stood rooted to the spot. I felt a touch as she urged us forward and we stumbled the last few steps in a daze. We looked straight into the piercing blue eyes of a *"young foreigner, fair, good-looking and tall."* The next thing I knew I was kneeling at Baba's tomb with tears streaming down my face. Stifling huge sobs, I placed my head at Baba's feet. No words can describe how I felt and there was nothing coherent in my thoughts.

When I came out, "he" was still there, his hand outstretched as he gave me two little orange sweets, the *prasad*, always the custom I believe, after visiting Baba's Tomb. After that, he put his arms around me and said softly, *"Jai Baba."*

The world stood still.

Having taken Baba's *darshan*, we sat together, each of us deep in thought and "he" sat with us as if he naturally belonged. His beautiful eyes were closed and he remained motionless as if his thoughts were far away asking his Beloved Master for blessings for us, his family.

Leaving him reluctantly and only because we had no choice, we walked to Mansari's home to introduce Jimmy to the unusual lady. Mansari had company, an American lady who arose to greet us enthusiastically, "Oh, hello Mrs. Umrigar, how are you. I have been waiting to meet you, actually, wanting to meet you," she said.

"I heard your story from Meherabad friends and I am so deeply touched by it." Puzzled with the familiar manner in which she talked to us, I wondered who this over-friendly American could be. She continued to share a little about herself, whereby we learnt of her own tragedy, the death of her young husband in a car accident. She explained that since this was to be her last day in Meherabad before returning to America, she had not gone with the others to Baba's home. We sat and shared a cup of tea with Mansari and as we stood up to leave, the unknown guest put her arms around me and said, "I have found so much peace here my dear, that I just know you will find the same."

We walked out of Mansari's little home and saw the boy in the red shirt leave the *Samadhi* and walk towards us. As he walked by with head bowed, a strange dry breeze seemed to pass with him and I noticed Jimmy fidgeting with his right shirt sleeve, pulling at it in confusion and complaining irritably about the static. Though momentarily distracted, my thoughts remained with the young boy, till I suddenly realised that it was time to leave and that I had still not asked the all important question. I begged of Neville to catch up with the red shirt and ask his name. "Don't push it Mum," he replied, "you have seen more than enough – it could not get any better." But seeing the imploring look in my eyes, he went to do as I asked.

His name was Patrick. Slightly disappointed that the name was not what we expected to hear, the "*Hamma Maklane*" of Karl's message, we walked the last few steps to the car and reluctantly drove away. We looked back to see him standing there atop the little hill, a solitary figure in a red shirt, hand outstretched in farewell. Our hearts stayed with him even as the car wound its way down the road, till finally, the last curve hid him from view. There was no way I would ever forget the overwhelming emotions of that day.

We drove to Meherazad in silence, except for Dolly, who continued to chatter, quite unaware of what we had experienced. In spite of my thoughts that were filled with the wonder of what had just taken place, I asked her more about the boy, Patrick. She confirmed that he was an American, currently living at the centre and one of Baba's very devout followers. Then she went on to tell us more about Baba's home which is situated nine miles north of Ahmednagar. I wanted to be alone with my feelings after the experience of "Patrick," but there was no time, for we soon entered the beautiful gardens of Meherazad.

In the middle of a drought-ridden area, lies an oasis of great beauty and tranquillity. I must describe the incredible delight that filled me when I first laid eyes on Baba's home.

Huge trees spread their shady branches over a single-storeyed baby cottage, with outhouses that once used to be stables and barns, belonging to a time long gone by. A garden, filled with plants and flowers, haloed this cottage with vibrant and deliberate hues. Little white daisies and big yellow sunflowers danced, whilst bougainvillea shrubs cascaded down in waterfalls of pink and fuschia. Blossoms lay scattered around like a carpet and cacti mingled with mango trees bearing lovely big green fruit. The soft fragrance of custard apple blossoms filled the air. Butterflies and bees danced amidst pale pink and yellow roses and birds twittered in the distance.

As we approached the ivy-covered cottage, we noticed a group of people sitting together on the porch. As we climbed the steps, a lady arose graciously and came towards us. "Welcome to Baba's home," she said softly, "I am so happy you have come."

I looked at a vision of loveliness. Brown hair curled softly over light grey eyes and a finely chiselled nose. Her serene face was lit by a gentle half smile. There was a mark in the shape of a perfect little heart on her forehead. This was Mehera, Baba's most beloved disciple.

Meherazad – Meher Baba's home

"Come and sit by my side," she said, as old Baba friends shifted kindly to make way for new ones. We sat with Baba's *mandali* and other Baba lovers and listened to stories and soul-searching songs that touched my heart. As if they all sensed our sorrow, they included us in their discussions till we found ourselves sharing our story of how the writing had led us to Baba. Many responded with sympathy, a few with tears and some even wondered if it was the right thing to do. But Baba's *mandali* were touched by the story.

As we prepared to leave, for we had a flight to catch, there was just one more thing I had to do. Jimmy and Neville were on their way to the car when I approached Heather, the lady who was then in charge of the pilgrim register, and asked her the vital question.

"Can you tell me please, if there is a Maklane registered in your books?" I looked on anxiously as her finger sped down the list of names she had on hand.

"Oh, no, Mrs. Umrigar, we have no Mr. Maklane but, wait a minute," she hesitated, recalling, "we did have a Mrs. Maklane, but I am afraid you missed her, for she must have left Meherabad this morning."

Excited, but disappointed at the same time, I could not wait to share the piece of information with Neville and Jimmy. But first, we had to say our goodbyes. As we trooped towards the car-park, some of the *mandali* and volunteers accompanied us. Our taxi soon started off amidst waves, cheers and shouts of *"Jai Baba"* and *"Avatar Meher Baba ki Jai."* We were barely out of the gate when I told them of what I had learnt from Heather.

A few miles down the road, Neville's face lit up with a smile, for he had remembered the friendly American who had found herself naturally drawn to us – the lady we had met in Mansari's house. "Do you think she could have been Mrs. Maklane?" he questioned.

"Oh Lord!" I groaned. "We didn't even ask her her name!" I could not wait to get home.

Sabita and Tina were waiting anxiously. "What... what... what?" they asked, their voices rising as they sensed our excitement. I left the men to do the talking and hurried to the phone and dialled Dolly's number in feverish haste. I asked her if she could possibly tell me the name of the lady who met us at Mansari's home. I poised pen over paper and waited with bated breath. Over the crackle in the receiver, I heard her reply. "Her name is Mrs. Maklane," she said and then quickly added, "Actually, you know she has two names – she calls herself Mrs. Maklane Carlson."

Five pairs of eyes were glued to the paper as I wrote the name down. As I came to the last word, CARLSON, my fingers began to shake – the room spun around and the receiver fell from my hands.

We collapsed on the sofa, too stunned to speak.

I recalled Karl's words, *"Come to Meherabad and you will see the difference in your life, for when you go back home, things will have changed, and happiness will always be there for you."*

This chapter would not be complete if I did not mention that two years later, Mrs. Maklane came back to Meherabad in her quest to adopt a baby. This is when she solved the remaining part of the puzzle.

Mrs. Maklane sent word that she very much wanted to meet us again as Karl's story had always been uppermost in her mind. She had heard the first part but now wanted to hear about what had since transpired. So she came over for dinner. I was telling her about that incredible day in Meherabad and the boy at the *Samadhi* in the "red shirt, brown pants and no shoes," when she stopped me in mid-sentence.

"Why didn't you ask him his name?" she inquired.

"We did," I answered, "his name was Patrick."

There was pin-drop silence. Her face registered shock. Then her mind seemed to race furiously till something slowly dawned on her.

"Oh, my God," she said, in an awed whisper, "my husband's name was Patrick, Patrick Carlson! I find the connection simply amazing – someone up there has deliberately picked this out for me to remember, and for you to connect. Furthermore, I have to point out one more amazing coincidence – I too had dressed him in his favourite red shirt before he was put to rest!"

Note: Some years later, a chance meeting with Kristine Maklane in Meherabad, solved the mystery of 'Hamma'. She said that what Karl actually must have said was "Huma" – the pen name Baba used when he wished to write anonymously. During auto-writing, it is usually the sounds in one's mind that get translated through the hand on to paper. Hence, my hand may have written 'Hamma' instead of 'Huma'.

CHAPTER 9

The Awakening

There are now no words to sufficiently describe the lift in our hearts except to say that the days seemed brighter, the sky more blue and the flowers appeared to bloom again. Our windows were flung open, and the blinds were swept apart to reveal a world that promised another glorious beginning.

Meherabad and Karl's words filled us with intense love and happiness. It seemed as if the morning "race" sessions had resumed, with everyone eagerly gathered around Karl, each vying to ask a million and one questions, or share their thoughts and love that had been suppressed for so long.

We spoke to him of our normal day to day affairs, of family cousins and friends, of our problems and difficulties. We would speak of the present, the future or sometimes remind him of the fun we had in the past. On one of these occasions, Jimmy teased him about something. He retaliated and said, *"Daddy, you must not say that to me for I am a saint now."*

Jimmy laughed incredulously. We reminisced about the days when Karl got into trouble over some hair-brained scheme, or was punished for not completing his home work... saint? Indeed! We were simply not prepared to believe that our scamp was on his way to becoming a saint (unless souls were given some sort of opportunity to progress even after death)! Maybe, we thought, he had become a good boy now, but that did not necessarily mean he had sprouted wings!

Wanting to find out more, I asked him a thousand questions. I inquired whether he could describe what the other world was like and what work he was doing.

"Where are you now at this moment Karl?" I queried.

"I wait at the gate for you Mum," Karl explained, *"till you call me in the morning, I wait – and then after I have spoken to you, I go about my daily work with Baba."*

I wondered about the whereabouts of this *"gate"* that Karl spoke of, till one day I made my way to the Meher Baba Centre in Bombay. I found myself staring at a chart titled "The Evolution of Consciousness," drawn under Baba's specific instructions. It was all so strange to me. The chart explained the various stages that the soul passes through on the way to becoming one with God. In my efforts to understand, I slowly traced my finger along the path, beginning with the pictures of the soul in the mineral or stone form, followed by the vegetable, worm or reptile, fish, bird and animal forms and finally to man. On reaching the stage of consciousness as man, the soul then begins to evolve or find its way to where it originated from – God. The pictures suggested that there are many lifetimes of birth and re-birth. In this way, the soul covers innumerable experiences. My finger traversed through the many planes or stages depicted on the chart till suddenly, it stopped at the threshold of what looked like a green gate. Startled, I wondered whether this could be the place where Karl waited.

I went home deep in thought. Although reincarnation and God-realisation were words that I had heard of, they were not concepts that I had needed to understand or follow as part of my religious beliefs. The chart I had just seen, detailed a pathway that I had never come across before. I was not familiar with anything that the chart suggested, let alone the *"gate"* that Karl talked about. What was Karl trying to explain to me?

"Mum, I am aspiring to go higher up in this realm and I am going to travel higher and higher up every day, till I reach the highest level. I want to go up and up and up and still further up." From these words, we gathered that Karl's ambition to win and be the best had still not left him. It seemed he had really set his heart on being Meher Baba's *"right hand man"* and was working hard at it.

Karl tried his best to prove this to me in a number of ways. One day he said, *"Do not write to me for six days Mum, for there is a problem and I am going to Israel to do some work for Baba."* We shared this new development with Neville at breakfast. He looked at us in disbelief. "Karl! In Israel! Can you imagine what he will do to

Meher Baba's plans Mummy?" he said, as he picked up his briefcase and left for the office.

It wasn't long before I heard his voice on the phone. "Mum, I have had a rude shock," he said. He went on to explain that on reaching the office, he came across a friend of the Bhavnagris, who knew of our contact with Karl and who was also into communication with the spirit world. He stopped Neville on the steps and suddenly asked, "Where is Karl?" "What on earth do you mean," said Neville, taken aback. He was even more astounded when the friend replied, "Oh, I just wanted to know because my spirit guides have all been sent to Israel to deal with an emergency."

It wasn't much later that the newspapers reported great unrest in Israel and a threatened war with Palestine.

On occasions such as these, I felt elated, for although I could not see Karl, I could definitely feel him with me. He would so often describe himself and also what was around him. *"Mum, there is no night and no day here. We have no food, no hunger, or thirst – only love and fresh air. Everyone is happy. We can talk and laugh and sing and pray together and say hello to all the newcomers."*

At other times, when Karl would speak of the painful past, I would go back to despairing and feeling lost and alone. *"On the day I left you Mum, you really had to bear the terrible burden of my loss and show a brave front to the world. I do realise how much you had to go through for my sake, but my darling Mummy, you cannot imagine what it felt like to suddenly leave everyone and go away. There was a blinding light and I saw God clearly standing there. Then my spirit began to see everything and feel only happiness. He came to greet me and took me by the hand and led me to all my loved ones and I felt so good. Meher Baba came to me, saved me and looked after me. He has made a beautiful life for me, and I am really very happy here. This world is like you have always imagined – beautiful, tranquil. Life has taken on a new meaning now, to look after all whom I love best in the world. I feel so happy again, and Meher Baba is happy that I am happy that you are happy and all of us are happy to be together again."*

I received pages and pages of such conversation from my son, the words sometimes legible, sometimes not. It was becoming increasingly clear that Karl was trying to convince us to pay close attention to Meher Baba, a man he described as being kind, gentle and compassionate, and totally dependable. It did not matter what time of day or night we chose to call upon him.

And so the days flew by, till a restless need to be sure about my feelings made me return to Meherabad. I needed these few days by myself to be near Karl. Soon I found myself climbing the hill towards Meher Baba's *Samadhi*. I sat outside the Tomb in silence and watched the sun rise in the dark blue sky. Though I had everything to be grateful for, I could not figure out why I was sometimes in pain or why I felt so alone. The family was together again, yet there was a sense of grieving within me. How could that be, I thought to myself – why couldn't I make any sense of my thoughts? Once more I cried out to Baba as his name trembled on my lips. I did not question Meher Baba's favour and asked for nothing except peace for Karl and the will to understand Baba's glorious love and compassion.

The Baba lovers, who could not help notice my grief, came forward and hugged me in silence, lending me their strength. With faces full of love, they assured me that life would prove to be different with Meher Baba always there to help me. I looked around, wondering what manner of man Meher Baba was to have attracted so many followers who expressed such deep love and devotion to him.

I spent time with Mansari, who explained that Baba's life work was to use his deep love to free souls from the shackles of many lifetimes and to bring them closer to him. In loving Baba more and more, we, in turn, would learn to ease ourselves off the pathway of negativity and lead more caring lives. I tried hard to understand all that she had to say, but to be quite honest, it was all very confusing to me.

That evening I spent an hour walking outside the grounds of the centre, and then sat on the stone parapet looking up at the *Samadhi*. "Karl, where are you?" I cried, "Why are you with this spiritual Master, this stranger? Who is Meher Baba, what is he and where is he?" The questions echoed in my mind till the shadows fell. A full moon slowly made its way through the clouds and tinted them a dull silver. A small measure of peace crept into my exhausted mind as I walked down the hill.

So the day passed. I lay in my bed in my little room in the *ashram* and listened to the monsoon break with the dawn. I heard the raindrops pattering and the wind in the trees. I heard the frogs croaking and the birds fluttering. I was able to listen to the sounds of the world again for I heard the trucks hooting and the trains rumbling as they disturbed the early morning silence.

I climbed the hill again and again until I found I was able to listen to the beautiful voices singing Baba's *aarti* and found comfort in the rhythmic hum of the prayers.

I began to see a little light through the dark mist around me and somehow I knew in my heart, that one day, Baba would help me find a way of understanding everything. Till then, I resolved to try to be happy and grateful for what I was being given – an opportunity to begin again with Karl and his loving Master, Meher Baba.

CHAPTER 10

Lights Through The Mist

We were well into 1985 when one of Karl's school friends, Laila Quereshi, paid us a visit. She had kept in constant touch with me even after Karl died. On finishing school, she had gone abroad for her further studies, where she met an Indian boy, Vijay, who captured her heart. For a long time, she nursed a hope that the relationship would lead to something more permanent, but somehow this did not happen and he had called it off.

With a forlorn expression on her face, she poured out her little tale of woe, whilst I listened and watched the effect it was having on this lovely child. I found myself impulsively reaching out to Karl, wondering if he remembered her and also if he could help her resume a happy life.

As the thought entered my mind, she asked hesitantly, "Aunty, have you heard of the Bhavnagris who talk to their sons?" Startled by the coincidence, I smiled and nodded my head. I told her that I had already been to the lady and had made contact with Karl. Excitedly she pleaded, "Do you think we could talk to Karl?" I don't know why I did not have the courage to tell her of my personal experience with the writing. Instead, I quickly offered to get her a message through the medium, Mrs. Bhavnagri.

The next morning, I apologised to Karl for my shortcomings, but ignoring this, he came straight to the point. *"Tell her that this is the best thing that has happened to her. She will soon find someone better who will care for her and give her a happy life. Very soon now, in a month's time, she will get to meet him. I will arrange it. He will be a boy from abroad who will be here on holiday. She is my dear friend and I will always make her happy. She will always remember my words."*

I sat back, astonished. How was I going to give her this

message? Somehow I did, and as expected, she reacted by shaking her head in disbelief and dismissing the contents of the message. "This is absurd, Aunty, how can it be true?" she declared tearfully. "There can never be anyone else, for I am counting the days for Vijay to return to Bombay. I cannot stop thinking of him."

It was not up to me to say that she was making a mistake by hanging on to a love that was not reciprocated, nor could I force her to believe Karl's words – only time would tell. And so it did, for exactly twenty days later I received a call.

"Aunty," said her shy sweet voice, "I am getting married." I held my breath as she continued to tell me that her marriage was to be with a fellow student from abroad who was on holiday in Bombay.

I did not know whether to laugh or cry! I just could not figure out how Karl could be so accurate. Either he played cupid or he could see into the future!

"I am the king of the sea and the skies," he exulted, *"king of heaven and earth, the sad and happy, of above and below, of the good and the bad, the lonely and the lively. I can laugh and cry, be happy and sad at the same time – I am free! You can call me whenever you need me Mom, it's easier than a phone call. Just say Karl come to me – and I will be there in a matter of seconds. I will come flying from the ends of heaven for you."*

I wonder if Laila will ever know how happy it made him to be able to do something for her from another realm. I was pleased, very, very pleased, but my complacency was shattered by the next directive from Karl – *"Now that you believe, I think it is time to tell the rest of the family about Baba."*

I sensed trouble! Karl and Baba seemed to be setting me up. What did he expect me to tell the family? How would I explain the presence of Karl? What if they did not believe me? Worse still, what if they thought I was crazy?

I had not long to wait for the opportunity presented itself in the form of my younger sister, Silla Dubash, who arrived from Delhi. She dropped in to see me and we talked at length, mainly about her daughter, Abie, who was determined to marry a man from another faith. Unfortunately, her father was equally determined not to give his consent or blessing. Silla was torn between the two. She respected her husband's orthodox viewpoint, but also felt that her daughter's happiness and request to choose its source merited some importance. I listened to a very worried sister and somewhere in the middle of the lament, I decided to talk about Baba. I expected an explosion. I thought that she would tell me that I was indulging in fantasies. I expected her to tell me that I should not disturb Karl's soul, but Silla surprised me with her very natural acceptance and enthusiasm.

"So much has happened, such wonderful things have taken place and you haven't told us," she declared. "How could you do that? We have to tell the rest of the family immediately." And with that, a determined Silla rushed off to arrange a family gathering for that evening.

I was terrified, yet propelled by a force I could not describe. My elder sister Tehmi Shroff, her husband, her three children and their husbands, Silla and her entire family – all listened to my fantastic tale with eyes wide open. But I need not have spent so much time worrying, for without hesitation they said, "We want to go to Meherabad."

Luck seemed to be on my side for Jimmy's sister-in-law and his nephew, Kekoo, came to Bombay from Sydney at that particular time. We thought it only right that they should also know of the wonderful happening. After hearing the story, they got so carried away that they picked up the phone and dialled Sydney, urgently summoning Jimmy's brother to Bombay.

"You have to come," they said.

"Why?" he asked.

"Because it is something about Karl and it is impossible to tell you everything on the phone."

"Karl?" he queried astonished.

"Yes. Trust us, you have to come."

And so he came.

That March morning the train compartment was full of our family – from Sydney, Delhi and Bombay – all wending their way to Ahmednagar and Meherabad.

"I will be there," said Karl, and I shivered with anticipation. *"Yes – you will see me clearly. I will be there in a blue flowered shirt – it will be a blue shirt with huge, big flowers on it."*

My confidence was once again put to the test. We spent an hour at the *Samadhi*, each with our thoughts and reasons to be there with Baba. I prayed hard to him and called upon my son, Karl, not to let me down. I squirmed and fidgeted and made excuses to myself. The hot sun beat down upon our heads as we looked mournfully at the deserted *Samadhi*, for there was not a soul around. I eventually took them all to meet Mansari, hoping to prolong the time there, but I knew we would soon have to leave. Had I brought them all on a wild goose chase? Intensely disappointed, we said our goodbyes. With head bowed, I dragged my feet across the gravel and began to follow a part of my family who had already descended the hill – so I was really not prepared for what followed.

A lone figure came striding up the pathway that leads to the *Samadhi*. I saw him on the curve of the hill and was struck by the electric blue of his shirt and his big balloon pants. He had long flowing brown hair, like Christ, and as he drew nearer and nearer, my heart pounded, for on his shirt were huge, blue flowers!

The family members who had already gone down the hill were seen running up behind him, hands waving frantically and fingers pointing, their faces flushed with excitement and joy. Nothing disturbed him for he walked past us without an upward look. Literally falling over one another, we followed him into the *Samadhi* where he prostrated himself flat on the ground before Baba's Tomb. We sat quietly around as he lay there for a full five minutes, motionless and in absolute devotion, his forehead touching the foot of Baba's grave.

We sat in silence as our eyes lingered lovingly over his form. Our time together came to an end, for he suddenly got up, stepped out of the *Samadhi*, and with eyes lowered and head bowed, he walked back the way he had come. Back into the stillness without an upward glance, without a word, he walked, straight down the hill and out of our sight.

My family had made contact with Karl but I had no idea of the effect that it was going to have on their lives.

One day, Silla called from Delhi. She was frantic with worry. She had lost a container of embroidered garments, a consignment to the U.K.

"I would never have asked you," she said tearfully, "but a large investment has gone with it. I know I should not ask for this kind of help, but I have nowhere to turn."

I pleaded her case to Baba and Karl the next morning.

"It is not lost," said Karl, *"it has broken on the way, and it has gone back to where it started from."*

They searched everywhere – they called the agents, but to no avail. There was no trace of it. They called London. They combed all the possible areas again – but there were no signs of the container.

"It was broken on the way and has gone back to where it started from," insisted Karl.

Silla's son, Raiomond, played with Karl's words till it suddenly dawned on him. Since Karl said it was broken, could it possibly have gone to the repair yard? They followed up and eventually found the container exactly where Karl had said it would be! Not only that, but with Baba's grace, every single garment was intact in its packing.

But Karl did not stop there.

There came another phone call from Delhi. Silla's husband had suddenly, for no apparent reason, consented to their daughter's alliance and we were all invited to the wedding.

An Indian family is usually a large one, and no function is complete without each member being there. We really missed Karl and I told him so. *"Why should you miss me, Mum,"* he declared, *"I will be there. You will hear the sound of a horn – not a horn but a horn-like noise and you will know that I am there."* Not likely, I mused smiling, for the marriage ceremony was to be held in an air-conditioned flat on the second floor of a high-rise building. There was not much chance of a horn being there, let alone being heard there.

The gathering was small, the guests sitting around in an array of multi-coloured apparel. The bride and groom looked resplendent in their traditional attire. Abie was draped in a gorgeous pink chiffon *sari,* embroidered with gold thread. Her forehead was dotted with a vermillion *tikka* and she held a coconut and flowers in her cupped hands. The bridegroom, handsome and tall, was in a white *sherwani. Diyas* sparkled and the sweet fragrance of sandalwood and sticks of incense created a beautiful ambience.

All too soon the wedding was over and the bride left for her husband's home amidst a shower of rose petals and good wishes from everyone who had gathered there. But there was something, rather, someone missing. We did not hear the sound of the horn as promised. We returned to Bombay.

Late one night, the phone rang and an excited sister yelled into my ear. "I am sending you something with a friend but I am not telling you what it is. Oh, the wonder of it!" Abruptly she disconnected the phone.

The next day, a parcel arrived for me. It was a video cassette labelled "Abie's Wedding." We watched the ceremonies with great curiosity till the very end, when the bride bids farewell to her parents and is received alone at the doorstep of her new home. Her husband's family waits to welcome her with a silver tray, little lighted *diyas*, a coconut, *kumkum*, flowers and rice. Suddenly we see Abie turn in response to someone or something – and then we hear it! From the distance there comes the sound of a horn. It is not a horn but definitely a horn-like sound. We hear it loud and clear like a clarion call. It is the sound of a conch shell, blown by someone unknown and unseen. Abie smiles with silent acknowledgement.

Abie confided to us later, that this special moment with Karl was, for her, an awakening and she knew in her heart that no matter what was to be in her future, Meher Baba and Karl would always be there for her.

One more family member, who came to Meherabad that wondrous day to make contact with Baba, found herself being drawn irrevocably towards him. My cousin, Tanaz Bharucha, was facing a major problem in her life. She was unable to sustain her pregnancy to full term and had suffered repeated miscarriages. *"Meher Baba says to tell her to have hot water and mustard seeds, squashed in ginger paste every morning for a week,"* said Karl, when I approached him with the problem. We grinned at the thought of Tanaz imbibing this unlikely combination of herbs, but she decided to humour him and saw no harm in following his advice. Much to our surprise and delight, she was soon pregnant. Unfortunately, she did not complete her pregnancy and so, back we went to Karl.

"She has a cyst at the bottom of the womb," revealed Karl. Although tests were taken, no cyst was discovered till much later when a curettage was done. Sure enough, Karl had been right, for the cyst was discovered and removed.

There were some harrowing times for Tanaz and her husband, but their faith in Baba remained steadfast. We hoped that Karl would continue to give us as much help as he could – and so he did.

One day, he suggested that she go to America for a check-up as he now felt the problem went much deeper than we had earlier thought. As luck would have it, or rather, as Baba would have it, a relative invited her for a visit. Before she left, Karl said to me, *"Mum, today you will find something."* The conversation ceased abruptly and I was left with the pen in my hand and no clue whatsoever as to what I should look for.

Still intrigued, I sipped my morning tea and began to read the newspaper. As I turned the pages my eyes were directed towards an article that highlighted a newly-discovered injection to help couples conceive children. "This must be it," I thought excitedly and dashed to the phone.

Tanaz and Sohrab left for the USA. Intensive tests were carried out in due course, but the results were not encouraging. They had almost given up hope, when the result of the last test made them eligible to go to Philadelphia for a course of injections. While packing, they glanced through their medical files and their eyes fell on the cutting I had given them. To their utter delight, they realised that the injections they were going to take were none other than the ones recommended in the article. Better still, and totally amazing, is the fact that the doctor who was going to administer the treatment was the very same lady who had signed the article published in Bombay.

They flew to Philadelphia with hope in their hearts, but in this case, it turned out that destiny played an even bigger part than wishes and dreams. Although Tanaz and Sohrab still continue to hope, they have accepted the fact that sometimes you win, sometimes you lose. But, the presence of an unseen guide attempting to help them along the way is what definitely keeps them buoyant.

CHAPTER 11

Precious Moments

There was one particular question that I had been wanting to ask Meher Baba for a long time, and on November 9, 1986, I received a really beautiful and meaningful reply from him. Normally, Karl would answer on Baba's behalf, but this time, it was Meher Baba who made a rare "personal appearance" on paper. He finally put to rest the terrible memory that I had always carried with me – the memory of Karl's inert body and the dreaded hoof mark on his chest.

I wanted to know why, when he loved the animal so much, and spent all his waking hours and most of his sleeping ones dreaming of the horse, why did it have to end like it did? Why, Baba? Why?

> ***"Karl has a stamp of horses forever on him because of life in another life – but he can never be hurt again. I have taken him to Me so he never will have to go back to life again. He is with Me and I will take care of him forever. He will never leave Me now,"*** replied Baba.

I asked Baba why he had come forward to help my son and all of us when we never had any previous connection with him, or for that matter, even knew his name.

> He answered, ***"Racing, I love it Myself, I used to come and watch from the outside and I have seen Karl many times riding a horse. I have watched him and admired him as a small boy and I knew I would look after him forever if anything happened to him. I always knew he was destined for great things, but his career was cut short. I was as sad as all of you. I was crying from here. You may not believe this, but it is true. I cried as the***

world cried with you, and I took him immediately. He loves you all very much and is near you all the time. He knows Me and loves Me now. I have him safe with Me. Please believe Me, I am there for you. I will ease your pain and help you along the pathway. I will be your good friend through life and bring you to Me after life. Look forward, never backward – just think ahead. Dear family, I wish you all the very best in the world and beyond.

Meher Baba."

I was touched by this simple message.

Our son Karl had been the source of much joy, happiness, and pride. Could the memory of those agonizing days and nights of willing Karl to fight for his life be truly over for me? Who was this man who had stood outside the racecourse keeping a watchful eye on my son? Who was he and why had he come forward to give me this message. Where was Karl? I would give anything to know that he was truly safe and happy. Could all that he had just told me really be true? Could Meher Baba, with his gentleness and compassion, remove the agony that lay deep within my soul? I wanted so much to believe in his promises. I wanted to keep faith in him, and prayed that some day he would reveal his purpose in reaching out to us. Till then, I resolved to move forward and really try never to look back in pain again.

My husband and I drove up to Meherabad many times to drink in the peace and love that vibrated through the hills. Almost every time we went, Baba brought Karl to us in a number of different ways.

Once Karl said, *"Mum, I will be a voice."* On the day in question, Mehera and the *mandali* drove up from Meherazad for a special mid-morning *aarti* at the *Samadhi.* As Jimmy and I approached, we heard a beautiful melodious voice echo through the hills singing "Begin the Beguine." The singer and the song pulled at our heart strings, for the words emphasised a renewed beginning with our son Karl, more so when we were told that it was Baba's favourite song.

Another time, Karl said that he would be a *"butterfly"* and again, as we stood in line for *darshan* outside the *Samadhi,* a butterfly fluttered along a ray of sunlight towards us. We watched as it gently circled around the two of us, once, twice, thrice. I closed my eyes and "willed" Karl to come to me. I felt a tiny movement over my heart and looked down to find that it had settled on my shirt. Gazing at its rich blue colour, I longed to stroke its soft wings, wanting so much to say something special but, before I could say "thank you," it lifted itself off in farewell and flew towards Meher Baba's Tomb.

To date, Karl continues to demonstrate his love for us in so many wonderful ways that there is absolutely no doubt in our minds that he is with us and also with his beautiful Master.

To keep us alive to the faith of an existing spirit world, little demonstrations took place in our home – the home that Karl had loved so much. The clicking sound of switches would suddenly be heard – the lights would come on or the fans would start to whirl. Without warning, the cordless phone would ring loudly or the intercom would keep interrupting our sleep. The mobile over my grandson's bed, in what used to be Karl's room, would play its soft tune to the sound of happy gurgling and laughter.

On one occasion, when Sabita was expecting her baby, the lampshade over her bed exploded. Her eyes flew up to the huge piece of painted glass that hurtled towards her reclining form. Suddenly, it changed course as if an unseen hand had swept it aside and it smashed into the doorway, breaking into a thousand pieces. She stared at the shimmering pieces of glass, her dark eyes widening with fear as she began to realise what a providential escape she'd had.

One day Karl said, *"This evening I will be coming to the house to meet you – I will be a foreigner with a companion."* Just like that, as if it were a normal everyday occurrence! As we sat down to dinner, the doorbell rang. The family, lounging in informal attire and not used to strangers dropping in at dinner time, scattered in all directions. I was left gaping at two foreigners who stood at the door. One of them held out a cassette and asked whether I was interested in buying the same. With trembling hands, I gave him the money, which he gratefully accepted and then disappeared down the staircase. My heart still pounding, I stood speechless and stared at the box in my hand. It read, "CALLING YOU." There was a picture of a boy of about Karl's age with hands outstretched to a lady walking through the clouds towards him. Sun, moon and stars – all the elements of divinity were pictured around them. On turning it over, my eyes fell on a collection of songs entitled, Heaven's Magic. The tears spilled over. I read the names of the songs: Earth has no sorrow... More than a friend... It's better to have loved and lost... Why is that tear in your eye? ...How did you know... If you are far away I still hear you... I'll do it your way... I am born again.

We could not finish our dinner.

I think that Karl, by then, was overexcited with his success. He knew that we were beginning to believe him more and more. Everytime he told us that he was near, we would hope to sense his presence, but it was never the way we imagined. He would always surprise us.

Picture on the cover of the cassette

One morning, he declared that he would be coming to see us during that afternoon. *"I will be there in a white kurta-pyjama and you will definitely know it is me. You will all be there."*

Now this, I thought, was going too far. This, I would definitely like to see! Neville always returned late from the office and no one in the family was in the habit of wearing a very Indian dress like the *kurta-pyjama.*

My husband and I were resting in the afternoon when Neville rang to say he was having some bankers over for tea. At about four thirty, I suddenly awoke with a thought – where was Karl? Could he be one of the bankers, I wondered. I peeped through the doorway of the living room, but was too late, for they had already left. When Neville joined us, I asked him whether any of the bankers had worn a *kurta-pyjama*. He grinned, shaking his head in denial and looked at me as if to say, "Are you going cuckoo?" We mused over Karl's message as we sipped our afternoon tea.

There was a knock on the door. "May we come in?" sang out Sabita. "Someone has come to see you." We heard the patter of feet and little Zahan, aged three, came running into the room. "I have come," he called out, his little arms stretched out towards us. He was dressed in a white *kurta-pyjama*!

The impact that Zahan made on us was electrifying. Neville, lazily tilting his chair back and forth, suddenly lost his balance and almost fell over backward. Jimmy gasped. His eyes widened with disbelief as he clapped his hands over his mouth; they opened up to let out a loud cry, "Karl has come!"

Sabita stood transfixed. She looked from one to the other and thought we had all taken leave of our senses. She was unaware of Karl's morning message as she had already left the house to go shopping. Seeing a white *kurta-pyjama* in a store-window, she purchased it on a whim. Little did she realise the lasting effect that it would have on all of us!

One morning, we got a particularly strange message. It read, *"A call will come for you and you must answer it."* As we watched a programme on television that night, a newsflash appeared, requesting viewers to donate blood for a lady who was critically ill. We thought that maybe this was the call for us to heed, but strangely, none of us had her blood type. The next day, we heard that she had not survived the crisis and had passed away in the early hours of the morning.

Not thinking much of it, I was stunned when, a few days later, strange writing moved slowly across the page. She introduced herself as the lady who had just passed over and wrote, "Dear Mrs. Umrigar, God has chosen you to help me. My heart is heavy with pain. Please help me to contact my husband. Karl is my help in time of trouble – take me to my baby."

I was not aware of a baby! Was this the call that Karl had wished us to answer? What were we to do? How could we approach a stranger with an even stranger story. I somehow managed an appointment and amidst hundreds of mourners made our way to her husband and identified ourselves. He graciously took us aside and listened patiently as I stumbled through a short version of Baba and Karl and finally read out his wife's message. To my surprise, he asked me to tell her to rest in peace and that he would always be with her and look after the baby with great care. With that, we returned home, praying for Baba to give them peace.

Each morning, before starting my communication with Karl, I would say my prayers and often wonder if, one day, I would be blessed enough to see Baba's face. One afternoon, I awoke from my slumber for no apparent reason at all. I looked up at the tiny crystals dangling from the lights on the ceiling. In the darkened room, a shaft of light drew my attention to a beautiful face that had formed amidst the rainbow-coloured glass – it was Baba's. Strong, beautiful and complete with mustache, eyebrows and flowing hair, Baba smiled down on me as I lay mesmerised. I held my breath in awe as the precious moments ticked by and finally the vision faded from view. I was left with the darkness and the gentle swaying of the crystals as they tinkled merrily. I then realised that it was January 31, *Amartirthi* – the anniversary of the day Baba had dropped his Body.

It was not my imagination, for I know he was really there.

CHAPTER 12

1987

There could have been times when we permitted ourselves the luxury of imagining a spirit presence, but I must be fair and say that Karl's attempts to convince us were linked with times or with events that were totally unexpected and beyond any contrivance on my part. The dominant fear that always lay within me was one of being carried away by my own thoughts and imagining words from the spirit world. Karl made sure that this was not so. Also, I would never have pushed my way through without the moral support of my family. But this was not enough. By now, my interest and curiosity were thoroughly aroused and I wanted to know more – much more about the spirit world and life after death. I wished to know if I was the only one experiencing the unexpected or did others also know of this kind of contact with the unknown.

I needed to find the appropriate person who could point me in the right direction. I could only think of one – Mrs. Bhavnagri. This time, her door opened to admit me into a room full of people, being guided by her and learning how to communicate. I stood there overwhelmed by the realisation that there were so many persons wanting to contact their loved ones. For further insight, Mrs. Bhavnagri recommended that I see a Mr. and Mrs. Phiroze Kapadia, both mediums of many years standing, who were also closely connected to Mrs. Rishi, the medium that I had met on an earlier occasion.

Mr. Kapadia and I had long discussions on my experiences and doubts. Although he had his own interpretation of spirit phenomena, he could find no explanation in the ambit of spiritualism for Karl's representations in different forms and shapes. However, he had no doubt about the reality of my experiences and strongly urged that I trust the guidance as it was also being controlled by a spiritual Master. Not many people, to his knowledge, had this advantage. Besides, the person that I was in direct contact with was none other than my own son.

"Let this communication grow," he entreated, "and most important of all, always use it for the benefit of others." As I was about to take a trip to London, he suggested that it would be in my interest to visit the Spiritual Centre at 33 Belgrave Square in that city.

Once there, not only did I pick up and read books avidly, but also made appointments with mediums who held demonstrations – each more fascinating than the other. I was introduced to clairvoyants and clairaudients – mediums who can see and hear spirits. They can even describe what they wear, tell us their names and convey messages that they wish to send their loved ones and friends in the audience. I learnt about psychometry, where a medium psychically reads into objects or articles belonging to sitters in the room. From the vibrations surrounding each object, she determines its source, detailing the time and place of origin, and finally identifies the owner.

And then, there was the demonstration by Coral Polge of her psychic drawings. A lady strode firmly onto a stage at the centre, said a short prayer and turned to an easel. With chalk in hand, she proceeded to draw a picture and simultaneously describe the nature of the portrait that seemed to be taking shape. She completed the character description of a sweet-looking old lady holding a pair of knitting needles, by saying that she could hear the name Margaret and that she came from somewhere in Lancashire. A young lady in the audience exclaimed that her "Aunt Margaret" who had just passed away a few months ago, had resided in Lancashire. I was amazed! Coral Polge drew eight pictures in a matter of half an hour and all were claimed by someone in the audience. I sat fascinated, hoping the artist would draw the next one especially for me!

At the end of the demonstration, I requested the secretary for a private appointment. "Oh no," she said, "this is Coral Polge, you know, and she is booked in advance for two years. She is one of the best in the world today."

Not willing to give up easily, I called again the next morning, and to my utter delight, there was a cancellation and I was granted a sitting for the very same day.

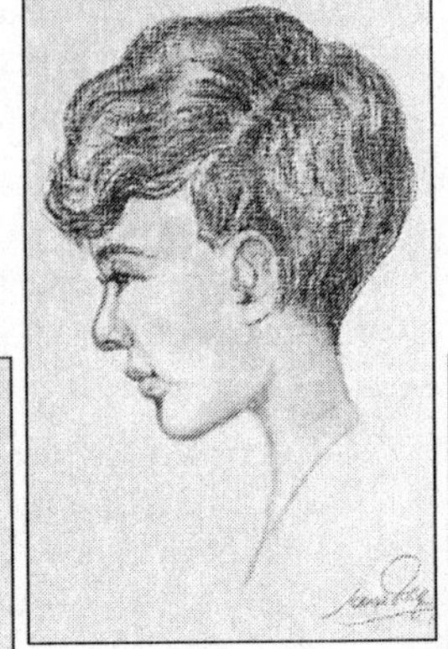

Nan Umrigar's guide souls

Coral Polge did not ask me my name. She held my hands to feel the vibrations and quickly proceeded to draw the first portrait. A lady with a very strong face and hair drawn back in a soft bun slowly took shape. Her chiselled nose and eyes reminded me of someone, but I was unable to identify her. The next picture was of an old man with a striking headdress and a wise and learned look on his noble face. The last picture was that of a little boy.

"Are you trying to make this picture fit someone?" she asked, looking up at me for the first time. I nodded my head. She gently told me not to be overly keen to have a particular person's portrait, but to be content with the picture of those who wanted to reveal themselves to me as my "guide souls" who love and watch over me. I had really been hoping for a picture of Karl, but that was not to be.

The next morning, I asked Karl why he had not come to me when I so longed to see his face, and he replied, *"I am with Meher Baba – I will only come to you through Meher Baba. Why do you need to go anywhere to learn anything when we are there to teach you?"*

Ignoring his admonitions, I asked him who the three "guide souls" were. He replied, "*The first is your mother's mother's mother. The second is the first descendant of your father's family – his guidance is priceless to you. Strength flows from him and he gives you lots of love and affection. The little boy is your father, he looks after you.*"

Actual picture of the author's father

I was fascinated and decided to photograph them for each member of my family as Coral Polge had advised. It was just as well that I did, for much later, my sister Silla from Delhi sent me a photograph of my father as a young boy. It was an exact match of the portrait done by the brilliant psychic artist. It really was my father as Karl had so correctly pointed out. I was thrilled.

"Karl, why can't you draw something for me?" I asked him the next day. But the results were so hilarious, that I broke into hysterical laughter and soon gave up trying, quite aware of the fact that the only exam Karl had ever failed was art!

I cannot deny that I longed "to see" my son and "to hear" his dear voice, if only just once more, but no matter how much I tried, I never did succeed. I was depressed. If so many others were able to do so, why couldn't I? It took some years for me to come to terms with the fact that with some, these are specialised gifts; but with most, they are mediumistic abilities that are not easy to develop.

My second invaluable encounter was with a medium of the College of Psychic Studies, Ivy Northage. Browsing through some books one day, I came across her book, "Mediumship made Simple." Her biography was impressive, for not only was she a teaching medium of fifty years standing, but also a trance-medium with a Chinese guide called "Chan." I met this marvellous eighty-year-old one day, and placed before her my experiences with Karl and Meher Baba.

She sat down politely to hear me out, but as I progressed, she became so interested and involved, that she requested me to stay on after working hours so that I could complete my story. "No, I would not advise you to join any classes," she said, "for what you have is most beautiful. I have never in all my years heard anything so beautiful and I would not change it. When you have a Master spiritual guide like Meher Baba, you don't need someone like me. I can't teach you anything. Just continue as you have been doing and do exactly as they ask you to do. You can never go wrong. Your son is there to look after you."

I went home a grateful person.

There had really been no need for me to go looking for proof or confirmation of my experience with the spirit world. In spite of all Karl had said and done, I had tried to know more about what I was doing, for I was only human and not ready to accept things without looking deeper into them. What Ivy Northage said went a long way in putting my inquiring mind and heart at rest.

CHAPTER 13

My Family

Jimmy and I met as children in the late 1930s. We used to play in the stables, a meeting ground for our families who loved horses with a passion that surpassed that of any other hobby or sport. My sisters and I were trained to ride by an adoring father, who, in his devotion and caring, left no stone unturned. Each outing that he organised was always a special treat and the discipline that he exacted from us paid dividends, for there were many trophies adorning our living room.

The saddle was my second home. There was not a hurdle I could not jump, or a race I could not successfully participate in, or a polo game that would not excite me – everything and anything to do with horses was, for me, a permanent passion.

The natural red mud tracks in the hills of Matheran provided an ideal setting for Jimmy and me, two young people who were happy to be together. We competed fiercely, yet shared a love for each other and the animals that we rode on. We covered every inch of the horse-beaten track, spending many hours overlooking the valleys covered with luxuriant green trees. This idyllic haven was ultimately the setting in which we decided that we would spend the rest of our lives together.

As a collegian, Jimmy bought his first horse, Moghul King. This horse won many races for him. After we were married, we began investing in a string of racehorses, hoping to continue the trend of winning many more races. But somehow, it was not to be, for the horses perished on the race track in quite unusual circumstances.

Carnival, a beautifully-bred chestnut, broke his fetlock while jumping out of the starting gate in his very first workout. Twinkle Toes, a classic filly, out for her final gallop before the 1000 Guineas, threw her jockey and dashed headlong into a tree. She fell dead on the spot. Caesar Augustus could not bear the intense heat of the Pune track and collapsed after winning his race. Zorba, a huge bay, fought a stirring duel down the straight, lost by a short-head and fell dead opposite the stands. Each tragic death tugged at our heartstrings, for we really loved our animals.

We were soon blessed with our children, three lovely babies, Neville, Karl and Tina. Besides having a normal childhood and school career, each one of them grew up to be good riders, joining us in our daily morning rides and enjoying all the other activities connected with horses. We all fitted in so comfortably with one another as well as Jimmy's way of life, for horses filled his entire existence. We spent days and nights in the stables, working our horses, feeding, petting and grooming them – but when they all died so tragically, our dream of owning a Derby winner slowly faded into the distance – till our son Karl began to show promise as a champion rider. His name flashed like a meteor across the newspapers. "A Star is Born," they said. We were so sure that our son would make our dream come true – we had such great plans.

Neville and Karl had been very close. They were not just brothers, but companions, friends and competitors. All their lives they had shared one room, which had always been full of noise, chaos and much activity, interspersed with *ayah* Mary's shouts.

And then there was the silence!

Neville had always held an unshakeable belief that Karl's indomitable spirit could never be broken. When Karl was desperately ill and fighting for his life, Neville held onto this conviction and did not allow himself to think that Karl would ever leave us. But he did. It took him a long time to really get over the hard reality of Karl's death. The years passed and just when the pain had somewhat eased, Karl suddenly "returned." Neville's first reaction was shock, but it wasn't long before he got over his reservations. He was always aware of his brother's extraordinary ability to overcome anything. But this reappearance, the way it happened, took his breath away.

When Sabita came on the scene, she was quick to remind Neville of the crush that she had had on Karl. She talked about the many trips to the racecourse, accompanied by her cousins. She remembered her young heart beating rapidly as she watched Karl ride. As all teenagers do, they were carried away by their enthusiasm and would run to the winners enclosure to wave, trying to draw his attention. She never thought, even in her wildest dreams, that she would marry his brother!

On the day of their engagement, we had reserved a table at a restaurant to celebrate with Sabita's family. At this time, Karl had only just begun proving himself, so we never gave it much thought when he declared, *"I will be present – you will see,"* dismissing it as the fervent hope of a boy who loved his brother. A table had been booked for ten, but when we trooped into the restaurant and settled ourselves around our table, we discovered an extra setting and chair. Intrigued, I asked if anyone had changed the reservation for ten people to that of eleven, but no one had! So there we were, with one place suggestively empty throughout the evening. Somehow it was not unusual for us to look at the chair lovingly and Neville knew that his brother had manoeuvred the situation to show him that he too wanted to celebrate the occasion.

Sabita had no reservations in believing in spirit phenomena. Therefore, she accepted Karl's return with a natural enthusiasm and excitement that surprised me. She became enamoured with the pranks of her spirit brother-in-law and soon developed a beautiful relationship with him, taking his side whenever we said he was wrong or when we thought he had misguided us in some way. Since then, he has helped her over many rough patches and she has total faith and belief in his spirit presence. It took a while and many proven episodes for her to totally accept Meher Baba.

Zahan, her baby son, was just about two years old when he began developing bruises all over his little body. At first, we presumed they were the result of the usual knocks and falls of a normal child, but when they became alarmingly frequent and dark in colour, we took him to the doctor. That night, Sabita came home and wept.

The tests that had been carried out showed a sudden drop in the platelet count. The doctor warned that a further drop could prove to be a danger to Zahan's life. Hearing this, names of diseases like haemophilia and leukaemia jumped to mind as, once more, our thoughts flew back in time to a hospital that held the memory of Karl.

I desperately went back to the writing, asking help from Baba, begging of him not to put us through another ordeal. I implored him to continue to be father, friend and guide, and to let us have faith in his love for us. Inspite of many assurances from Karl that we were not to worry, the platelet count kept steadily dropping and frequent visits to the doctor confirmed the diagnosis – Zahan had ITP, a condition involving the platelet count, which is responsible for blood clotting; an accidental fall could lead to an internal haemorrhage.

For the next year, Zahan was watched over carefully. He was not allowed to play any games or take part in any rough activities. But in spite of all our efforts, there was no appreciable change in his condition. I rushed to Meherabad and begged of Baba to do something – anything!

On the day of my return a friend, who was in the habit of exchanging books with me, sent me an old tattered book called "Healing Hands" by Bernard Hutton. Somehow, I could not get rid of the feeling that Karl had found the book for me. I read far into the night. The book was about spirit healing and the cures affected by George Chapman, a medium, guided by the spirit of a Dr. Lang. There was a passage that said, "distances were no barrier to the spirit world." Hoping that this was Baba's way of sending help for Zahan, we decided to write to George Chapman.

A few nights after we had received a positive reply, Sabita awoke for no reason at all. When her eyes became accustomed to the dark, she turned her gaze towards Zahan's little bed. To her amazement, she saw a kaleidoscope of silver and lilac lights around his head. Fascinated, but not trusting her eyes, she moved closer and glanced down into the cot. Zahan's whole face was bathed in a light that resembled an X-ray plate, red and glowing, whilst the coloured lights still flickered around it.

Could this really be someone doing the healing?

The topic of conversation at breakfast the next morning, naturally hinged on Sabita's "night wonders." Karl had warned us of *"ups and downs"* with the platelet count, but kept reassuring us that we were not to worry as *"Dr. Lang"* was looking after Zahan. Secure with this knowledge, we eagerly awaited the results of each blood test, and found that he was getting better and better. The doctor, pleased with his progress, reminded us once again that Zahan must never have a bad fall, for he could bleed internally and we would be none the wiser.

It was Sabita who recalled Karl's warning two days before Zahan was born – that the baby would be a boy and the one thing we would have to be careful about was that *"he should never ever have a bad fall!"*

Karl explained, *"You see, here we understand much more than you can fathom. You see a little around you, we see all around you. This is the difference and we are helping you to see more than you could if we were not there."*

We continued to call on Baba who, in turn, continued with the absent healing, whichever way he chose. Although Zahan still suffered from nosebleeds, he steadily improved. One day, Karl said, *"Now he is well and you need not worry about him."* A visit to the doctor confirmed that Zahan's count had touched normal once more. You can imagine how happy we were.

"Look up, not down," said Karl. *"Always look higher and you will go higher."*

Sabita, I feel, has a kind of intuitive power, and is very sensitive to pick up Karl's thoughts and feelings. In her own way, she has drawn many to Baba and helped them to understand him. She has sat with me many times for the writing and has encouraged me when I was diffident and unsure. Of all my family, she has given me the greatest support.

Neville and Sabita always feel very close to Karl and now the little children, gentle Zahan and their precocious daughter Zara, feel joy and comfort in knowing that their "uncle" is there to sort out all their little problems. They have all made trips to Meherabad and keep Meher Baba in their hearts in their own way.

My daughter Tina had a very different relationship with Karl. Although five years his junior, she loved teasing him and had an uncanny knack of distracting him when he least expected it. Yes, he was a successful jockey, but also her brother. So, she treated him as such. She put the pressure on, especially after he started winning all the big races of the season. This irritated him all the more because he had great expectations of looking every inch the professional and had nursed dreams of waving and acknowledging the cheers of the crowd. But, there was one major drawback – he still wore braces on his teeth!

"Kala daant... kala daant (black teeth), don't smile!" Tina would sing out as he was being led into the winner's enclosure. She would

hang over the railing and wave her arms wildly to attract his attention. Then she would clap her hands over her mouth to indicate that he should keep his closed. Karl would grit his teeth, close his lips and give her a fierce look. Of course, he, in turn, would bide his time till he found something equally rude to say to her. His nature was so affectionate that he would soon forget and run off to see her in school during her lunch break. He would buy her mountains of sweets, which she shared with all her little friends, who would crowd around him. He had become quite a hero by this time and Tina would hug him and feel so very proud. He loved her dearly.

As a child, Tina was delicate and extremely timid. It took her a long time to come to terms with the tragedy of losing Karl. But by the time he "returned" to us, she had grown up into a young girl with quite a will of her own. She resumed her relationship with her brother as if he had not gone away at all.

An important time in Tina's life was fast approaching. She was soon to tie the knot with the love of her life, her cousin Pesi, by now, one of India's leading jockeys. "Please Karl, come to my engagement," she begged.

"I will be there," he replied, *"of course I will be there. I will be the gold thread on your head!"*

All the ladies were dressed to suit the special occasion. There was gold in the sarees, bangles and necklaces, on the wrappings of presents, gold dust on the sweetmeats and gold in the beautiful setting sun, but no gold thread could be found anywhere near her.

I was beginning to get used to Karl's capers, but these were never at the time or in the way we anticipated. So I was always disappointed. Sadly, I watched Tina searching silently for his presence. For two days she pouted, "Mum, he promised to be there, he promised and he did not come." Just then Sabita raced into my room, excitedly holding out the engagement photographs.

There, in full view over Tina's bowed head, lay many gold threads, delicate web-like threads from the beautiful rose garland that Pesi's mother had placed round her neck. They sparkled like tinsel and that was not all. For, between them, was a faint outline of a face. Could it perhaps be Meher Baba's? Tina's eyes swam with happy tears as she clutched at the proof before her. Not only had Karl been present at her engagement, but maybe Meher Baba too!

Tina with gold threads on her head

This became Tina's special little "miracle."

Love, laughter and grateful tears soon dried up, when a few days later, she discovered that her little diamond earrings were missing. Being a particularly meticulous person, she had no idea how she could have misplaced them. She searched high and low, muttering how certain she was that she had put them away carefully in their usual place. They were not very precious in terms of money, but they were in sentiment, for she had worn them every day of her life since I had given them to her on her very first birthday. "Please ask Karl to find them for me," she requested. "He is not here to find things for you, Tina," I admonished. "I think there are more important things for him to do."

My advice fell on deaf ears, for the next morning, Tina descended on Karl and asked him herself. *"Look in your drawer – they are in a piece of cloth in your drawer,"* he replied. We rushed to the drawer and turned it upside down, but with no success. Karl repeated the same message over and over again and this time, we were sure he was wrong.

"He is lying," she screamed, "he is purposely lying, he is supposed to be our guiding spirit and he cannot even find a small pair of earrings. If he is not careful, I'll call him *kala daant* again!" With that she flounced away, furious. I was hoping he did not hear her last remark.

Two months passed and Tina really missed her earrings. "Please Karl," she begged one last time, "find them for me."

"Look in your drawer," came the reply.

Later that morning, I went to a drawer which I open every single day of my life. This drawer also holds Karl's little mementoes, his small favourite red transistor, his watch, jockey licence, mouth organ and finally, a plaster cast of his teeth. I unlocked the drawer to get hold of my house-keeping money, when a small piece of cloth caught my attention. "Hello! Who put this here?" I thought to myself. I opened the drawer a little further and there – staring up at me like two twinkling stars were Tina's diamond earrings! It seemed as if unseen hands had cleared a small place right next to the teeth and placed the earrings neatly, side by side.

There was only one incredible explanation – Karl! It had to be Karl's special way of teasing his sister to get back at her for her crack about his teeth.

"Tina, come quickly," I screamed, and she came dashing into my room. She was ecstatic. "How could they have been placed there?" It was some time later that I learnt of a term called "apportation." It is given to any kind of physical levitation from one place to another by a spirit form. Well, you live and learn.

Flies drop in her soup, lights dim and sparkle in her room. Tina blames Karl for everything, for they have a very special relationship, these two.

Karl was 5'7" and rather tall for a jockey. Although he had slender bones and weighed only 46 kgs, he still had to watch his diet and go easy on his favourite foods – the Goa curry and rice and the *gulab-jamuns*. Tina, who always had a hearty appetite, was the target of his envy, for she ate up what he could not and there was always a major scrap. An incident took place that literally took her appetite away!

It was nine o'clock one Saturday morning, and breakfast time for Tina. Knowing that it was also the time when I normally "talked" to Karl, she walked into the room, plate in hand, and sat down opposite me on my bed. This was always my special place for communicating with Karl. She deposited the plate on my right and looked greedily at the contents – crispy white potatoes sprinkled with fresh coriander and green chilly, topped with a lovely, soft golden egg.

She suddenly had the urge to tease Karl. "Look what I have here. Can you see what I am about to eat – your favourite egg, Karl," she taunted playfully, not realising that he was still capable of losing his volatile temper – and how!

The pen that I had been writing with came to a dead halt. It began jumping on one particular spot on the paper, slow at first, and then faster and faster until it propelled itself to such a speed that my hand took a flying leap from the book – smack into the middle of the plate by my side. Splash went the yellow egg yolk as it flew together with potato slices, coriander and chilly, all over my clean, white bedsheets!

"Oh my God!" shouted Tina, as she fled, leaving her delicious breakfast behind her. I could imagine hearing Karl's victorious cackle of laughter, as out of the room she went without a backward glance. She left me sitting there, book in my lap, and my hand and pen dripping with egg yolk.

Tina prepared to go to Meherabad. She wanted to take her fiancé to Baba. Tickets were purchased and reservations made, but something came up and they had to postpone the visit. She picked up the telephone to speak to a friend but, before she could dial her number, there was a cross-connection and she heard an exchange of voices on the line, "You must come to Ahmednagar," insisted one. "You must come to Ahmednagar... you have to come to Ahmednagar!"

When I opened her bedroom door, I found her sitting there, staring stupidly into space, the telephone receiver dangling from her hand! So they decided to put aside their other commitments and continue, as scheduled, to Meherabad.

It was a lovely monsoon day, the sky was overcast, threatening to open up and pour heavily over the earth below. Tina and Pesi climbed the hill to the *Samadhi*, only to find it absolutely deserted and quiet. As they seated themselves, Tina suddenly felt Karl's presence. "I am sure that he is somewhere near," she confided to Pesi, but could not explain the reason for the urgent feeling. She looked around, but there was no one in sight, except for one of the village locals who sat quietly in a corner on a stone parapet some distance from the *Samadhi*.

Tina and Pesi entered the tomb for *darshan* and then sat quietly, knowing that the few precious moments spent with Baba are worth a lifetime of treasures.

Still, Tina could not shake off the feeling that Karl was close, very close.

As they came out of the *Samadhi*, the lady from the village arose from her seat in the distance as if she had been waiting for them to finish paying their respects to Baba. Drawing her bright yellow *sari* over her head, she started walking slowly towards them. She headed straight for Tina and, putting her cinnamon-skinned arms around her, she said, "Jai Baba." Surprised, Tina looked up and saw the wide beaming smile. She stepped back in a state of shock for, in front of her, gleamed the most gorgeous set of "black teeth" she had ever seen! They shone black as coal in a dark face that was otherwise completely covered by her yellow *sari*. The only other part of her that was visible, were her large eyes, full of mischief and laughter.

A clap of thunder startled them, and a torrential downpour completely drenched the three figures left staring at each other on Meherabad hill.

CHAPTER 14

The Net Widens

Father, mother, brother, sister, in-laws, aunts, uncles, nieces and nephews were all entrapped. It was time for Meher Baba to throw his net into deeper waters and catch another part of the family, with Karl as bait.

My cousin, Arnavaz Dubash, is as dear to me as a sister. I now thought that the time had come to share everything with her and her husband, Jangoo. Both cherished very dear memories of Karl, for our children grew up together as one big family. I expected a strong reaction from Arnavaz, as her father had fanatically opposed any mention of a *sadhu, guru* or *baba*. I expected them to get up and walk away, but to my delight, both patiently heard me out and accepted what I had to say without question.

It was during one of our vacations in London that I sat down to talk to Karl. Arnavaz came and sat near me. *"Hello Arnavaz Aunty,"* said the writing, *"I am so happy to meet you again."* Overwhelmed, she asked if there was really any way in which Karl could prove to her that he was back with us again, and the following incident occurred.

The pen that I was holding stopped in the middle of a word and we were left staring at each other in surprised silence. Suddenly the faint sound of hoofbeats could be heard coming towards us – clip clop, clippety clop. They became faster and more distinct till they rang out loud and clear beneath our window. I sat frozen with the inert pen in my hand. Hardly able to believe what she had heard, Arnavaz ran to the window to see a solitary figure sitting erect on a beautiful horse, riding majestically down the main road in the very heart of London where we lived. The hoofbeats faded into the distance and the sudden buzz of street traffic transported us back from our private thoughts of this wonderful happening.

"Now do you believe me?" asked the writing.

How could we not? A horse, the animal Karl loved best in the world, had been chosen by him as his symbol of proof. It could not be any other way.

Just behind Meher Baba's *Samadhi* is a beautiful banyan tree. It spreads its branches, heavy with plump green leaves, over pure marble slabs that cover the personal effects of Meher Baba's mother and father, Shirinmai and Sheriar Irani; some of the women *mandali* as well as the pet dogs and peacock that belonged to Meher Baba. This peaceful setting became Arnavaz's special place of retreat. Whenever she visits Meherabad, she finds herself drawn to this tree, with its small blossoms and red berries. The gnarled roots offer her a comfortable seat as she rests her head against the broad tree trunk and watches the sun setting behind the hills of Ahmednagar.

She listens with rapture to the melodious strains of Meher Baba's evening *aarti* and looks up at the four symbols on the dome of the *Samadhi* – a temple for Hinduism, a mosque for Islam, a cross for Christianity and the *afurganyu* for Zoroastrianism. All religions are housed in Meher Baba's heart, telling us that all are one to Baba.

Meher Baba's *Samadhi*

Her thoughts fly into the quiet serenity of Baba's *Samadhi* and in her mind's eye she sees the rose-covered shrine. Imprinted in gold letters on the white marble are the words, "I HAVE COME NOT TO TEACH BUT TO AWAKEN." These words are a prelude to Baba's Universal Message that tells you the exact purpose of His recent advent as *Avatar* of the Age.

Arnavaz continues to sit under her tree till the last strains of a guitar, playing one of Baba's favourite songs, Ocean of Love, fade away. The *aarti* is over, the voices are quiet and a hush descends over the hill. Slowly, one by one, all those who have felt their souls stirring with Baba's love, make their way down the hill gradually, and the first star winks and sparkles in the now darkening sky.

For Arnavaz, that star has a very special meaning. She feels it is Meher Baba telling her, "I am there with you," and very soon he will be surrounded by myriads of other little stars, until the whole universe is glowing with their radiance.

She is the last to go down the hill. The shadows fall, the sunflowers close their yellow petals, the little sparrows and mynahs fold their soft brown wings as she slowly walks down the slope, recalling her first trip to Meherabad.

She remembers how she felt when she first met Baba's sister Mani, his faithful Mansari, and all the rest of his *mandali*. She smiles as she recalls the kindness of those who live there and serve Baba; the conversations, the sharing of views and ideas with the many Baba lovers, the early morning hot tea and the cleaning of the Tomb at 6 a.m.

But most of all, she remembers the time, when on her return to Bombay, she made a permanent place for Meher Baba's picture next to those of her beloved mother and father. A great worry had been on her head at this time and she wondered if there was any way in which Meher Baba would be able to help lift this burden from her soul.

One night, the *diya*, placed next to the pictures, had extinguished completely. In total darkness, she tossed and turned and drifted off into a troubled sleep. Suddenly, she was wide awake, for above her head was a circle of light. She stared fascinated, wondering where it had come from. She heard a crackle, and her eyes turned to Meher Baba's picture on the bedside table. It was fully illuminated by the *diya* that had lit itself once again – without fresh oil, without a new wick. It cast a golden halo on the ceiling and around Meher Baba's smiling face.

Arnavaz's son Phiroz was Karl's closest friend, confidante and "partner in crime!" The two of them had been inseparable. They used to fight, wrestle, swim, ride and date girls together. One summer, just after Karl had received his jockey's licence, we had all gone to Ootacamund, a hill station in South India where races are held during Bombay's hot summer months. Ooty, as it is popularly known, nestles in the Nilgiris or the "Blue Mountains," so called because of the abundant growth of the eucalyptus tree with its blue leaves.

Karl had, by then, been retained to ride for the well-known Goculdas family who owned a stable of more than thirty horses. On that day, Karl was scheduled to ride a strikingly beautiful filly, Minivet, in the Kunigal Gold Cup, one of the most prestigious events of the Ooty Racing Season.

"We will be back soon," shouted Karl and Phiroz as they ran out into the early morning mist. We had not missed them till lunch, when we suddenly realised that it was almost time for Karl to leave for the races. Frantic with worry and anger, we went looking for them.

As we approached the boat club, what do you think we saw? Astride local ponies and careening around the pathway, were the two scamps. With legs dangling out of stirrup irons, sticks waving and shirts flapping, they were gleefully chasing a couple of Gujarati ladies out on their morning ride! The poor victims took off in fright, their screams shattering the air. We saw flashes of *saris, salwars* and *chappals*, buns that had loosened and plaits that had opened out into wild streaming hair.

What if Mr. Goculdas had seen that!

Without a smattering of guilt on their flushed faces, the boys continued with the day. Karl went on to win the Gold Cup, while Phiroz looked on with pride from the crowd. They had shared many such memorable days.

Phiroz never thought his friend would leave his side. His heart ached for a long while till the day he heard of Karl's "return." Not knowing what it meant, but excited nevertheless, he lay on his bed that night with his eyes fixed on the doorway, expecting Karl to walk in. At dawn, he fell into a deep sleep.

He dreamt that his childhood companion was wrestling with him as of old – they were tumbling over and over, hugging one another, spitting at one another and racing each other around the world. When he opened his eyes, it was morning and time to sit with me and communicate with Karl for the first time.

"How did you like the fight?" began Karl!

The years have gone by and many questions and answers have passed between Phiroz and Karl. The friend from beyond continues to send messages that demonstrate a rare quality of comradeship. They have a ring of familiarity and a closeness that distances cannot sever. Phiroz will always be his pal, a kindred spirit.

Karl with his cousins at the Gymkhana Races

In turn, Phiroz's devotion to him is extremely touching, and not a day passes without him looking upwards and saying, "Hi, Karl."

Now Phiroz is married to a lovely girl, who, to his delight, is called Meher. Although she had been his childhood sweetheart, there was a brief period when their paths almost went separate ways. It was a bleak time for Phiroz, a time when he missed the physical closeness and support of his best friend – a time when even mothers cannot help. He found it very hard to accept the fact that he might have to spend the rest of his life without Meher. He spoke to Karl many times, asking for his guidance and suddenly, one day, the sun broke through. Phiroz found himself riding the waves with happiness. The separation was only to show them how much they really needed one another. Though Meher had grown up amidst a family who loved Baba, she was never really drawn to Baba till she got to hear of Karl's story and felt the love and compassion of a truly great Master. Now, in her own time, she has become an ardent and sincere lover of Baba.

When they were expecting their first child, a worried Phiroz would "talk" to his friend frequently, and say, "Karl please look after my baby." All went well for seven months till a day in August when Karl said, *"This baby is having difficulty in finding its feet for takeoff. This is the baby's problem and you will not understand it."* Difficulty in takeoff! We laughed. "Karl, this is a baby, not a rocket," we admonished.

One October morning, Meher was driven to the hospital for the delivery only to discover that there was a small problem. The baby was a breech case, and the doctors had to do a Caesarean section. Little Janine was born with a foot that had locked itself behind her head. There was no real emergency but it was obvious that the little baby had *"difficulty in takeoff."*

Why hadn't we given more thought to what Karl had told us?

CHAPTER 15

Nicol

Meher Baba decided that now that my family was convinced, it was time to include the rest of the world. I begged of Karl to keep our communication private. I was terrified of public opinion. "*No,*" was the reply, "*Meher Baba says you should not be afraid, you must love all people on earth, be of good cheer and help all those that need you. He says, tell people more about Me, and more, and still more, so that they might find their burdens lighter and their lives brighter.*"

This was the most important message that had come through to date. I was beginning to see that Karl had come back for the purpose of having Meher Baba shine light on darkness and despair, and to help people carry on with their lives. He was there to help the bereaved and the downtrodden, the sad and the lonely, and to give hope and compassion to those that could not face the thought of tomorrow.

"*Baba hopes you can try to enjoy life, for tomorrow is not far away and yesterday is gone.*" says Karl. "*Those who cannot help themselves have to be helped. Happy will be the man who will do all he can for people who have no one to make happiness for them. Remember that.*"

It was August 26, 1987. Arnavaz called that morning. A friend of hers, Amie Rabadi, had recently lost her little girl, Nicol, who was eleven years old. She had had an unexplained fever and after much suffering, the little girl passed into spirit and took Amie's broken heart with her. Arnavaz suggested that I talk to her about Karl and that perhaps Baba would find a way to help her.

I panicked! How easy it was to receive Baba's beautiful messages. But to take others into confidence? That was a different story! I was filled with trepidation.

I began to recognise what a brave lady Mrs. Bhavnagri must be. What confidence she must have in her own children to publish her article in the papers – to face the criticism and sometimes hurtful remarks from people who may not understand how beautiful it was for children to want to "return" to their parents with love.

I agreed to give it some thought.

Karl had been a public figure, the darling of the racing world. In his short span of riding, he had achieved more than any other jockey in the history of racing. His tragic accident had moved so many to prayers and eventually to tears. What if his story were misunderstood? What if some paper published it without knowing its beauty, what if this stranger did not respect my privacy, what if... what if..?

The doorbell rang.

On the landing stood a lady. She was dressed in black trousers and a crisp, white shirt. She had a swarthy complexion, lovely black curling hair, red-rimmed glasses but, such sad eyes!

"May I come in?," she asked softly. "My name is Amie."

Many questions and doubts raced through my mind. What could I tell this lonely lady? Quick to sense my discomfort about a subject that is not ordinary everyday conversation, she initiated the discussion by telling me not to worry and promising to keep my confidence. There was something about her... a directness and a poignant grief perhaps? But whatever it was, it prompted me to go ahead with my story.

"Dear Meher Baba, please help me," I implored.

I started off hesitantly, but eventually found myself sharing the initial turmoil that I had experienced and how it had changed to feelings of peace after Meher Baba entered my life. She listened quietly and never once questioned anything, but it was her tears that told me everything I needed to know. It was as if Meher Baba had called her and she had answered his call. He wanted her and she had come! I sent her away promising that I would speak to Karl. Hadn't I been in her position too?

The next morning Karl was exultant!

"I am Karl Umrigar, I am with Meher Baba," he said, *"and I will do whatever I am going to do with great care. We are mother and son and we have a very strong bond, Mum, – you and I. Call me whenever you wish,*

call whoever wishes to come. You must not be afraid or send them to anybody else. Have faith – we are there to help you. You must go ahead. Nicol will have the best care as Baba is a wonderful friend and teacher. She will learn everything from Him about life in this world of ours. We are so happy here. Tell her Mum, she is safe now. Meher Baba is looking after her. She will be explained that there are ways of life, and people come and go according to a pattern. They must fulfil whatever they have to."

Amie returned the next day and we talked our way into the afternoon. She expressed an easy willingness to communicate if Nicol so wished. She promised to visit Meherabad, hoping in her heart, to experience a "visitation" from Nicol. Though she had no knowledge of spirit matters, she found Karl's representation and foreknowledge of actual happenings very beautiful and natural.

On October 31, a small group of seven accompanied Amie on her first trip to Meherabad. Karl said, *"Bells will ring when you come and when you go, and you can be sure it is all of us around you. I will be a white bird with lovely big scaly wings and a head as small as a dove's."*

I worried about the pain so evident in Amie's heart, and prayed that Baba would bring back the light to her eyes. Just as we checked into the Pilgrim Centre and deposited our bags in the ladies' dorm, the door flew open and a little girl came charging in and jumped onto Amie's bed. We could not help but notice that she was a child suffering from Down's syndrome, about the same age as Nicol, with the same smiling face and dimpled cheeks. She gazed at all of us curiously until her eyes fell on a pendant, a *farohar*, hanging around my neck on a small gold chain.

"What is that?" she asked politely, holding the *farohar* in her little hands. "It is a bird," I replied without consciously knowing what I had said. Suddenly it dawned on me – was this the *"bird with the big scaly wings and the small head like a dove's?"* It fitted the description so perfectly. Was this what my son had been trying to convey to me? However, I wasn't to find out till a few months later.

In the meantime, Frenietta, the little girl, in all her innocence, attached herself to Amie and spoke incessantly to her. I felt strongly that this was Baba's way of comforting the mother through a little stranger's instant love. It was Baba's way of stretching out his arms to gather Amie to him.

Being intent on solving the puzzle of the bird, we were late for the *aarti* that evening. We dashed around – someone forgot their shoes, someone a torch, someone a scarf and so on. "Hurry," I called, "or we shall miss the prayers." By the time I led them all out of the Pilgrim Centre, we were almost running, only to come to a dead halt beneath a huge tree. We heard the loud clanging of a bell high above our heads. Time and the world stood still as we reflected on Baba's welcome. *"Bells will ring,"* Karl had said, *"and you will know we are there."*

The next morning, with much lighter hearts we made our way to Meherazad, Baba's home. We spent many hours speaking to Meher Baba's *mandali* and then waited for Mehera to make her appearance on the porch. We were lost in the capable hands of Divana and Kaycee, two lovely ladies who live there and have dedicated their lives to Baba. They took us into Baba's room, where, in subdued tones, they pointed out pictures and portraits of Meher Baba and plaster casts of His feet and sensitive hands.

A gentle breeze wafted in through the window as we sat and listened attentively to the story of Meher Baba's hair. On a dresser in Baba's room, pressed between two plexiglass sheets, lay His hair, which Mehera had lovingly collected from combings over the years. After Baba had dropped His body, Mehera sent His hair to America for preservation. The story goes that one day, when the *mandali* were feeling particularly low and missed Baba very much, Mehera's eyes fell by chance on the plexiglass sheets. She found, nestling amidst the strands, a face that peered back at her. It was as if God had sculpted Baba's face out of the hair, especially to comfort Mehera and all his beloved disciples. Eyes, nose, mouth and flowing hair, the face still remains there for all to see.

We then sat among the devotees, marvelling at the love that they had for him, till it was time to go home. I lingered with my goodbyes, and as I turned away to join the others, Phiroz came running up to drag me excitedly to the little passageway leading out from Baba's garden. "Nanny Aunty, listen, just listen," he cried. There, suspended from a beam, swaying melodiously in the wind which seemed to have sprung up from nowhere, were little Chinese bells. The wind-chimers tinkled furiously, dancing and swaying above our upturned faces. It was Baba's way of saying, "Goodbye and I am glad you came."

Amie's best friend and closest companion, Neville, also came along for his first Meherabad experience. The following is what he has to say:

"Meher Baba is a name that I vividly remember being argued about by my grandfather, father and uncles, when I was eight or nine years old. Angry voices told me that He was not a favourite topic of conversation, but little did I know that the Godman that they so vehemently discussed, was none other than the *Avatar* Himself, whose reputation of always being surrounded by women devotees upset my grandfather greatly.

"My family believe strongly in religion, but my uncle also believes in the Masters, Upasni Maharaj and Sai Baba of Shirdi. Photographs adorn the walls of our home, and books of the saints, spirituality, the paranormal and life after death line many shelves in our home. Though I have read many books and know of the experience of spirit contacts, I myself never showed a keen interest in the subject till Nicol passed away and the story of Karl was slowly unfolded to me.

"When Nan took us on our first visit to Meherabad, its ambience, together with that of Baba's home, Meherazad, the simple stories told by the *mandali,* and the experience of Frenietta all told me intuitively, in a flash, all that I needed to know. 'This is it', I said, 'after many years, my search is over'! Little did I realise that I was making an inner contact with the Master of all Masters, Meher Baba.

"Frenietta gladdened my heart by playing with me in a way that Nicol used to, for Nicol and I had shared a few games of our own that we both enjoyed. Frenietta had raced into my dorm and had refused to leave in spite of the entreaties from her Mum who was not allowed to enter my room, one of the strict rules of the *ashram*. With a little persuasion from me, Frenietta climbed piggy-back and I delivered her into the anxious arms of her mother. This incident, and others, brought back the memory of Nicol for me.

"Though I have a long way to travel, I discovered a direction with Meher Baba whose loving hand I hold in mine – for I know that only He knows the way. Outward thoughts are no longer important to me, inner ones and the love I have for Meher Baba are the only thoughts that matter.

"And so they will, forever be."

On January 29, 1989, a day when Amie felt particularly unhappy, Meher Baba sent her this message through Karl:

"Meher Baba says you must forgive everyone and do work that will make you think highly of yourself as someone left in this world. You must work out your own salvation, by thinking you are someone chosen by Baba to help others go through life with a smile. That is what Baba wants you to do. Others must be made happy and you are the one to make them so. So you have to read, study, find out everything about Baba, so that when you speak to others that know nothing, you have all your facts straight from Baba. Baba has asked you to love and teach all those that come to you. BOOKS ARE PAPER LETTERS, BABA PREFERS HUMAN LETTERS, the difference is so great. So work will stop if you cannot think with laughter. Tears do not wash away your sad thoughts and these will only go when Baba takes over. So laugh sometimes, heartily and loudly – we love that, and do not feel lowly for you are a star for us and you have to shine, not just shine but sparkle, and that has to be done by polishing all your points and then leave the silver lining to Baba."

Amie followed Baba's instructions as faithfully as she could and this is what she had to say about herself and her experience with Meher Baba:

"Everyone watched closely whilst I pretended to be calm; some believed I was strong, others that the flood-gates were still to open, but none knew of the inner despair, the inner coldness that was based on no calculation at all – an experience of detachment from reality. Nicol had shut the door – she had defied the doctors, she was no more.

"Alone and guilty, I relived every moment of the preceding year, avoiding eyes that accused me of not being clever enough to have saved my child or being stupid enough to have made the arrogant mistake of losing her. I had trusted myself, I used to be in control, or so I had thought.

"Was I someone who believed in God? Yes! But did I think He would intervene to help? NO! I would argue this with a conviction and the backing of my ego which told me I was the only one capable of creating the reality around my life. I was responsible for the decisions and choices that I had to make, and when there were mistakes I looked at them as lessons to be learnt, sometimes not even learning from them. God did not play an active role in my life – I was my own master. Till Nicol.

"Death defies logic and death destroys illusions. I was left with nowhere to go and nothing to hold on to. I felt worthless as a human

Nicol

being. Nothing seemed to matter till the day I met Nanny and was introduced to the world of Karl and Nicol. All Karl said was that she was in the hands of a beautiful, kind and loving man and I was touched – I wanted to know more. Karl's story was like a dream, his Master's home was a place that spelt love and safety – it felt right, it felt real. Mine was a world that should not exist! I needed to escape – I had no doubts.

"Before long, I was communicating and learning about a Being called Meher Baba, the likes of whom I had neither heard of nor experienced before. The words were Nicol's, but the energy Baba's, for only He could direct me to read and study and be with every living situation I was in. He said one day, that I would learn to love Him and I rolled over the carpet with laughter, throwing a challenge at Him saying, 'that will be the day'! But it was not long before I learnt to trust Him, learnt new words and new terms and began to understand that He was no ordinary human being, He was beyond that and much much more.

"Doubts came up for me from time to time, for there was a difference in the communication – I was denied the personal help with problems and matters concerning day to day living. Nicol strictly adhered to Baba's rule of teaching me and guiding me with the reading I had to do, always reassuring me of Baba's continued love that would never leave me, she said. Bit by bit I surrendered to Baba, and was made to see the futility of living with the pain of the past and its guilt. In the beginning, I did not realise I was truly a seeker, but as time went by, I learnt more of Baba's spiritual truths and once convinced, there was no turning back.

"The next step was to begin cleaning up a life that was a mess. This required inner trust and inner faith I was not sure I had, but once the decision was made, it was up to Baba to pave the way. I sat back, terrified that everything would fail and that I was escaping deeper into a delusional experience. But Karl convinced me beyond the shadow of a doubt. In Meherabad, he gave me the most beautiful message and representation of Nicol that I have ever had.

'Nicol will be in gold all the time but in the gold will be black and blue lines and she will be the helper of the poor. You must look inside of her for signs that will make you feel – Nicol, yes she is here. She will be in sober colours. She will be the gold of love in everything and this will be prominent throughout your stay'.

"I remember the time vividly. There was no 'appearance' of Nicol till the last day, the morning after a particularly joyful and raucous evening in the dining room. My dearest friend, Freny Peddar, and I were standing for *darshan*, least aware of a lone figure who had made her way towards us. I was the last in line and sensing a presence, I turned and there stood a foreigner, a lady with a blue *sari* that had black vertical lines! Startled, I turned back to Freny and clutched her hands, beseeching her with my eyes to look behind me. She did, and responded with a wide and happy grin – Nicol had 'arrived'.

"Needless to say, the *aarti* was beautiful, but as we walked down the hill we tried to figure out the next step – how was I going to approach her with what I needed to know? The opportunity presented itself after breakfast. I went up to her, introduced myself, hummed and hawed, but got through to asking her about her work involvement. Tripura had this lovely translucent skin and clear eyes that gazed quizzically at me as she said that she would tell me, provided I told her what was behind my curiosity. With no choice in the matter, I told her a little of Karl and Nicol and inwardly prayed for belief and understanding.

"In spite of hearing an abbreviated story, Tripura's expression displayed a wealth of compassion and her tears convinced me of her open mind. She finally got around to telling me that she and her husband were returning to America to look for jobs as both were currently unemployed. She smiled apologetically as she saw disappointment writ all over my face and just as an afterthought she said, 'We are also on our way to the north, a place near Hardwar, where we will be attached to an orphanage, teaching the children for two months'. She gasped and we both realised the significance of what she had innocently said. She was talking of being *the helper of the poor*.

"Without any reservation, she clasped me in her arms and we both cried unashamedly, smiling at the same time. I felt her bones through a body that was as thin as Nicol's and looked over her softly-lined face that spoke of a maturity and sensitivity of a person who seemed to know much. I gazed at her and suddenly realised that of all the foreigners in the dining hall the night before, she was the one who had unobtrusively joined in on the fun and game of "Up Jenkins." She had been in my team that won!

"That afternoon, I was preparing to leave Meherabad and as I placed my bag in the taxi, I felt strong hands over my eyes. Startled, I turned around to look into the mischievous face of Tripura who lovingly gathered me to her. Looking into her eyes, I saw a million more things than goodbye.

"Now, my life has become centred around Meher Baba. With respect to all the beliefs in the world today, none of the scriptures provided me with an insight into the Truth as Baba did – through His books, and "teachings" that came in every day. With each life experience, I was taught by Nicol the meaning of 'surrender' and after a long struggle, I discovered that it was easy to let go of time, completely and absolutely, so much so, that no matter what the experience, good or bad, I am drawn closer and closer to Baba. I found that though my intellect and logical mind is used to play an important role in delving into the Truth about life, it is my heart that has been captured instead. This was the only thing that mattered to Him, and now to me.

"I happily concede that Meher Baba has won His bet!"

My prayer for Amie was answered, for after many visits to Meherabad, I now see a different person. She has conquered her sad thoughts by giving them all up to Baba. She has become well versed with Baba's teachings and has now become my source of confidence. Whenever I have a problem in trying to figure out Baba's ways, I turn to Amie. Whenever I need to discuss how to help someone, there is always Amie. It is as if Meher Baba had brought her in to help me along in every way, and I look back at the time when I almost turned her away.

According to Karl's messages, Nicol seems to have retained her impudent nature and her *"bouncing curls,"* and although she defies Baba sometimes, she has been inspired by him into generally obeying him and loving him greatly. She has the single-mindedness of her mother who has linked inwards in total and absolute devotion for Meher Baba.

CHAPTER 16

Pilloo

It wasn't long after Amie had begun communicating that a fascinating turn of events took place. Being fiercely straightforward and headstrong by nature, Amie had, in the past, been quite intolerant towards some members of her family, and had alienated herself from almost all of them. She had a cousin, Pilloo Ghasvala, who unfortunately found herself at the receiving end of Amie's cool indifference and ire. This, of course, had gone on for many years.

I had known Pilloo in my school days and always remembered her as a lovely girl. But she was the target of much envy, for she led a charmed life, almost like a princess, with a beautiful home, many friends and a kind and loving mother. She married early, but her husband passed away in 1965, leaving her to care for two small daughters, Laila and Anita. After a while, life settled into a comfortable routine of whirling parties, champagne and glitter, card sessions and holidays abroad, for money was never a problem.

There suddenly came a time in Pilloo's life, when her luck changed. Both her daughters were faced with marital problems. Her beautiful home was filled with tears and gloom, and her frustration increased over the fact that there was nothing she could do to make things better for her children. She was uncomfortable about facing her own set of socialite friends, who wasted no time in letting her know what they truly thought. Desperately, she shared her helplessness with Temi Randeria, Amie's mother, who had been living with Pilloo for many years and was a dear companion to the family. It naturally turned out that a suggestion was made to ask for Amie's help through the channelling with Nicol. In spite of her reservations about Amie, Pilloo decided to take the chance.

When Amie heard of the appeal, her immediate reaction was

to shy away so as to not disturb the truce. However, she thought of Baba and his messages to all of us. Was it really her place to decide who should receive his love and help? She didn't think so. So, she called me.

Frankly, knowing how ladies can gossip, I was terrified. As we mulled over what should be done, I had distinct visions of all my beautiful experiences being torn to shreds and tossed around between the aces and queens and jokers of the card players! It was the last thing that I wanted.

Finally, I turned to Karl, and as if he was punishing me for my thoughts, he said, *"Tell her everything."* I could not believe it.

"Everything?" I queried. "How will I do that, Karl?"

"Just take Meher Baba with you," he said.

I was scared, really and truly scared! I went to Pilloo's house and we sat over coffee, biscuits and paper-thin sandwiches. After the initial niceties, I made a conscious effort to compose myself and began to tell her Karl's story. My voice finally levelled off from a whisper and my hands stopped shaking as I recalled Karl's words – *"Take Baba with you."* Soon, I came to the part where Maklane Carlson had to be mentioned and that, together with Karl's appearance at the *Samadhi* in a *"red shirt, brown pants and no shoes on my feet,"* had Pilloo dissolve into tears. She cried unashamedly at the wonder of Karl's efforts at renewing his contact with his parents and family.

"However did you leave him there and come away to Bombay?" she sobbed.

"I left him there with Baba," I answered.

Pilloo's attitude towards life changed rapidly as did her affection for Amie, and both were more startled by the sudden change in themselves. I thought I'd wait a while for her new-found enthusiasm to abate, but she proved me wrong. She flew through her problems with flying colours, and the bitterness quickly disappeared with Baba's love and support. She voiced a desperate need to serve Baba and promised to try hard to do everything that was right. She continued to go to parties and play cards, but these activities were no longer a priority. She had found Baba.

She shared her new-found happiness with her children, grandchild and friends, and fervently recited Baba prayers every morning and evening, sang the same songs and started attending *satsangs* or spiritual discourses. She did her level best to be conscious of the way Baba would have wanted her to live and tried to follow Baba's advice as to how to love God:

> "To love God in the most practical way is to love our fellow beings;
>
> If we feel for others in the same way as we feel for our own dear ones;
>
> if instead of seeing faults in others, we look within ourselves;
>
> if instead of robbing others to help ourselves, we rob ourselves to help others;
>
> if we suffer in the suffering of others and feel happy in the happiness of others;
>
> if instead of worrying over our own misfortunes, we think of ourselves more fortunate than many, many others;
>
> if we endure our lot with patience and contentment, accepting it as His will;
>
> if we understand and feel that the greatest act of devotion and worship to God is not to hurt or harm any of His beings, we are loving God.
>
> To love God as he ought to be loved, we must live for God and die for God, knowing that the goal of life is to love God and find Him as our own self."

In the middle of 1989, Pilloo made a surprising declaration to Temi. She said that her life was completely in Baba's hands and that she had no doubts or fears as to its direction. Very shortly thereafter, she suddenly passed away, and joined Karl and Nicol to be with her beloved Meher Baba.

I hark back to the time that I was told of Pilloo's need to talk to Karl – how could I have been afraid to tell her?

Pilloo's story did not end here, for Meher Baba seemed to make it a point to collect families around Him and let His compassionate love reach out to more than just one.

Pilloo's daughter, Anita, initially found it inspiring to know that her beautiful, butterfly mother, had fallen for the charms of a spiritual Master. When Pilloo passed away, I worried. I expected Anita to react with resentment towards this person – this Master who had promised so much. I would have thought that Anita would question why he had not been able to take care of and protect her mother, whom she loved so dearly and depended on so greatly.

Maybe you should listen to what Anita has to say.

"I thank Meher Baba for coming into Mummy's life at the right time. Just before she died, she was always reminding us of the fact that her life was in Baba's hands. Mum talked about her deep feelings for Baba and the remarkable manner in which He had captured her heart. I have accepted that it was her time to die and that there is no better place for her to be, than with Meher Baba.

"Karl is a guiding light, always keeping me in touch with Mum. Thanks to him, I know where she is and what she is doing. I feel her closeness and ask for her blessings every day and ask her to look after me and mine, the way she always did.

"Although I had heard of Meher Baba before, I found the wonderful stories about Karl and his connection with Meher Baba absolutely fascinating. I sat and listened to Nanny Aunty, and was like a sponge, absorbing it all without a blink. The fact that little Nicol was with Baba and that He was looking after her, was really something that hit home.

"I was going through a very difficult time in my life and though I was putting on a very brave front, I didn't really know how to deal with it. One day, without prior intimation, Amie dropped in. I took her hand and I found myself pouring out my heart to her.

"From then on, I never looked back. We went to Meherabad and it was an experience I will never forget. Everything Karl said came to pass – it was like a dream. I instinctively knew that life would be different after Baba had touched it. I know now that I am never alone, even in my darkest days, through ill health or sorrow, Baba is always there, and it makes life so much more beautiful."

* * *

Baba was soon to reach out to Amie's mother, Temi, who was totally stunned by Pilloo's untimely death. Her sadness was writ all over her face as she bade farewell to her friend.

Temi had first been drawn to Shirdi Sai Baba and as a measure of her faith in him, she always wore a Sai Baba ring on her finger. Because of her closeness with Amie, Nicol and Pilloo, she found herself wending her way to Meherabad – but a feeling of guilt persisted and she would not allow herself to sufficiently feel Baba's loving arms around her. Was she being unfaithful to Sai Baba by accepting Meher Baba?

The answer soon came to Temi, when on her return to Bombay, she discovered that she had left her Sai Baba ring at the Pilgrim Centre in Meherabad. She was very disturbed by her carelessness, till Amie gently reminded her that it was perhaps Sai Baba's way of telling her that it was time to make Meher Baba hers.

There are many facets to a diamond and they can all shine together – it does not mean being unfaithful in your love and devotion. It just means that it is time to move on. It means acknowledging that all Masters lie in the One and all point in one direction only – towards God.

CHAPTER 17

Africa

Africa was a land that had always held a strange fascination for me, more so, because the word Africa conjured up a frightening picture of dark jungles. I was terrified of wild animals.

As a child and sometimes even now, I used to dream of lions and tigers stalking me in the dead of night and carrying away my family. I would wake up screaming, in a cold sweat. Even the loud snoring of my old *ayah* in the still of the night, would sound like lions roaring.

My father was a *shikari* and loved the call of the wild. My sisters and I would listen avidly to the stories of his encounters with wild animals, especially lions and tigers. He took us to every film about Africa – "Hatari," "Watusi," "The Wild and the Free" and "Born Free." We saw "King Solomon's Mines" almost twenty times! He wanted us to love the hunt as much as he did, but I had mixed feelings. I was drawn to it but at the same time, very afraid.

I remembered all his stories as we took off on a holiday to the wilds of Africa. My husband Jimmy, Arnavaz and her husband Jangoo said a silent prayer, but I, on the other hand, had Baba's picture tucked firmly away in my luggage.

We landed at Nairobi and spent two enjoyable days in the shops and superb restaurants, dancing to the rhythmic beat of the bongo and tasting all the delicacies of the fascinating cuisine. Soon, it was time to embark on our safari. A combi with an adjustable top transported us to the Tree Tops, a beautiful hotel located atop the trees, overlooking a water-hole which attracts buffalo, deer, leopard and the prize beast of them all – the African rhino. It was a gorgeous sight! The next morning, we drove miles to William Holden's Hunting Lodge with its exquisite gardens filled with myriads of vividly coloured flowers and wild pink cactii.

At about four o'clock in the evening, we set out with ten other lodge cars on a safari looking for lions. There is safety in numbers, I thought to myself, as we headed from a place called KeeKoroc that had just received unprecedented rain. Suddenly, for no apparent reason, our driver veered off the beaten track, away from the others, and we found ourselves alone in lion-infested country.

My heart lurched as the combi took a dip and slithered to a stop at an alarming angle. "What's happened?" I cried in panic. The driver, realising that the wheels were caught in the thick slushy mud, suggested we get down and push. How on earth were we supposed to move this huge wagon? Jimmy suffered from kidney problems and Jangoo was a small man with a weak back. Arnavaz, of course, had a keen mind but not much muscle and last of all, yours truly – I was terrified of being eaten alive!

The driver turned to look at the sole occupant of the car and raised his eyebrows in question. "No way," said I, as I covered my ears and crawled under the seats, whilst the others gamely put their shoulders to the car and tried their best to push. It did not budge an inch! We were well and truly stuck – stuck in the mud!

Four o'clock became five o'clock and then six o'clock. We sat huddled together hoping that someone would come to help.

"Don't you have a walky-talky, don't you have a radio that you can use to send out a SOS?" I pleaded in desperation. The driver shook his head. "We have to wait," he declared.

Slowly the sunset red of the skies changed to purple and then to black. Small grunts and groans could be heard amidst the tall grass. I closed my eyes to shut out the visions that crowded my hallucinating mind – visions of stampeding tuskers pounding our combi, of the fierce rhino whose horn would surely rip us open, of buffalo crushing us with their iron hooves and, finally, the lion entering the car and crunching our bones!

"Meher Baba," I cried, "where are you?"

The clock pointed to seven. "We are finished," I thought, for now there was really no way out of here. We were five stranded beings with no help for miles around. My nightmare had finally become a reality! Arnavaz, now truly rattled, turned to me and urged me to pray to Baba. I closed my eyes and clenched my hands together in prayer and reached out with all my might, begging him to lend a helping hand, to get us out of this wilderness.

A minute passed. "Aha," said the driver, "What's that?" My eyes flew open. It must be a lion I thought, the end had come.

A small glow of light appeared in the distance. The driver responded by feverishly flashing the combi's headlights. The glow became brighter as another light became visible and then another and yet another and soon, to our tremendous relief, the glorious headlights of eight combis focused on us. They came from all different directions like beacons from heaven to help us and lift us out of our hell.

All the drivers jumped down, and amidst happy shouts, the passengers joined them to put their shoulders to the wheel and heaved us out of the bog. Hands clapped and voices cheered us as if to say, *"Meher Baba ki Jai,"* and we were free!

It was almost 8 p.m. Tired, but happy, we got into our cars, started our engines and began to cruise back silently. The cavalcade must have moved about 100 metres or so, when the lead combi suddenly came to a halt. There, before our incredulous eyes, stretched out across a flat rock, lay thirteen lionesses, their beautiful amber eyes glinting in the darkness. We sat in awed silence, staring at the proud cats who seemed not to be disturbed by the curious eyes of another species. Some gazed back at us whilst others continued to lick their sleeping young cubs, their soft paws shielding the deadly claws that could have been the end of our lives if it hadn't been for Meher Baba.

It took us a few days to recover from this experience and pluck up enough courage to agree to a balloon safari! We left our tents in the Governor's Camp at half past five one morning, circumvented a large herd of buffalo and reached the balloon point at daybreak. Africa was extremely beautiful at this hour of the morning.

This time, it was Arnavaz's turn to be nervous. She hated the thought of being pulled up into the skies by ropes and a balloon. "Please ask Meher Baba and Karl to be with us," she begged. The huge basket, connected to a deflated balloon, stood before us. As eight of us clambered into the "Masai Rainbow," I wondered if we would complete the flight safely or find ourselves descending among a herd of tuskers or drowning in a hippo pool.

The pilot began walking towards us and he smiled. "Looks dependable enough," I thought to myself, scrutinising his handsome features. "Baba bring us back safely," I continued in prayer. I closed my eyes for a quick connection with Karl, only to open them to stare directly at the blue and gold letters of the name plate on the young man's chest – KARLSTROM!

We flew over the jungle as if Baba had given us wings – we were fledglings who knew not the perils of the earth or skies. Far down below us rumbled herds of elephant, buffalo, and wild beasts. We soared over the wide mouths of hippopotami languishing in their still pools, and delighted in the frolic of gazelles as they romped and played beneath the early morning rays of the sun. Birds began to stir as they stretched their gorgeous plumes to take off at will over the thick green carpet of trees. For the first time, I envied their freedom as I looked through their eyes at the vast expanse of beauty around me and felt the freshness of the cool air against my cheeks. Except for the soft whoosh of the wind, nothing could be heard – the silence touched my soul.

I turned to look at Karlstrom and gave myself upto his gentle loving care. For the earth and the skies belong to Baba and I was just a trusting passenger, along for the ride.

CHAPTER 18

Stanstead Hall

Karl had worked hard to quell the many doubts in my mind, but I still worried a great deal and constantly tried ways and means to justify my experience. There were many who reminded me of the pitfalls of such a preoccupation, and some who disdainfully said that I was clutching at straws and using the communication to fill the void in my life. I wondered again and again whether I was just imagining all this. I would withdraw, puzzled and confused, despite reassurances from the small, loyal group around me. Amie struggled to keep afloat, relying on Karl's messages, for she too had embarked on a journey totally alien to her.

Still chasing shadows, in June of 1988, I had asked Amie to join me in London where I was preparing to further investigate what the western world had to offer. I had no idea what we were going to find, but I was hoping for some advice that would strengthen the way we were communicating. So far, our experiences had been limited to each other, the Bhavnagris, the Kapadias and Mrs. Rishi. As such, we were not sure where we fitted in, if at all.

We could not have been guided to a better person than Ivy Northage, whose acquaintance I had made before. She is a renowned teaching trance-medium, of fifty years standing, who can also "see" and "hear." That evening, she sat and listened carefully to all the developments that had taken place since I had last met her, and then enthralled us with the many supportive things she had to say. She gave us an endorsement that I have recorded, but for the sake of brevity, I have only included a portion here.

"Your experiences are most remarkable" she said. "I have never heard of anything like this before. I wouldn't change what you are doing, you are so beautifully controlled and you have had the most remarkable results. You don't know how fortunate you are – it's almost miraculous. It's beautiful, dear, and if you want to know if it is a genuine channel of communication, the answer is a positive yes. I have never heard anything so beautiful and so absolutely convincing. You are wonderfully blessed. Karl is definitely there and he is part of a community that is very powerful. It has got a lovely purity – it's beautiful.

"You've got something unique, you really have, so treasure it! It's got a kind of glory. It's like opening the lovely gates of light and power. His aura and yours are blended and of course Meher Baba is there Himself. The emanation that comes from you is quite exquisite. It's like someone with lovely jewels and they do not know what they are worth. It's amazing, unique and absolutely remarkable."

With our heads floating in the clouds, Amie and I prepared to leave the lovely lady. At the door, we mentioned our plans to visit the Arthur Findlay College of Metaphysics at Stanstead Hall. "No dear, I would not if I were you. I think that you would be wise to discontinue your search, for some would not fully understand," she said with raised brows. "It is difficult to understand the natural guidance of a spiritual Master such as Meher Baba." Suddenly closing her eyes, she concluded, "No, no, Nicol and Karl seem to think you may not even stay the full week."

Of course we were not prepared to listen, for we were too excited about our impending visit. We had to live and learn.

The Arthur Findlay College, to which we finally made our way, was recommended to me by the world famous psychic artist, Coral Polge. It is a lovely old manor house called Stanstead Hall in Mountfitchet, Essex, about an hour's drive from London. It is a college that dates back to 1096 A.D. and was founded by J. Arthur Findlay, MBE, JP, to advance the study of psychic science. It is administered by the Spiritualistic National Union as a residential centre where students can study spiritualistic philosophy, psychic unfoldment and kindred disciplines. People from all over the world come to visit.

As our car drove into the spacious and breathtakingly beautiful gardens, we were faced with an imposing mansion. After registering, we walked through the portals into a high-ceilinged hallway with a lovely polished and carpeted wooden stairway leading up to well appointed bedrooms. Amie and I were to share one of these for seven days. We quickly unpacked, checked on our scheduled lectures and meal timings, and walked down to explore some more.

We strolled into a majestic lounge which housed a grand piano whose melodious notes must have enlivened several musical soirees in the years gone by. Ladies in billowing gowns must have waltzed gracefully to the music of Johann Strauss and many a gavotte must have been danced between the pastel and gold walls of this elegant room. Wooden fire places once warmed old carved furniture, and portraits of the Findlay family looked down sedately from their gilt-edged frames. Chandeliers glittered over our heads, lighting up the blues and purples of the old carpets beneath our feet. We stood totally in awe, drinking in the charming old-world ambience.

What I loved most were the beautiful gardens that stretched up to a distant lake dotted with ducks and graceful swans. Fat English cows stood lazily chewing the cud and white rabbits gambolled between huge old trees with hanging roots. The hedges were overgrown with sweet smelling wood roses, whilst bluebells clustered below, looking like pieces of fallen sky. Rain drops glistened on rose petals and butterflies flitted around. A stately chapel looked out over the lawns, and as the evening drew to a close, we made our way to the service where the organ peeled out and our voices joined the choir in thanksgiving.

The next morning, we drew our minds away from all this beauty and settled down to our lectures, the most inspiring of which was by Gordon Higginson, MSNU, also the Principal of the College.

Mr. Higginson was one of the most powerful mediums of present times, a spiritualist and teacher par excellence. It was enthralling to listen to him. I was amazed at the skill with which he reeled off messages from the departed. To give further proof of survival, he added addresses and even phone numbers. He exuded a suave charm and absolute self-confidence. We learnt later that his mother, Fanny Higginson, was one of the greatest mediums of her day and he had inherited her gift.

During one of our breaks, I read an interesting story about Gordon Higginson. It appeared that he had a number of spirit children with whom he used to play. One of these was a little girl. He had a rubber ball which he used to throw to her, and she would throw it back again. This mystified his brothers, who, of course, could not see his companion. One day they asked their father to watch and he, in turn, called some neighbours. When Fanny returned home, she saw them all crouching on the floor, watching this odd performance in fascination.

Gordon's father often found his son's behaviour somewhat strange, but his mother realised his potential and knew that he was extremely gifted. Therefore, from the age of three, she trained him with great discipline and care.

As he grew, so did his psychic ability and this saved him in many difficult and dangerous situations especially during World War II when he joined the army. On one memorable occasion, he was hiding with his colleagues in a farmhouse in German-occupied territory. His commanding officer shouted, "Higginson, are you going to be killed?"

"No Sir," he replied.

"Are you going to be taken prisoner?"

"No Sir."

"Then take as many men as you can and get the hell out of here!"

Taking forty men with him, Gordon ran till he came to a halt on the banks of a swirling river. It was pitch dark at the time and he had no idea how he was going to get the men across. All he could do was kneel down and pray. "I'll help you," said the spirit of the little girl with whom he had played ball when he was young. He saw her clearly in the darkness. "If you get me out of this, I'll serve the spirit world for the rest of my life," promised Gordon, as he followed the little girl into the dark and deep waters. The child led them, without faltering, following a zig-zag path where the water was shallow. Shivering with cold and fear, they reached the other side.

Gordon kept his promise to his little spirit friend and a few years later, he became the President of the Spiritualistic National Union, eventually making his headquarters at Stanstead Hall.

Gordon Higginson believed that spiritualism is a philosophy which has a great deal to teach us about this world as well as the next. "The aim of spiritualism," he said, "is to make men spiritual, more loving, more caring, more responsible towards each other and the world we live in."

In the college, we mingled with people from different countries and shared beautiful experiences over typically English meals. Tea time was a time for chatter, with crunchy biscuits and mugs of steaming Earl Grey tea. When the end of the day was upon us, it was time to go to the Sanctuary to witness demonstrations of spiritual healing. After dinner, at nine o'clock, we would congregate to share "spirits" of another kind and the bar would ring out with songs and laughter.

We read abundantly in the stately library, and also purchased many books to share with our friends back in India. Several mediums demonstrated their skills as clairvoyants and clairaudients. Though we learnt that the aim of a medium is to give proof of survival and a measure of happiness to those left behind, I must mention that somehow we found a difference in our way of working as compared to theirs. There seemed to be a competitive spirit that did not appeal to us. We did not really seem to fit in anywhere for we were not mediums in the true sense of the word. We could not "see," "hear" or "speak." Our work was not only to give proof of life after death, but primarily to learn the universal truths through Meher Baba and to make *"burdens lighter and lives brighter."* As Karl once said, *"We are nothing, Baba is everything and we are all drops in the Ocean of His Love."*

I recall that it was on a Thursday that we had completed the day's lectures, and as usual, retired to a basement room that had been converted into a bar. By then, we were quite familiar with the students, guests and practicing mediums, and although they had asked me many times to share my experience, my inherent fear and reservation prevented me from doing so.

I do not know why I suddenly found myself wanting to narrate Karl's story to them. So we settled ourselves in a cosy niche below the staircase of the hall and I began to tell them about Karl and Meher Baba. Oblivious of my intentions, Amie tripped happily along barefooted until she noticed the hushed group around me. Intrigued, she came closer, and discovering that it was the story closest to her heart, pumped her arms in a gesture that implied support.

As the story reached it conclusion, I looked up, quite unprepared for the reaction. There was pindrop silence.

A deep and hostile voice suddenly sliced through the silence.

Jane Smith, a fellow student, but also a medium by profession, unfurled herself from an armchair and took the floor. With a practiced leadership quality, she tore holes in our story and expressed serious doubts as to the validity of our guide, our children, as well as Mrs. Rishi and her ouija board. I felt Amie's nails dig into my arm as we heard her denigrate automatic writing and the ouija board, both of which, in her opinion did not measure up to her "high" standards. She ended her tirade by saying in an arched voice, "Why don't you read what the great Red Indian guide, Silver Birch has to say. He will show you the way."

Too stunned to react, I looked anxiously to the others for some verbal and moral support, but found none. Realising that Jane Smith had chosen the perfect moment to steal the attention away from me and assert her dominance, I mumbled an inaudible "good-night," whilst Amie, very near to tears, kept a stony silence. We excused ourselves and retreated to our room for the night.

The next morning, we were scheduled for a group sitting. We filed into a large room and sat on chairs that were placed in a wide circle. On the floor, in the centre, was placed a tumbler full of water encircled with flowers and dried acorns. We were then asked to concentrate our energies on the glass of water and try to send a telepathic message to anyone in the room. I closed my eyes and willed with all my might. I willed the impossible, for I was still smouldering. "Dear Meher Baba, show Jane in some way that you are present. If you are really there, please turn the water in this glass into wine!"

After fifteen minutes of meditation in absolute silence, we were asked to take turns at sharing any telepathic receiving of thoughts. Jane was the first to rise and she seemed very agitated as she said, "Why do I get this distinct and urgent feeling that someone wants to turn this water into wine?" All eyes riveted on me as I fell off my chair. I sat on the floor stunned – and then the laughter bubbled up inside of me as I silently thanked Meher Baba.

Later that day, we were sitting around as usual in the niche. Amie, still rankling from the episode of the night before, had an altercation with one member from the group, who did nothing but talk about herself and her prowess as a medium. In spite of Meher Baba's teachings, Amie's temper got the better of her. She berated them for their discourtesy, ignorance and pride in showing off. She said that we did not profess to be mediums – we were newcomers who only wanted a sharing of experiences. The centre stage had shifted and they did not relish it. "For five days," Amie yelled, "we have listened to you and you and all about you – we do not want to hear any more." With that, she practically dragged me out of the college and back to London, a full day ahead of schedule!

The laughter only came back into her eyes when I recounted what had taken place during the sitting earlier that morning. We had been forewarned by Ivy Northage, Karl, as well as Nicol, but as I said, we had to learn an invaluable lesson – to trust ourselves and our children and above all, Meher Baba.

Al Catternach, a Scottish medium, was also instrumental in restoring our confidence in ourselves. She made it a point to visit us for a private meeting and reaffirmed our experiences with Meher Baba and the children, and I slowly watched the light come back into Amie's eyes.

Imagine our delight when we got back to Bombay and read Silver Birch, the book that Jane had recommended to "novices" such as us. We discovered a full chapter devoted to Mr. and Mrs. Rishi. Silver Birch personally acknowledged them as being mediums of international renown and rated them as being among the best spiritualists in the world.

We had strayed a long way from home, thinking erroneously that answers would be obtained in another land. We were indeed wrong, for we were to find that the answers lay in our hearts and in the faith we had in our children and Meher Baba.

CHAPTER 19

Is Baba God?

"Mummy, I want you to love Meher Baba more than you love me, for Meher Baba is God. Karl."

Confronted with words that I had never wanted to hear or read, I sat dumbly staring at the communication and contemplated its meaning for many long hours. Since the time I came to know about Meher Baba, I had read many books on him but had firmly decided to ignore the passages where his followers have called him "God – The *Avatar* of The Age." As long as I could gloss over this fact, I was comfortable with whatever way I had decided to accept him. No one was going to convince me otherwise.

Yes, I was prepared to accept Baba as my guide, my constant companion, my protector and best friend. I even tried to understand his teachings – to bow down for his love and grace, for in my heart I knew that Meher Baba was an exceptional soul. I even sensed that he was beyond being human – an enlightened being whose love and compassion was so beautiful, that I was convinced he had made it possible for my son to return to me. But, I could not accept him as God – no, not God! Never God! For me, God did not exist.

"No Karl, I am charmed by what you always have to say, but this time I will not agree to your request – I am not ready yet," I cried out stubbornly.

"You feel I was badly treated by God and that is why you are against Him," he replied. "I know how you feel, Dad and Mum, but so many good things come out of bad. Just think how we are now together and doing things that we never thought possible. I am here to make you happy – that is all I wish for, and I will do all that I can for that. I will do more and more, so that you will say, Karl is near always, nearer than he was before. I am with you forever."

Thus began Karl's crusade. Every morning, my son would give us a new message and continue with his efforts to make us believe that Baba was always there for us.

"God is everywhere and in everything. He is big and He is good. He does not want to hurt anyone. He loves everybody and does not wish to make them unhappy. Just think that Baba is God, and God is Baba. He is all of me, and all of you – He is everything and all people who love Baba, love God, and we are all one.

"Baba is the kindest person on earth and in our world He is considered to be the most helpful soul ever created by God – and that is why He gets the name of Meher. What is the meaning? Meher means 'my heart is in the right place'. So Mum, He is a person who gives His heart to people in order to see that they find peace – He gives them His heart.

"Meher Baba is not there to preach or teach religion, faith or anything that is against what people think. All He wishes for is happiness. Baba is God to me and to all those who need Him, He is God. Happiness in any form is necessary, so God, Baba, can give them happiness – therefore He is God. God means a father who gives. All you have is from Him – all you need is from Him – nothing matters except Him."

Karl's messages were always simple and direct, but I was still unwilling to give up my position – sometimes I accepted what he had to say and sometimes I rejected his wisdom. I wanted to understand Baba for I knew that all he really wanted to do was to reinforce what my religion and faith had taught me all along. I appreciated that Baba laid down no rules as to whom you should worship and how, whether you folded your hands in a temple, mosque, or agiary or knelt in a chapel; whether it was Ram, Krishna, Buddha, Mohammed, Zarathushtra or Christ whom you loved – it was immaterial as long as you loved God. But who was God? How could I love him? How could I do the one thing I had sworn never to do again? How could I truly explain what it felt like and what it still feels like to have lost my child? How could I believe in God?

Where was God when a mother's heart cried out in anguish and begged him to save her son's life? Where was God when I needed him most? Where was he when I asked for his grace, his love, and his help? I sat in agony as Karl's slim figure swam before my eyes – his love of his animal, his excitement, his dash, his verve, his will to win, had all filled me with joy. But then I saw a figure being carried off on a stretcher, a motionless figure with a small white face, the red hoof mark on his chest and his beautiful eyes closed forever – and I cried aloud in pain.

How could I ever believe in God?

But now, on the other hand, I was introduced to a compassionate soul called Meher Baba, whose love is said to be so total that it helps to relieve the suffering of life's burdens and, who had, in the most unimaginable way, allowed my son to come back to me. How was I now to relate the thought of God and Meher Baba together – how?

One day, many months later, on one of my trips to Meherabad, an episode took place that went a long way in convincing me of the powers and the love of the soul born into this world as Merwan and then called Meher Baba.

In my ardent desire to help someone, I had told her something that was not entirely true. By the time I had reached Baba's *Samadhi,* the lie had grown to huge proportions in my mind and I begged him for forgiveness and understanding. As is the usual routine, we continued from Meherabad to Meherazad, where everyone gathered on Mehera's porch.

Mehera began reminiscing about her beloved Baba. She told us how Merwan, as a young boy, loved to sing and act. He used to wake up at 5 a.m. and in his sweet voice, sing *shairies* and *ghazals* that awakened all the neighbours in the *mohalla* where they lived. Nobody objected to the hour as they sat listening, entranced. "Merwan is singing," they would say in ecstasy.

Mehera went on to tell us how Baba mixed with his companions and was both God and man to them. He gave spiritual discourses with the same love and enthusiasm as he played cricket or seven tiles with them. Equally, he enjoyed a simple game of cards. She lowered her eyes, smiled shyly and added, "...and you know, he even used to cheat sometimes."

I gasped as I realised the significance of what she had just said – casual words to all present, but for me, they were the words I most needed to hear. I had asked Baba for understanding and he had answered me with more.

Another favourite story related that day, referred to one late afternoon on July 15, 1969, just after Baba had dropped His body. Mehera was standing by the east window of her room at Meherazad,

Meher Baba – 1925

looking at some newly-planted shrubs and thinking of her Beloved. Suddenly, her attention was drawn to the umer tree, just a few feet away from the window. She saw, to her amazement, the likeness of Baba's face etched on the tree trunk. At first, she thought that this was due to the way the light played on the tree trunk, helped by her imagination – but no, it was BABA'S FACE – in all its beauty, serenity and compassion. Mani and the *mandali* shared this wonderful sight. News spread among the villagers who came from far and near to pay homage to Baba's image on the umer tree. "What a compassionate gift Baba

The umer tree outside Mehera's room

has bestowed on us," concluded Mehera. With a sweet smile, she proceeded to pass around pictures of the tree with Baba's face clearly looking out at the world.

I sat in Baba's garden staring at the umer tree and the image of God as I had always pictured Him swam before my eyes. We are followers of Zarathushtra the Prophet, who had lived in the hills of ancient Iran in South Central Asia some three and a half thousand years ago. Zarathushtra or Zoroaster as the Greeks referred to him, had humble beginnings and lived in a pastoral society in which He taught His people to revere the seven creations of *Ahuramazda* (God); namely the skies, waters, earth, plants, animals, man and fire.

Zarathushtra was the recipient of the *Gathas* or hymns that were divinely inspired and which formed the basis of our religion. When this revelation was accepted by the people of ancient Iran, it became a religion, the tenets of which were good thoughts, good words and good deeds. This made Zarathushtra the first prophet priest of the oldest revealed religion in the world.

We never had the urge or need to delve deeper into the books of learning and so, our understanding of Zoroastrian teachings was very fundamental. Visits to the Fire Temple on festive days to ask for the blessings of God were a normal practice for us. The *dasturjis* or priests of our religion keep the fires perpetually lit by burning sandalwood and *loban*. This is a practice used to spread harmony in the world, whereas the lighting of *diyas* is to keep us aware of the path of truth and enlightenment.

There are many pictures of Zarathushtra that have come down through the ages, but the picture of Zarathushtra on the walls of our fire temples was the image that I have always carried with me – a figure dressed in a long white robe, standing amidst billowing clouds, and with hand upraised and finger pointing towards heaven. I imagined Zarathushtra to be the (God) source of what He preached – good thoughts, good words, good deeds, as these became the tenets of our religion after His work on earth was over. I did not consider God to be a punishing God or a God that I feared, but someone like Zarathushtra that I looked up to and worshipped from afar with reverence and love. I always bore in mind my grandmother's words, "Do good, child, and good will come to you. Remember God will always help you." How then, could He have ignored my anguished cry for help at the time that my son was fighting for his life? This was my simplistic reasoning, and I lived by what I believed.

But a new thought struck me – was I protesting too much?

The image of Meher Baba that I now had close to my heart, was someone I could relate to. He was approachable, laid down no laws, allowed my son to come back to me and, He even cheated at cards! His teachings seemed to be no different from those of Zarathustra, but this time around He went by the face and new name of Meher Baba.

Was I beginning to see a similarity between the two Masters?

I continued sitting, lost in thought for a long while. Deep in my consciousness I heard the voice of Baba repeating the words that he had used in his very first communication about Karl and his fall.

"Racing – I love it Myself. I used to come and watch from outside, and I have seen Karl many times riding a horse, I have watched him and admired him as a small boy, and I knew that I would look after him forever if anything happened to him. I always knew he was destined for great things but his career was cut short. I was as sorry and as sad as all of you. I was crying from here – I cried as the world cried with you, and I took him immediately."

Impulsively, I went to Mehera and asked, "Did Baba ever go to the races?" "Oh yes," she answered readily, "we used to go and stand outside the Pune racecourse, for Baba and I loved to see the horses passing by. I remember one particular racing day, when Baba asked for a race card. The four o'clock race was about to begin, and the horses cantered by on the way to the start. Baba's eyes fell on a particular animal. His cheeks glowed with pleasure and his eyes twinkled with delight. He put his fore-finger and thumb together to indicate to us that He loved this particular horse the best. I even remember the name of the horse," concluded Mehera, "the name was Moghul King."

"Oh my God!" I shouted, interrupting Mehera in mid-sentence. The startled *mandali* turned and looked at me quizzically. How could they know why the name, Moghul King, had triggered an immediate outburst from me; that the animal had belonged to my husband Jimmy; that it was the first racehorse he had ever owned in his life; and that somehow it was the one horse that Meher Baba had picked out in appreciation that day.

It is true, it is true, I thought to myself joyously, Baba must have seen Karl riding, he must have known and loved Karl and finally, when Karl had reached his destination, Baba went to receive him. I knew also that Baba's care is planned with meticulous detail leaving no stone unturned. Right from the beginning, he had Karl set out on a conquest and, despite my stubborn, unreasonable stance, Baba knew that one day he would touch my heart and so win over my mind.

I smiled to myself as I allowed the new awareness to seep through my being and my thoughts flew to Karl, acknowledging his efforts to convince me – that Baba is God, and that I was to love HIM more than I loved my son Karl.

Instead of simply accepting the fact that I had at last conceded to his request, the onslaught continued. Karl was bent on driving his point home. After the revealing session with Mehera, we all made our way to the hall, where sat Eruch Jessawala, one of Baba's *mandali* and most trusted companions. As is the normal practice in Meherazad, he was ready for a question and answer session about Meher Baba. I settled myself in an empty space just as Eruch was about to begin. His kind, bespectacled eyes swept the room and came to focus on a group of newcomers. I heard his soft voice say, "I have an unusual request today – I am going to tell you, in brief, the story of Meher Baba's life." Without further preamble, he plunged straight into the narrative.

"Merwan Sheriar Irani was born in Pune, India, of a Persian family on February 25, 1894, at 5.15 a.m. His father Sheriar was a seeker of God, and at the age of twelve years, he left his family and began wandering through Iran, in search of spiritual truth. Failing to achieve the enlightenment that he sought, his steps eventually led him to Pune, to the home of his sister, Piroja, who urged him to marry and settle down. It is said that a dream or inner voice assured him that one of his children would become a great spiritual leader. Following his sister's advice, Sheriar married a girl in her early teens, Shireen Dorab Irani, who eventually bore him seven children; the second son was Merwan."

"Did he know he was God the day he was born?" asked one of the newcomers.

"Oh, no," answered Eruch, "He followed a normal course of life, attending school and having fun with his family and friends. He grew up benevolent and kind, always helping the poor and needy. He took a great pleasure in games, especially cricket, but He was also a good runner and strong walker. He was a natural leader, but never craved for name and fame. He had a happy childhood, loving those around Him and revering His parents wholeheartedly. He was a soft-hearted and mystical child, untroubled as yet by any sense of His own destiny."

"And when and how did all this change?" asked a voice from the back of the hall.

Eruch paused – there was a faraway look in his aged eyes. "Ah," he said, "it was a day that changed the course of His whole life and that of so many others." It was a day in May 1913. Merwan was riding His bicycle on His way home from the Deccan College where he was studying. He noticed an old woman seated under a neem tree. Her name was Hazrat Babajan. She was known to be a Mohammedan saint, a Perfect Master. That day, as Merwan passed by her tree, she suddenly beckoned to Him. He got off His bicycle and walked towards her as if He had been drawn magnetically. She embraced Him lovingly and said, "My beloved son!" Merwan was dazzled by Babajan's embrace and walked home forgetting his bicycle.

"Weeks and months passed, and gradually Merwan lost interest in everything. He was unable to concentrate on His activities and unable to explain His feelings. He would walk off to visit Babajan under her neem tree and sit long hours by her side, sometimes till late into the night. Life was now totally empty except for one person – the old woman. A link of divine love had been established between these two souls.

"This is my beloved Son... He will one day shake the world, and all humanity will be benefited by Him," she declared – and then Merwan felt her kiss!

"The kiss Babajan gave him, carried him into the bliss of God-realisation. He was no longer human conscious – He was in that state to which very, very few go."

There was a hush in the hall. Eruch continued speaking. "His mother worried endlessly as cruel neighbours jeered at Merwan's vacant looks. What had happened to her Merog? His father looked on with patience and sympathy at His young son. Merwan's eyes were open but they did not see, His ears were there but they did not hear. He was in the world but not of it. He had gone somewhere far, far away. For nine months He lived without sleep, staring vacantly into space, pacing up and down in His little room until one day, something began to change. Merwan found himself walking towards the river again and resumed his visits to Babajan. There were days when He seemed to drift back to normal consciousness, but there were other days when He would sit in solitude and in total darkness in his home. He began to sing again, Persian songs with deep fervour – He sang to the glory of God, for He felt his true self as one with God. The glow on His face became a halo for He was absorbed in the highest state of spiritual consciousness.

"It was only in November 1914, when it seemed that some degree of normal consciousness began to return. Gradually, His hold on life strengthened. He began conversing about God, the inner path, the need for a Master and other spiritual issues. He decided to live the life of a *fakir*, renouncing worldly things and practising austerity. He began to visit the other Perfect Masters in turn.

"His first steps led him to Narayan Maharaj of Khedgaon. From him, He began to feel the glory of His Godhood. Next, he went to Nagpur to visit Tajuddin Baba, once a soldier in the service of the British, but now a God-realised soul. Then it was the turn of Sai Baba of Shirdi, who was seventy-seven years old at the time. Eventually, when Sai Baba passed by, Merwan stretched himself, full length, on the ground in front of his feet. Bowing down in reverence to the youth, Sai Baba, in a deep, resounding voice, uttered the word *"PARVARDIGAR"* which means God, The Almighty Sustainer. In that instant, Sai Baba gave Merwan Infinite Power!

"It was the month of December 1915. The young Zoroastrian wandered in a daze to Sakori village. Sadguru Upasni Maharaj was sitting on the steps of the Khandoba temple. As the young man approached with folded hands, Upasni greeted Him, so to speak, with a stone which he threw at Merwan with great force. It struck Him on the forehead, at the exact place where Babajan had so lovingly kissed Him. With the force of this impact, Merwan began to come back to life again after nearly two full years of divine absorption – but it took almost seven more years and a great deal of suffering for Him to completely return to human consciousness. The intensity of His suffering was due to his unwillingness to descend into human consciousness, which was necessary for the work that He had to accomplish."

The hour flew by. I sat quietly in my corner of the hall, listening to everything that Eruch had to say. My inner voice said to me that surely this was no ordinary man – He was different – yes definitely, He was something other than a normal human being.

"The five Perfect Masters did all that they could to help Him through this period of His life," continued Eruch. "He travelled to their homes again and again and learnt all that they had to teach Him. He became a great speaker on spiritual subjects and gradually, His divinity spread throughout Pune."

"The day finally arrived. The *Avatar's* divine mission was to begin! In January 1922, Merwan was destined to leave Upasni Maharaj of Sakori and begin His universal work. A few minutes before Merwan's departure, Upasani Maharaj called Him into his hut and, with folded hands, proclaimed 'Ah, Meher, you are *Adi Shakti* – the Primal Force! You are the *Avatar*'! Merwan wept tears of bliss and bowed down at the feet of the Perfect Master. For a long time, until the *tonga* was out of sight, Upasni Maharaj gazed as the dust stirred on the road. As Merwan departed from the 'King of the Yogis' to begin His mission, silent tears caressed the Sadguru's cheeks. They were tears of joy.

"At the age of twenty-seven, Merwan had become MEHER BABA. He was young, strong and handsome and ready to begin His work for mankind."

It appeared as if Eruch had finished for the day, but we continued to ask him more and more questions, for our appetites could never somehow be satiated. "How did you come to be with Baba?" we inquired.

Eruch sat back again and stretched his cramped legs. He told us of the day when he was a little child of six and Baba had come to ask if his family would allow their little boy to be with Him. They had refused at the time, but as their devotion grew, they began to see the divinity in Baba. They left their homes and possessions and made their life with Him.

"This is how Meher Baba started in earnest to gather His close disciples and formed the nucleus of the *mandali*," he said. "This is how Baba established a community near Ahmednagar called Meherabad – this is where He wanted to have His final resting place and this is where, under His personal supervision, His *Samadhi* was constructed. Meher Baba spent many hours sitting in this vault, in prayer and meditation, to send forth the vibrations that have since brought much happiness and comfort to so many."

Eruch then spoke briefly about Meher Baba's work. This embraced a free school where spiritual training was stressed. He opened a free dispensary and hospital and gave shelter and food to the poor. Meher Baba made no distinction between high and low castes. Everyone mingled freely because of His love. He taught everyone to love God, increased their spiritual understanding and instilled in them a spirit of selfless service.

"And what about His silence? Please tell us about His silence," we echoed.

Eruch shook his head. His face reflected his feelings of profound admiration and wonder at the inner strength of his Master. He tried to express in words the enormity of the task that Baba had taken onto Himself, to explain to us how Baba had kept silence for the rest of His life, a period of forty-four years. Unbelievable as it is, this is what Baba did.

Eruch closed his eyes as he relived the days with Baba – "On July 10, 1925, Meher Baba began observing complete silence. His silence was not undertaken as any sort of penance, but it was a suffering that He took upon Himself for the benefit of all creation. Baba used an alphabet board to dictate His many spiritual discourses and messages, but He discontinued using this after 1954. Thereafter, His communications were in gestures that were beautifully expressive and easy to understand."

"And what about you Eruch, why were you called 'The Tongue of God'?" asked someone in the group.

Eruch peered at the questioner. Not wanting to dwell on his own personal role, he said briefly, "I joined Baba permanently in 1938. I became His interpreter and looked to all Baba's personal needs and comforts for the next thirty years."

Eruch went on to tell us of Baba's visits to the West and His many *darshans*. He told us about the latter part of His life, where He met *masts*, advanced persons on the inner planes of the spiritual path, who became spiritually intoxicated from the direct awareness of God. He regarded the meetings with the *masts* as most crucial to His work on the earth plane. He told us about His washing of the lepers and the distribution of grain, cloth and money to thousands of poor and destitute people. There followed two automobile accidents that Baba suffered through, as a part of His universal work.

"The intensive work which He did inwardly, together with His many large mass gatherings throughout India, His search for the *masts* and the even stricter seclusion that He placed upon Himself for the purpose of His universal work, finally took a great toll on His health. In September 1968, Meher Baba announced that He had completed His work one hundred per cent to His satisfaction."

Eruch looked around at all the upturned faces and the wide eyes of those sitting with him in the hall that day, for he had almost come to the end of his story. The love that he felt for Meher Baba shone through the very core of his being.

In a voice quivering with emotion, Eruch said, "On January 31, 1969, at 12.15 p.m., my beloved Master, Meher Baba, breathed His last and dropped His physical body. All those who sincerely love and have faith in Him can always feel His presence, be they scattered in the world or sitting with us here today – so let us join our hearts and lift up our voices as one to say His name and spread His love."

The tears shone in Eruch's eyes as he concluded, "I am reminded at this moment of the words of Bal Natu. 'The life of the *Avatar* is like the sky that we can see and move in but cannot fathom. It has a place for everyone and everything, yet this "sky" – this Beyond State – is ever incomprehensible. *Avatar* Meher Baba, in His all-encompassing compassion accepts whatever comes to Him from a loving heart'."

Eruch got up and slowly walked towards the door. He turned, looked straight at me, bowed his head, joined his hands and said, *"Avatar Meher Baba ki Jai."*

I have read many life sketches of Meher Baba but none of them seemed to have the same impact on me as the way it was narrated by Eruch that day. Maybe it was the mood that I was in, or that I was in His home, surrounded by His love. I really cannot say. I only know that it contributed a great deal towards resolving the doubts and resistance in my mind about God and Meher Baba.

Note: Eruch passed over to his Beloved Lord and Master, Meher Baba on Aug. 31, 2001.

CHAPTER 20

"The Thief of Hearts"

In Meherazad, there hangs a poster of a face with a mischievous look and twinkling eyes:

> **WANTED**
>
> ***FOR THE STEALING OF ALL HEARTS***
> ***AVATAR MEHER BABA***
> *Alias Merwan Irani*
> *Charming desperado who was*
> *once heard saying:*
> *"It is said that I am very slippery.*
> *I am the Universal Thief.*
> *I steal the hearts of all!"*

Unquestionably, one of the first hearts He stole was Mehera's, and she became Baba's beloved.

Mehera's mother was a devotee of Upasni Maharaj, one of Baba's five Perfect Masters. She brought Mehera as a young girl to Sakori and they lived together in Upasni's *ashram*. This is where she saw Merwan for the first time. Seeing the intense love He had for his Master, Mehera's heart was deeply and irrevocably touched. It wasn't much later that Upasni Maharaj instructed both Mehera and her mother to leave Sakori and "go with Merwan." Little did she know to what profound degree this move was to change her life and how destiny was to keep her at the *Avatar's* side as His chief woman disciple and beloved.

In May 1924, Mehera and her mother were among the very few women to make their home in Meherabad, in what used to be a one-room post office. Mehera described the day she spotted Baba coming across the fields – "His lovely hair, brown and golden at the tips, was shining in the sun." He struck her as exquisitely beautiful and this image was to remain with her throughout her life with Him. Whenever she saw Him, no matter the time, the place, or the occasion, His beauty always fascinated her – she never tired of gazing at Him. It is true to say that Mehera's relationship with Baba was always totally innocent of physical involvement, and therefore her love had a true clarity; the spirit behind her service to Him was one of absolute self sacrifice. In August 1925, Meher Baba reciprocated His love for Mehera by declaring, "From the first time I saw you, I recognised you as My Radha."

The years sped by and Baba's love for Mehera was amply demonstrated by His gentle devotion and acquiescence to every wish of hers. In spite of the arduous work throughout the various phases of His life, it was never really difficult for her; each day was filled with joy and satisfaction, only because she loved Baba so. She accompanied Baba on His travels, attending to all His personal needs. She enjoyed sleeping under the stars, walking in orchards and eating the meagre fare meted out by the poor villagers. But that was not all, for there were many other aspects of life that Baba was preparing Mehera for – obedience, joy in serving, humility and teaching her through the strength of prayer, the true spirit of loving God.

Mehera suffered with Baba through a major car accident and learnt to appreciate all the more, every moment spent with Him; His every little word, His every gesture and action was her command. Later in life, because of His health, Baba became restricted in His movements and so for His last twelve years, Mehera remained constantly by His side. Her devotion to Him was complete.

Finally, on January 31, 1969, the time came for Baba's last words to her. He said, "Mehera, be brave." After Baba dropped His body, Mehera's life changed. She was suddenly thrust into the forefront and she continued to be brave and strong, as day after day, week after week and month after month, thousands of Baba lovers thronged Meherazad. She stood on her porch to embrace each one lovingly to her heart.

Before my first visit to Meherazad, the concept of Baba having a beloved aroused no immediate question in my mind. My reasoning of who He really was and of everything about Him, was yet to unfold. I had imagined Baba's beloved to be old, wise and unapproachable, but to my surprise, I found instead a beautiful, serene and humane Mehera, who came out of her quarters at an appointed time, followed by the women *mandali*; she regally took her place in her favourite armchair on the porch.

And so it was that her gaze, so full of love and compassion, came to rest on my sad face as I sat with them on the porch that first day in Meherazad. I remember those gentle eyes shining with wonder as my strange story unfolded. It was the beginning of a friendship that was to blossom over the years into one of deep love and admiration from my side, and one of care, concern and true affection from hers.

On the many trips that followed, I used to sit transfixed as she shared her vast repertoire of Baba stories, some about His childhood, but most about His love for humanity. Sympathy and understanding would shine from her soft grey eyes as she bent over listening carefully to a sad tale or two – or sometimes her eyes would light up in happy recognition of a familiar face she had not seen for a long time. Even at her age, Mehera would make it a point to remember every detail of every person that visited. She would ask after family, friends and children and would share in their happiness and despair, and tears would come to her eyes when their suffering touched her heart, but most especially when she spoke of her beloved Meher Baba.

Mehera

I remember the animated face of another person who joined us on a day when the need for answers lay uppermost on my mind. She seemed to sense my sorrow and discomfort and decided to put me

The author with Mani

at ease by telling me her own story of how Baba had stolen her heart even before she was born. This was Mani, Baba's sister.

On December 15, 1918, when Merwan was twenty-four years old, Manija was born. Merwan was thrilled to have a baby sister and would return from His travels many a time, just to see her. He would often sit rocking her cradle and singing to her. Mani grew up loving her brother with a single-minded, deep and abiding love.

Mani schooled at a Pune convent where her class consisted mainly of Christian girls who would speak of their families and refer to their Godmothers and Godfathers. Proud as a peacock, Mani would tell herself, "They may all have Godmothers and Godfathers but I am the only one who has a GODBROTHER!"

Although Mani was a precocious child, reprimanded by Baba very often, He came to mean the world to her. In her book "God-brother," Mani describes the anticipation of spending her holidays with Baba. "And long before our train arrived at Ahmednagar station, I was leaning all the way out of the window to catch the first sight of the station's name. Ah, there it was, way up on that huge water tank, painted in large letters: AHMEDNAGAR. Oh the joy, the thrill of it! I would not have been surprised if they had painted PARADISE instead, because that's where I had come. Where Baba was, was Paradise for me."

When Mani was eight years old, her little heart nearly broke, for an incident took place which continues to live in her memory. Baba was seated with His followers and the *mandali*. Mani was so engrossed in just being there that she had no way of recalling exactly how or what had caused the misunderstanding to take place as it did. During the pin-drop silence, she suddenly heard her mother proudly say, "Well, Merog, if that's the way it is, I leave!"

Baba with His sister Mani

And Baba, His eyes still flashing, said, "All right, leave!"

His mother walked a few steps. Then she turned round and said, "And I'm taking my daughter with me!"

And Baba said, "Take your daughter with you!"

Mani's world was shattered! She reluctantly followed her mother down the long and lonely road to the station. Mani grumbled all the way, begging her mother to reconsider her position, and pleading with her to go back. Tired of the brisk pace and tired of her daughter's nagging, Shireenmai stopped under a banyan tree to rest. Mani, of course, did not give up! Suddenly, Shireenmai said, "Look, Mani. For God's sake, if you want to go and be with Merog, go! But please leave me alone."

Mani needed no second invitation – she promptly turned around and retraced her steps towards her brother, knowing in her heart that He would make everything alright. On and on she walked, till she saw a familiar figure in the distance. She referred to it as "an ethereal vision in white, gliding towards me." It was Baba. Her little legs began to run faster than they had ever run before and she flung herself into her Godbrother's arms, crying bitterly. Baba gathered her up and said, "Why are you crying? Everything will be all right. Come, let's go to Mother."

With His little finger clutched firmly in her hand, they approached Shireenmai who was still sitting sadly under the tree. Mani watched silently as Baba held out His hands to His mother – she in turn looked into His eyes, placed her hands in His and everything was forgotten. Not a word was exchanged. There was no need. Mani was ecstatic! She was once more with her beloved brother and nothing else mattered.

Mani never had any doubt in her mind that she was going to spend her whole life with Baba; and so she did. She travelled with Him, lived with Him and worked with Him. She was little sister, companion, friend and confidante, faithfully carrying out His every wish – but that is not all. To the end of her life she worshipped Him!

I realise now that both Meherabad and Meherazad hold the formula that heals broken hearts and sad thoughts. What I did not realise then, was that initially it must have been uncomfortable for Mehera, Mani and the *mandali* to accept that Baba had found a new way of drawing people closer to Him. The *mandali's* love for Baba was so total, that they never ever questioned His ways that go beyond limited understanding. With love, they just accepted everything that had taken place and that has since transpired. Baba had called me. That was enough for them. How and why did not really matter. I was a part of their family and they loved me. It was Mehera's acceptance and understanding of Baba's ways that paved the way for everyone else. They also received the many souls that found their way to Baba after hearing Karl's story and knew that though the "Thief of Hearts" had somewhat branched off in an unusual manner, His work was still being done.

Mehera looked forward to knowing about each and every event that took place. She read and treasured many of Karl's little messages about Baba, for they touched her heart. She would beckon the minute she saw me and indicate that I should sit by her side on the small cane stool near her armchair. Her eyes would sparkle with anticipation as I drew out the pages that held Karl's thoughts and Karl's love for Baba. She would wait eagerly to hear what wonderful things had taken place and how many more people had benefited by Baba's love.

Unfortunately, on May 20, 1989, Mehera's lovely eyes looked upon the faces of the faithful *mandali* gathered around her for the last time. Beloved Mehera went to Baba.

I drove up to Meherabad with a heavy heart, reflecting on all the special moments shared with this lovely lady. These thoughts were tinged with sadness, for her beautiful presence would not be there any more, but as I drew close to Ahmednagar, I could not but remember the special message she had for all of us, the one that I had read in her book "Mehera."

"You must keep loving Baba more and more, and make Baba happy with your love by remembering Him always. Think of Him and say His name and He will always help you. You love Him because He loves you – so be happy in His love, know that Baba is with you and know that He loves you – and so be happy. He is the God-Man and to be loved by the God-Man is so beautiful – How very fortunate you are."

After Mehera, everyone who went to Baba's home looked to Mani for comfort, help and guidance. Love for humanity shone out of her sparkling brown eyes for they were the mirrors of her bubbling spirit. She used to spread her hands and tell us hilarious stories in her own inimitable way; she wandered among the pilgrims, making everyone feel welcomed and loved. Joy in being with Baba and carrying on His work was her only role in life. She looked after His office work and performed the exacting and multifarious duties as the Chairperson of the Trust.

Mani could be a child with children, sit on the floor with them and entertain them with stories of Baba and His animals; she was old with the aged, sitting quietly with them for hours, giving them all Baba's love from her heart. On the other hand, she could also hold discussions on philosophical matters with scholars, and speak fluently on spirituality. She could laugh with you and cry with you, play the sitar and sing with you; she could act and she could dance – she was the very source of joy! Her smile, her jokes, her stories and her affection, in fact her very presence put cheer into the saddest heart, for I know it did in mine from the first day that I stepped into Baba's Home. Her care and concern for every single person who came to Baba was a lesson in itself; for, if every human being in this world had to show one hundredth of the *joie de vivre* and love that she shared with everyone who needed it, the world would be a far, far better place.

The Thief of Hearts took care to leave someone behind to help steal more hearts, for, till just a little while ago, August 19, 1996, there was Mani, a living family member, His own flesh and blood, who was loved more for being a part of Him.

CHAPTER 21

The Messenger

So much for Baba's own family, but what about mine? The very first heart to be happily given to Baba was Karl's. I have often wondered how and why, but the experience of Karl's representation as *"a bird with big scaly wings and a head as small as a dove's,"* leads me to the *farohar*. I began to question the significance of the little gold *farohar* that always hangs around my neck on a tiny chain. What is a *farohar*? What exactly did it mean? "Karl, my son, where do you fit into it?" I asked repeatedly.

It was at this time that I suddenly came across a book called "Reveal Thy Grace" by Meher Jamshed Patel. It stated that "A *farohar* is a messenger from *Ahuramazda* (God) to mankind and from man to *Ahuramazda*. ...To be able to stand in the presence of *Ahuramazda,* one must have laboured for evolution.

"To be a messenger to and from *Ahuramazda* requires qualification. ...What job one does, matters not, as long as one does the job entrusted to him with zeal, enthusiasm and with perfection.

"The job of a messenger is no small task. To carry the message correctly, to reach the proper destination in time and to be able to impress the message on the mind of the receiver is no small task. The messenger has to be alert to read the reply imprinted in the mind of the receiver and to carry it back to *Ahuramazda*. Only absolute dedication and devotion to duty can achieve the task.

"The task of the messenger is not just to carry messages, but also to guide the responsive individual to higher aspiration. ...So *farohar* can aid in evolution."

Amazed by what I had just read, I stopped to ponder its possible

The *farohar* – God's messenger

implication. It is true to say that Karl does carry Baba's beautiful messages to us and through them, gives our lives direction. He leads us to Baba and so to a better, happier and more peaceful life. Allowing for a mother's wishful indulgence, I smiled as I visualised Karl's lofty role in his new life!

Thus through the *farohar* or winged messenger, Baba has made one long daisy chain and each delicate white petal represents love, happiness, comfort, protection, faith and hope for the future. Karl has been a nucleus that has drawn people from far and wide, and the first that will be mentioned here is Dinoo Nicholson.

Dinoo and I met on the stage during our college days. She was an actress of repute and I, an aspiring fledgling. She played the elder sister Clementine and I, the younger one Josephine – that is how we became friends.

Life took us different ways till we met again at the racecourse and she became an ardent fan of Neville and Karl during their gymkhana racing days. When Karl graduated to professional racing, she continued to give him a great deal of support. After a win, beating me in fact, she would run down to the railings to cheer him and congratulate him, showering him with flowers and admiration. "Well done Carlos!" she would cry out.

When Karl fell and was taken to the hospital, she sat with me through that terrible dark night and was a constant source of support through the harrowing days that followed. I never did forget her kindness.

In the meantime, her son, Bomsie, had blossomed into an actor of great repute with many stage successes to his credit. He was also a well-known singer, dancer, director, professional hair-stylist and stage and television make-up artist. He too, was much loved by many of his peers and friends, for he was an extremely loving and giving person. There came a day when tragedy struck the Nicholson home. I heard that Bomsie had passed away on December 16, 1991. I contacted Karl immediately and asked him to look after Bomsie. Karl was only too happy to oblige, for he had found another friend.

On December 21, 1991, Karl told me – *"Bomsie is here and will say a few words to you."*

"My dear Nanny I have a very good person looking after me, your son Karl – I was so surprised to see him waiting for me, but when I heard the whole story then everything fell into place. Strength has returned to me already and I am so very glad to be here. My mother will wonder what I am doing here, so tell her I have so many new people here plus Papa and Mama and the old folks from home – but it is the new things that hold my interest, that is what I am doing, surveying the scene and looking at everything. Sherna will see you, also, to know about me. So, you tell her. Life is so good, it is unbelievable! Mum has to be told everything. She needs to know my whereabouts and whatabouts. Tell her not to be sad, for Baba is near me, telling me about the wonders of being with Him and so I have the best of both worlds so to speak – a loving mother, sister and friends and family and the love that comes from a Father here."

If Bomsie heard the whole story from Karl, then of course, Dinoo had to hear it from me and she had no difficulty in believing what, to me, has now become a way of life.

On January 19, 1992, Karl said to me, *"Meher Baba is very happy to know your friends for they are His family now. He will see to them from now on. For Bomsi has made a condition with Baba – 'My family is everything to me. If I am to serve you, you have to serve them'!*

Baba smiled and answered in His own gentle way – 'Bomsie, I do not need the man who has to make conditions – I do everything with love, so you must understand this'. And so they came to an understanding, but Baba loved his spirit."

Then Bomsie addressed his mother and sister Sherna, *"My Mummy and Sherna, love has made me come here to you. I am here but you must not cry. Sherna you will go home, you must go home – your family needs you. I am fine, I am absolutely fine – go home safely for*

I love you. Karl is very happy to see me. Love to all my friends, my cousins, my Diane and Phiroze, of course have the corner in my heart..." He wrote a few more things which, in context I knew nothing about, but which Dinoo and Sherna knew to be true and understood completely. The next day, Sherna received a phone call from her children in England, urging her to return soon. This so utterly convinced Dinoo and Sherna that Bomsie had been right there with us, that they requested me to arrange a trip to Meherabad as soon as possible.

Exactly a month to the date that Bomsie had passed away, Dinoo, her daughter Sherna and I were chugging down to Ahmednagar and Meherabad, armed with Karl's message which we read over and over again. *"To be with you we wish to be. Baba will send him to you within a few minutes of coming. He will come to you to sit near you and will be with you throughout the prayer time. He shall tell you not to be sad, not to be afraid and not to say how and why did this happen. Thoughts of happiness must be there. He shall come to you specially to give his best love to his mother and sister so that the peace that passes all understanding will descend on them."*

As always, I walked up the hill with legs that trembled and a heart that fluttered with nervousness. It was already prayer time as we silently took our places on one corner of the bench that faces the *Samadhi*. Who would come and sit near us? How would we know? We didn't have time to wonder, for at the stroke of seven, the *aarti* began, and with closed eyes, we stood to pray.

As soon as the prayers were over, we sat down once again and looking round, found ourselves flanked by two gentlemen. As we stared, one of them picked up a guitar, looked pointedly at Dinoo and Sherna, and sang a poignant love song with words that mirrored the exact sentiments of Bomsie's message – no further proof was needed. Clutching each other, Dinoo and Sherna dissolved into tears. With eyes lovingly resting on them, the young man sang the last refrain,

"Who says dreams can't come true,
I am here and so are you."

What further proof did they need? Their dream had come true – Bomsie was happy with Meher Baba and so they are too. What a glorious way the Compassionate Father had found to comfort the bleeding hearts of mother and sister – in the process of which they were also introduced to the Master – Meher Baba.

"There have been other memorable days and signs from above since then," says Sherna, "which have brought different feelings of comfort, peace, awe and elation. All these emotions have been felt sometimes alongside, sometimes in spite of the continuing ache in our hearts... since the time we have been in communication with Bomsie. We now know that he will always be with us. We talk about old times, happy memories, sometimes even laugh with each other. How would this miracle – for I can only call it that – have been possible without Meher Baba's love?

"Bomsie, Mummy and I thank Baba daily for this blessing and we bless Karl daily in our prayers."

* * *

Mohit Keswani raced in and out of his house on a Christmas day, happy with the spirit that Christmas brings and thrilled about the party that he was organising for that night. Little did his mother, Kamlu, know that she was to hear her son's laughter for the last time. That evening, fate intervened, and Mohit accidentally fell from the ninth-floor terrace and died instantly. Kamlu, her husband Shyam, and their younger son Sameet, were left stunned and shattered.

I had just returned from London when Amie brought Kamlu to speak to me. We shared as much of Baba as we could and I gave her the support and link that she needed to begin her communication with her son Mohit.

Their first visit to Meherabad, accompanied by Amie, will always stay in their memories. *"Mohit and Nicol will be there – they will be in identical blue," said Karl, "and I will be a head on your shoulder!"*

As usual, the butterflies fluttered in my stomach. Although escorting people was to continue to be my service for Baba, I never ceased to be nervous. As we walked up the hill to the *Samadhi*, I watched Kamlu searching desperately for signs of recognition, whilst Amie looked on quietly and confidently, for she had been through it all before.

The day stretched on and it seemed as if the heavens were having a last laugh at us, for *"blue"* flashed everywhere – aquamarine, turquoise, cobalt, royal blue and navy, but no two were *"identical"* and certainly no one seemed likely to put a head on my shoulder!

The next morning, soon after breakfast, we found ourselves relaxing and chatting on the parapet outside the dormitory. It was bath time and we were waiting in turn for the buckets of hot water. The loud clanging of a bell attracted our attention.

"Laundry, dirty laundry," sang out a voice.

"Laundry, dirty laundry," echoed another voice from the other side of the quadrangle.

Two cleaning women, dressed in *saris*, sauntered along, announcing the collection of clothes for laundering. Shyam, who had noticed them from his room in the men's quarters, came rushing along, excitedly looking from one to the other, shaking his head in disbelief. The two women finally converged in front of us, eyes sparkling and pearly teeth shining. They smiled, not in the least disconcerted by our open-mouthed stares, for they had come to meet their mothers and they were dressed for the occasion in *"IDENTICAL BLUE!"*

I watched happy faces as each shared special moments with the "children" and I gratefully closed my eyes and gave thanks to Baba. I knew just how much it would mean to them.

Now all that was left to complete my day was to have someone put his head on my shoulder. I sang out silently, "Where are you Karl?"

That morning, the hill had a festive air, for Mehera and the *mandali* were expected to attend a special *aarti* in Baba's *Samadhi.* The tiny cavalcade of cars drove up Meherabad hill and Baba's beloved slowly made her gracious way, beneath a gaily coloured umbrella, into the *Samadhi.* Baba's simple prayers were recited and sung by all of us and the voices of some of the residents – Ted, Heather and Debbie – took over to sing Mehera's favourite songs, written for Baba.

As soon as the *aarti* was over, we watched Mehera leave, acknowledging all of us with folded hands and a lovely smile. Suddenly she stopped and beckoned to me. "Come with me," she said and I followed her into a room near Mansari's quarters. Opening a small drawstring bag, she drew out a tiny brooch and pinned it on my shoulder. The tears came to my eyes. "Thank you, darling Mehera," I said, as I put my arms around her, "I will treasure this all my life."

I returned to the group and proudly showed them my gift. "Oh my," exclaimed Amie, always the first to understand Baba's signals, "Nanny, it's the HEAD ON YOUR SHOULDER!" Resting within the gold filigree that was encrusted with four tiny diamantes was a beautiful head of Meher Baba.

That night, overjoyed by the representations, an opportunity presented itself and we shared our wonderful story with some of the pilgrims at the Centre. We went to bed, secure in the knowledge that we were protected and loved. Baba had taken us all to His heart and made us His.

The next morning, I took up the pen and began my usual fifteen minutes with Karl. Wham! It came like a slap in the face! *"Baba says that He cares for all equally and makes no comparisons at all. He loves humanity and does not like people to think they are the best. He helps one and all equally – and that is the most important lesson you have to learn today."*

Just as abruptly, Karl disappeared, and I was left gasping. I recognised at once that I had indeed been on an ego trip the night before. The stern warning did not just deflate my ego – it punctured it!

I called the group together and read Baba's admonishment to them. It was a lesson that we all had to learn and remember – that everyone is equal in Baba's eyes and no one is special.

Kamlu and Shyam returned to Bombay happy that Mohit was in the loving care of the *Avatar* Meher Baba. Both decided to learn everything that they possibly could about Baba, through books and also the messages that began to flow in abundance from the other world. The communication with her son strengthened and began to provide her with the security that she needed and broken hearts were mended with much love and laughter. Her days were soon filled with opportunities to help friends and neighbours with their problems and drawing them to Baba.

As the years sped by, Kamlu found an increasing need to turn to the writings, for many more personal problems began to surface. Little did she know that she had fallen prey to two of the easiest dangers known to automatic writing – that of allowing the mind to control the channelling and that of depending entirely on answers from the spirit world. The situation warranted Baba's intervention and with a firm warning through Nicol, Kamlu was able to confront the truth. The truth was that although some of the answers in her communication had turned out to be correct, many were unconsciously being manipulated by her to influence decisions that had to be made in her personal life.

She battled with herself for quite a while, for it was hard on her, but her honesty prevailed and the following is what she has to say: "It was a difficult lesson to learn, for it showed me how easy it was to follow the dictates of my mind. Initially, the communication with Mohit filled the void in my life and he was responsible for giving me the love that I had missed for so long. Instead of only depending on him for the love I needed, I wanted more. I began to expect him to resolve my emotional and material problems that had escalated over the years. I unconsciously diverted the writings to focus on answers that relieved me mentally, but I found that the problems would not go away. Fortunately, before this went too far, I was pulled up by Nicol, who came forward, through Amie, to take on the role of my spiritual guide. It was she who was responsible for putting me back on to the road leading to Meher Baba."

After a while, slowly, but beautifully, from an inner working with Nicol, interacting with Baba people, all her trips to Meherabad and Karl's supportive messages, she learnt about a new love – Baba's Love – a love that has no strings attached.

Karl said, *"Baba is like an Almighty Rock. Hang on to Him. He will not give way to anything. He stands in the middle of storms. In the middle of heaven and in the middle of a great big hell. He stands firm and strong. He can never break or fail, and so if you hang on to Him, you go with Him everywhere. Tell everyone He has made them all part of His Love, and that Love will never fail them. So hang on to Him. He will take you through any pain or sadness. Happiness and joy are waiting for them all. JUST BE WITH HIM – that's all I have to say."*

With this message and a lot of thought, Kamlu resolved the inner conflict about her self worth. She has become a much stronger person. She has now learnt to express herself with clarity, freedom and the truth, and has given up her journey into the hands of Baba.

The writings have finally proved a bigger purpose. Kamlu does not feel the necessity to actively communicate with her son for she does not find the need to get answers any more. Mohit has convinced her that he is happy with Baba and will live on in her heart forever.

"The communication is what led me to Baba," Kamlu concludes, "but eventually my love and trust in Him is what I live with and my journey to Him is the only experience that matters to me."

* * *

Sushila and Utsav Kapadia did not come to me because of any personal problems – they are happily married, socially well-placed, have a lovely home and three beautiful children. What began as merely a wish to find out more about loved ones that they had lost, grew into a much wider and deeper issue.

It started them off on the inevitable question – why? Why do things happen the way they do? What is the scheme of things? Why am I here? What is really important? It is this quest for satisfying answers that led both of them to Meher Baba.

Utsav's keen mind sums up beautifully, the profound influence that Baba has had in his life. "My first reaction to Meher Baba was of guarded caution. Having been exposed to several religions, I was sceptical. But going to Ahmednagar was an experience I will never forget. I loved the peace and tranquillity. Added to all this, was the intrigue around Karl's manifestations. This made me inquisitive to know more about his Master, Meher Baba. And hence, I read not about Him as such, but His own writings.

"What first appealed to me was the simplicity of His language and lucidity of thought. Then suddenly, He opened up a spiritual horizon that I did not know existed, taking me onto another level of understanding which changed my way of looking at life.

"Indian Philosophy, as I had known it, became clearer to me. The very fact that there exists a separateness amongst men and therefore between religions, has always been an enigma to me. This whole concept of a division of mankind by religion vanished, and I could see or sense a commonness. It was not important whether you were a Jain, Hindu, Muslim or Christian. That was only academic. Each religion just showed a different way to reach the same goal – God-realisation.

"As for my personal attitudes, no longer was I viewing everything with suspicion and scepticism. I began to discharge responsibility, not with the purpose of achieving something, but more with the attitude of learning. I found I was able to relate better with people and project myself into the difficult situations that they might be facing. I was able to cope better with difficulties that came my way and somehow my mind was able to resist self-pity.

"These realisations, these changes in attitudes, this confidence to face difficult situations as a learning process is where my search for the answer to the eternal 'why' has presently led me.

"Meher Baba has also shown me that the power of prayer and meditation, of good thoughts, of clarity of vision, will one day lead me to a life of pure, selfless love.

"Hanuman is said to have told Ram, 'Lord, so long as I stand before You in my body, I consider myself your humble slave. When I approach You with my intelligence, then I think of myself as a part of You, but when I come to You with my soul, then I am indivisibly one with You. Then You are Ram, and I too, am Ram'."

With a profound understanding of life behind her, Sushila branched off into the field of healing. Those who suffer physical ailments may probably get some kind of hope after they come into contact with a spiritual power, for when neither medicine nor doctors can help, who else can you turn to but God? The fact remains though, that the faith in God must stand by itself and not because of what He can do for you.

It was Karl who revealed to Sushila that she had the ability to heal. He gave her instructions from time to time, when to use her head, when to use her heart and when to use her mind. With this encouragement, she looked deeper into the subject and says, "I read many fascinating books and found myself trying out techniques on family, friends and servants, who were willing to support my interest. When there is a struggle to focus on the divine source of healing within, I use Baba's prayer, 'Beloved God, help me to love you more and more, and more and more, and still yet more till I become worthy of union with You and help me to hold fast to Baba's *damaan* till the very end'. This prayer reinforces the link with the person I'm trying to help and I almost immediately feel the energy flow. Small successes have encouraged me and have deepened the conviction that the ability to tap the source of divine healing is latent in everyone and that seat lies in the heart."

The communication that started with a young boy wanting to be with his mother and his family, has progressed into a much wider network. The little messenger has indeed performed his task with zeal and devotion and definitely been instrumental in guiding the responsive individual to higher aspirations.

CHAPTER 22

The Dhuni

The *dhuni* is a beautiful ceremony that takes place under the trees just outside the Pilgrim Centre at Meherabad. Pieces of firewood are kept in a basket near a glowing fire, and as each Baba lover approaches, to the accompaniment of songs or poems, he or she picks up a stick, dips it in *ghee* or purified butter and throws it into the fire with a silent prayer to Baba. The ashes are collected and distributed among the devotees, who either apply the same on their foreheads or place a small portion under the tongue. The ash or *oodi* may also be used by the physically ill as it is believed to relieve their suffering.

Wondering what the ceremony signified, I was told that the fire is symbolic of protection and also of destruction. The one thing that causes immense suffering for mankind is the burden of having to go through life carrying your *karma* with you and having to deal with it successfully. I was beginning to understand that, besides the role of protection, the most important spiritual significance of the *dhuni* is to destroy *sanskaras*, or deep *karmic* impressions, so that the individual is freed and may be allowed to progress towards enlightenment and truth. Since the destruction of *sanskaras* is almost impossible to achieve without the help of a Master, it was explained that by participating in the *dhuni*, one could seek the help of Baba to secure the release of binding experiences or attachments.

The *dhuni* ceremony was initiated by Meher Baba as long ago as 1925. It happened this way.

It was in the month of September, at the tail end of the monsoon, that Ahmednagar district faced the imminent prospect of drought. Many villagers grouped together into a *bhajan* party and trekked to Baba for the specific purpose of requesting Him to invoke the rains.

Baba listened compassionately and sent them on their way. He then directed the *mandali* to make preparations for a *dhuni;* a fire was lit precisely at 5 p.m. and Upasni Maharaj's *aarti* was sung. Midway through the *aarti,* it began to drizzle and soon, there was a cool drenching shower. Thus the prayers were answered.

Baba subsequently ordered the *mandali* residents to light the *dhuni* fire on the twelfth day of every month. This custom continues to this day and all Baba lovers gather around the *dhuni* fire at Meherabad, under the faithful supervision of Jal Dastur, an ardent Baba lover and trustee.

There are many stories in Meherabad that are connected with the *dhuni.* I cannot relate all of them to you, but I am going to narrate one that followed the ceremony that I attended on February 12, 1990. I was very honoured to be one of the three requested to light the *dhuni* fire. After it was over, I took some of the sacred ash home with me.

A couple of months later, my aunt Ginger, who suffered from acute arthritis, developed a problem with her blood circulation which led to gangrene in the toes. She was taken to the hospital where doctors decided that they could do nothing for her except amputate both her feet. I was horrified, for Ginger had spent her entire life with my family and had looked after and cared for all my children. So I appealed to Karl to help Ginger, for her operation was scheduled for the morrow. *"No operation,"* he said, and instructed me to sprinkle some of the *dhuni* ash on Ginger's feet, say Baba's name and pray for the best.

So, I drove to the hospital and made my way to Ginger's room. I went to the foot of the bed, lifted up the cover from her feet and quickly sprinkled some of Baba's *dhuni* ash all over the infected toes. I turned my face away in horror, for the sight turned my stomach. The toes were dark black and oozing – they emanated such a nauseating odour, that I believed that there was nothing anyone could do to help. "Please Baba, help her," I cried out, for I just could not bear to visualise her without her feet.

The next morning, I reached the hospital half an hour before the operation was scheduled to take place, only to learn that the surgery had been cancelled for Ginger had lapsed into a coma! I wondered whether this was the end. But it was not to be. She actually recovered and to everyone's surprise, so did the feet! The jet black discolouration slowly faded to grey and then to normal, the terrible stench of rot disappeared and the toes took on a reddish hue.

The doctors were as mystified as my sister-in-law, Rutty, who could not believe her eyes. "It is a miracle," she declared. But Karl and I knew better! Till she died, not only did Ginger have the use of both her feet, but also her ten little toes.

The story of the *dhuni* ash reminds me about the oldest member of Baba's women *mandali* who still lives on the hill today – Mansari.

As a child, Mani Desai self-consciously nursed a skin disease on her hands. Medication did little to ease her condition and she continued to feel embarrassed by this infection, which was red and scaly from elbow to wrist. By the time she was seventeen, she had resigned herself to the fact that the disease was incurable, but her family and relatives never gave up hope and attempted, for over two years, to get her to see Meher Baba. Being very down to earth and pragmatic by nature, she argued with her parents and declared, "When the doctors cannot help me, what is an ordinary man going to do?"

With Mansari on *Samadhi* hill

The disease continued to haunt her till, at the age of nineteen, she reluctantly went to Lower Meherabad in Ahmednagar and stood in the corner of the Mandali Hall, amidst the thousands awaiting Baba's arrival. She watched as He made His way through the throngs. Suddenly, He stopped in His tracks.

What made Him turn towards a little girl in the corner? What made Him beckon to her?

She moved forward hesitatingly till she stood before Him and looked up at His face as He gestured, "What is the matter?" She explained the nature of her problem and Baba turned to one of

His devotees and asked for the *dhuni* ash. He told her to apply the same on her hands for fifteen days.

Mani Desai accepted the little packet of ash and although she had a spritely and defiant nature, she followed His instructions. She never really believed that it would do her any good, but with each passing day, she discovered to her delight, that the infection was becoming paler and less angry, until finally, at the end of fifteen days, the scourge had disappeared altogether. Everyone marvelled at the miracle.

In a month or so, the infection returned and friends jeered at Meher Baba. However, Mani Desai somehow stood firm in her belief of Baba, till the disease vanished, never to return again. Some six months later, she was told by someone that Baba had taken the disease upon Himself. Disturbed by this fact, she saved money so that she could see Him again and find out for herself whether what she had heard was true.

When she finally got to Him, He was seated smiling down at her. She looked into His eyes and was about to acknowledge Him, when her glance fell on His hands. They were covered from elbow to wrist with her infection! She broke down and cried.

What manner of man was this who would take on an incurable ailment from someone else and suffer it Himself? "Do not cry," Baba said with gestures, "You will be well and so will I. It will go away."

She decided then and there that she would dedicate her whole life to Him. She would do whatever He asked of her. Baba accepted this young member into His *mandali* circle and renamed her "Mansari" for little Mani came from the village of Navsari.

Today, you will still find tiny, bird-like Mansari, the only member of the women *mandali,* living on Meherabad Hill. This caretaker *extraordinaire* spiritedly watches over the domain of Baba's *Samadhi,* Baba's cabin and Upper Meherabad that also houses her living quarters. She has lived here for years, sometimes without water or electricity, braving the cold, the rain, the heat and the storms, fighting the only creature she has been mortally scared of – the snake. A few faithful dogs romp around and she refers to them as "her children."

Mansari declares that other than the "Wayfarers," which she has read thrice, she has not read a single Baba book, nor has she done any kind of meditation or special prayer. Meher Baba is in her heart always and her selfless love for Him has sustained her through all the hardships.

No one dare leave the hill without meeting Mansari. She meets every new soul that comes searching for Baba and talks to them in her own inimitable way. Often, you hear peals of laughter coming from her little room and you know Mansari must be relating one of her own special stories. There was one that she told me about St. Theresa, who, on a rainy day, had the misfortune of pushing a laden cart through muddy terrain. The thick slush made it all the more difficult, so she called out to Jesus to help her and in despair, asked Him why He had chosen her to be the bearer of this burden. "Because I only ask this of my chosen ones and my good friends," replied Jesus.

Mansari's mischievous brown eyes sparkled as she continued, "And do you know what St. Theresa answered? – 'No wonder You have such few friends'!" With that, she went off into cackles of glee and laughter. "I love it!" she declared.

Her continuous repertoire of stories gives you an insight into Baba's work, His nature and His love of humanity. She can show you innumerable pictures and sayings illustrating Baba's thoughts and explain to you, in her own simple way, Baba's wondrous love. For someone who lives alone, she radiates happiness and a joy that is difficult to describe – and yet, if you speak to any of the foreign pilgrims about her, they have this to say, "Ooh, Mansari... she is chilly!" I am sure this tiny and sharp little woman can be a little more than just peppery, whenever she needs to be. She is the only *mandali* member on whom Baba has placed a restriction – that of not crossing the railway line that separates the hill from Lower Meherabad and the Pilgrim Centre, except for emergency health reasons. She continues to lovingly adhere to His strict orders right to this day. Her devotion is complete.

Today, Mansari has become frail and does not have the strength to stand through the fifteen-minute *aarti* prayers, or sit through the devotional songs that follow. But I remember the times – as the sun was setting, you could see her bent little figure coming out of her home, lantern in hand and walking briskly to start the evening *aarti* of her Beloved Master – The *Avatar* Meher Baba.

Note: Mansari joined her Beloved Master on Jan. 12, 1997.

CHAPTER 23

The Ocean of Love

The Ancient Fisherman stands alone, His soft, ever-watchful eyes gazing into the far distance. Little boats bob gently over the swell of waves as His men begin to drag in His oft-repaired net. A young man with a head of strong dark curls, turns his face into the wind and smiles, for his work is faithfully done – another day, another catch from his Master's Ocean of Love.

The net that Baba had cast into the sea gathered more fish than I could cope with. The fish seemed to scramble to get into the net rather than out of it, attracted by the bait that was little Karl, who seemed to be swimming furiously from one to the other.

Over the years, I have had the privilege of meeting up with lovely people, who have arrived at my doorstep in most unusual ways. How Meher Baba gathered all these people around me, I still do not know. There was one time when I had to hire a large bus because twenty-four people wanted to make the trip together to Meherabad. I remember silently observing the eager but sad faces and wondered why each had turned to Baba – but then I remembered how the bus had rocked with song and laughter on the return journey, almost as if everyone had left their troubles behind on the hill, knowing that they were going to be taken care of by Baba.

> ***"I am All Knowing and All Seeing, I can see and know even if you do not tell. My love will make you grow, and all those around you will blossom with My love – yours are the hands that have to pass that love around – pass it freely and I will help that love to grow so that there is enough to go around. Pass it freely and lovingly and I will always be near you to help you – each and every one of you – BABA."***

Karl explained to us that when we go to the *Samadhi*, *"Baba comes down to touch each one of you. He really comes to you Mum – to each individual and touches your soul so that all your cares are taken away. You do not as yet realise what it is to have His caring love."*

Is it enough just to be loved, I wondered? I know that little miracles are constantly happening in people's lives, despite the onslaught of life's problems. I understood that Meher Baba is a Master who loves you no matter who you are, or what you do. So far, my role seems to be just to introduce souls to Baba – bring them to Meherabad, and then leave each one to develop his or her own relationship with Him.

Through Baba's love, mothers and fathers "returned" to their children, husbands to their wives and children to their bereaved parents. In this way, it became a novel method of drawing people towards Him and surrounding them with His light. He tried hard to demonstrate through Karl, that nothing and nobody is lost and gone forever.

To prove a point, I have to mention an incident that took place one day. I was approached by a lady who seemed to be compelled to tell me a tragic tale involving her sister-in-law, Betty, who was brutally shot whilst at work in her store in the USA. The fact that the team of investigators had, so far, failed to uncover any important clue, continued to frustrate her brother, whose mental anguish and pain was of much concern to her. She hoped that, through Karl, some light would be thrown on the investigation, so that the killers "could be brought to task and not harm again."

That is how I presented the problem to Karl. He answered promptly. *"The people who shot her are nomadic and cannot be found in any one place – but they will be found for sure. The clue to this is in the right hand slab of marble that is there in the shop. The right hand side has a bullet. You will find the bullet which will give you the key to them. The bullet is there in the shop. So look for it and you will find them. We will help you."*

This message was ultimately sent to the brother in Fairfield, Connecticut, with a prayer that it would be a pointer to the killers. A few months later, I was surprised to find a letter from Jonathan Starr, Betty's husband. "I wanted to let you know," he said, "that your writing has been substantiated in several ways. A bullet was found near a cabinet in the shop. It has been analysed and identified in make and calibre. Also, the local crime solvers group has a large reward out for information about this crime. If anyone local knew anything, I believe they would talk – to date, no one has, so we assume a transient did it. At this time, the police have no suspects and as time progresses, the chance of catching anyone from the clues collected, decreases."

Karl assured me otherwise and insisted that, *"They will be apprehended in a place far away from hers."*

On December 25, 1990, I received another letter which said, "There is good news. The man who murdered my wife has been arrested. He was caught a month ago in Boston." I was particularly happy to note that apart from getting answers, Jonathan was greatly comforted to know that Betty was with Baba and that He was taking care of her.

Later, Karl went on to explain, *"Those that come to us are those that cannot go further without the love of those they left behind – we look after them. My whole life here is to help them and show them how happy we can be together. Whether they write or not is not important. The fact remains that they are with us and are going to be looked after by Baba. This is the most important thing. The happiness that comes to both sides is because Baba brings it to them."*

* * *

There are many others who have found the cares of life ebbing away, washed by the pure waters of Baba's ocean of love.

Behroze Mody was an inquisitive child. She would always question Meher Baba's silence. It fascinated her and she could never fathom how He could teach people if He did not talk.

Over the years, Behroze was always amazed by the unexpected link with friends that were Baba devotees who told stories of Baba and His inexplicable ways. She never chose to be a Baba lover herself till she suffered a severe jolt. Quite unexpectedly, Behroze lost her husband Sarosh. After that, nothing seemed to go right and her problems were insurmountable. She missed his loving support terribly.

Behroze and I found a lot of things to talk about. Through the story of Karl, his power to help and his love for his Master, her interest in Baba was rekindled and over the subsequent years, she went beyond what she knew as a child. She soon discovered that all she had ever searched for was suddenly complete when she first visited Meherabad. She has now created a haven for herself with Baba – a place to which she retreats daily. Here is an extract from a note which she sent me on the occasion of her daughter Gita's wedding – "I really feel calmer within – and it's entirely because you have shown me the way to Baba."

At one point in time, due to personal reasons, Gita, the elder of her two daughters, became fiercely anti god-men. She turned a deaf ear when her mother spoke to her about Meher Baba, for she had no inclination whatsoever to listen.

When Gita gave birth to a little boy, Sarosh, there followed an emergency and she was operated on for a perforated intestine. That morning, she came out of surgery critically ill. Lying on her bed in the ICU, her eyes focussed on a vision of Meher Baba standing in a garden filled with beautiful flowers. A sense of peace descended on her, as over Baba's shoulder, she saw the smiling face of her father, who waved out to her. Baba put out His hand, smiled and said, *"Sabar reh, badhoo saroon thassay."* (Have patience, everything will be alright.) She knew it would be so, for her father would not be smiling if she were going to die. It was this vision that helped the family, that took away their fears and gave them the strength to pull through Gita's life-threatening ordeal.

As Navaz, her younger sister, confirms, Baba never fails to respond in times of need.

* * *

The ocean is indeed vast as well as wide, for the next person who had Baba's gaze wash gently over her was Zenobia Banaji, who had just lost her dear and wonderful husband. She was heartbroken, for she loved him dearly. All I could do was tell her of my own experiences and try to impress upon her that her doctor husband would always be there in spirit to lend her his support.

Thus it was that we spoke about Karl as we chugged towards Ahmednagar and Meherabad. When we reached Baba's home, she was drawn naturally to chatting with Dr. Goher, who looks after the free dispensary run by the Trust in Meherazad. Call it coincidence or call it Baba's way, but it was Dr. Goher who remembered and pointed out that there already existed a connection. Her late husband, Pil, a leading ophthalmic surgeon, had once been called to attend to Baba's eyes. It was then that

Zenobia recalled her husband's words, "To look into those eyes was one of the most remarkable experiences of my life."

I must also add one more astounding detail. The kind, gentle and humane Dr. Banaji left his practice one evening to answer the call of a little boy whose pony had gone blind. That little boy was Karl and the pony, his beloved Fury, who had pierced his eye when he ran into a nail on a wall. Although Karl was a child of nine, he bravely held his pony's head, whilst Dr. Banaji stitched the torn eye. Both of them spent the entire night with the animal, nursing and keeping it still. Who knows, they may have formed an alliance at the time, only to resume it in the world beyond.

Zenobia has since developed a quiet and close relationship with Meher Baba.

* * *

Sharon Prabhakar, an intense and attractive stage actress, has a singing voice that tugs at your heartstrings. She had a sad story to tell.

She could not find the words to sufficiently describe the sense of abandonment, despair and helplessness that she experienced when her mother suddenly passed away. She told me about a dysfunctional childhood. She had grown up amidst financial difficulties and a lack of love and harmony in her home. This had caused great heartache to this sensitive child.

There came a time in her young life when Sharon developed a throat infection. Because of financial constraints she was admitted to a municipal hospital and was operated upon without the support of any anaesthesia. This remains forever in her memory, for it caused her tremendous pain but cost her mother only one rupee.

There followed many days and nights of fear and silence, for Sharon could not utter a single word. But, out of that pain, emerged a voice that was to rock the nation. Sharon became a singing star – a sensation.

As many successes followed, she wanted very much to share all this with her mother, but before she could shower her with physical comforts and find time to tell her how much she loved her, her mother fell ill and passed away.

"Why did God do this?" says Sharon. "What was the hurry? I was left with so many unanswered questions and so many unsaid emotions. Who could I talk to – who could help me? It was with this despair that I went to Nanny.

"I was not prepared for the story that unfolded. I was touched beyond words listening to the power of a love between mother and child. It was here that I came to understand that if love was sufficiently strong, there was very little that could not be achieved. Maybe, it could also happen for me."

Clinging to this hope, Sharon travelled with me to Meherabad and the *Samadhi*. She sat alone in Baba's room, begging for forgiveness and for an opportunity to convey to her mother how much she loved her. Says Sharon, "I left with no pots of miracle balm or magic potions, but I felt that somewhere in that room there was someone who said, 'I have made a note of it'. Somehow, I knew my Mummy was now in the midst of protection, love and people to guide her."

The healing process took time as Sharon began to lean more and more on Baba. She rested her weary face on His shoulders and listened to His voice. It was much later that she understood what the voice seemed to say, "Learn to accept – no man can change the course of destiny, what has to be, has to be!" So she accepted that her childhood was perhaps a debt from a previous life, she accepted that her Mummy's troubled life was also something that she alone could account for. At last her debts were over – she was free!

My meeting with Sharon brought back memories and queries, for there are many like me who are not emotionally strong enough to deal with death. When Karl died, I was left totally bereft. The answers kept eluding me and God's role became intensely questionable. There are some who resign themselves to the inevitable finality of death and do not accept the ongoing journey of the soul. There are others however, who believe in reincarnation as outlined in Hindu philosophy – the existence of a spirit world or God is never questioned. I belonged to the first category, becoming fiercely agnostic after Karl's death. The passing on of a person who has led a full and complete life was acceptable to me, but the untimely death of a young child made me very angry and emotional.

Baba has changed everything for me. I have the unusual and rare privilege of entering into His new world of treasures and in doing so, have received His Love that will always be unreservedly shared with all who come.

* * *

One morning, Bombay was suddenly rocked with stunning news. A leading industrialist, his wife and daughter were among the many who tragically perished in one of India's worst air disasters. Fate had willed that their son, Yash Birla, was not to take the flight with them that unforgettable day.

Philosophical by nature, Yash held on to his pain with a stoic demeanour that belied his youthful years. Instilled with the teachings of the Bhagavad Gita, he firmly believed that somewhere his family still lived on. His calm acceptance of the pain was a real lesson to me, for he is so beautifully in tune with spirituality and his acceptance of Meher Baba's love was also beautiful in its simplicity.

"How will I know you Mama," he had asked when he was scheduled to go to Meherabad.

"By the smell of flowers," she answered him.

Yash made his way up Meherabad hill, accompanied by an unpretentious little Maharashtrian girl, Avanti, to whom he was engaged. As we stood with folded hands, reciting the evening *aarti,* his eyes suddenly flew open. "I smell flowers," he said in a hushed voice. There were no flowers around us except those inside the tomb, but the air was suddenly filled with the powerful fragrance of God's blossoms. Yash knew in his heart – his mother had arrived.

Every song at the *aarti* that evening was about flowers and gardens, about roses, marigolds and blue gardenias. Yash and Avanti were transported into another world by the beautiful voice of Jim Meyers and were totally overwhelmed by the feeling of simplicity and love that they felt.

In the silence of the *Samadhi,* Yash had made an urgent request to his mother. He wanted to give his lady love something that had belonged to her – her *rudraksha.* He also wanted to give her the watch that his mother had purchased especially for her daughter-in-law to be. Both were nowhere to be found. Though he had carefully checked the inventory made at the time of the deaths and emptied the drawers of her cupboard, there seemed to be no sign of the watch or the *rudraksha.*

On his return to Bombay, Yash pleaded with his housekeeper, "Lilaben, please look once more in the cupboard."

"Beta," she replied patiently, "I have looked a hundred times and all the servants have agreed that the *rudraksha* was last seen around your mother's neck the day she left on that fateful flight."

Not willing to give up, Yash coerced Lilaben into looking for them one last time. Avanti closed her eyes and prayed fervently to Baba. Lilaben began her search once more. She opened a cupboard and – in the top drawer was the watch – in the drawer below was the *rudraksha*!

Says Karl, *"Meher Baba makes the whole world happy! He makes people have mercy on the poor. He makes people who have lost dear ones come to Him in order to show them His love of mankind. Baba means Grace, Love and Happiness and His unbounded Mercy has made lost souls want to live. When all hope is lost, He revives you, He nourishes you, He succours you. He is the Soul of all, the Father of all, and the Lover of all."*

* * *

Baba's love proved invaluable to one more person, Zarine Mistry, who lived in Pune. She needed help and strength to cope with a disease dreaded by all human beings – cancer. Listening to her speaking bravely of her long line of surgeries, thyroid, breast cancer and a hysterectomy, my heart went out to this brave lady.

Although she was experiencing excruciating pain at the time that I met her, she was positive about her recovery. It was this fortitude in the face of her illness, that made me tell her of the spiritual healer, George Chapman, and his intended trip to India. Zarine closed her eyes and listened carefully and by the time I finished, I knew she would be drawn through him to Meher Baba.

Very soon after the healing session in Bombay, Zarine found a lift in her morale and a great lightness of heart. The blood flowed strongly in her veins and an energy seemed to have returned to her. She went back to her job at a bank and the next thing I heard, was that someone had seen her disco-dancing!

She eventually found her way to Meher Baba's home in Pune, on Dastur Meher Road – the home where He had spent the early part of His life and where He had received God Consciousness from Babajan, the wise old spiritual Master. Zarine went into Baba's room and sat there in peace, experiencing His Divine Presence and receiving His strength to carry on with her life to the very end.

A few months later, Karl delivered a message for her. He wanted me to convey that there was a gentleman in a long blue coat who was her family guide and helper, someone who was watching over her, looking to her welfare and wanted her to know it. This made Zarine really happy, but she was very curious about his identity. Who could it be?

My next call to her was answered by a lady who introduced herself to me as Gulrookh, Zarine's sister, from London. She informed me that Zarine had just passed away. It was April 1991.

I had lost a friend, but I was happy for her, for it meant the end of her suffering. She had found her way to Meher Baba. I was also happy to learn that Gulrookh and Zarine had found time to be with each other, talk about life and Meher Baba. They discovered from an old photograph, that the gentleman in the "long blue coat" was none other than their grandfather, who, during his earthly life, had been a judge and had always worn a long blue coat!

Zarine sent a message to her sister through Karl – "*Do not be sad, for you do not understand how limitless are my opportunities and you will not know the extent of my bliss even if I had to explain it to you for a million days – but I will tell you in short – just two words – Having Fun*!" This beautiful message touched their hearts, for Gulrookh linked it instantly with Zarine's last few words before she passed into spirit – she had told her younger sister that she was going to "conquer her pain, throw away all her cares, travel around the world and just HAVE FUN!"

CHAPTER 24

Meher Baba Centre – London

It was the summer of 1991.

We boarded a plane for London, and this time I had prepared for the long hours of the flight with "God Speaks," a book dictated on the alphabet board and through hand gestures by Baba Himself. Had I known of the heavy reading ahead of me, I would not have been so ambitious, for together with the hypnotic drone of the engine, I soon found myself day-dreaming. Every now and then, I'd turn a page or two, determined to struggle on, but as the minutes dragged on, I was unable to focus on Baba's words. I ultimately found myself fiddling with the jacket cover of the book and there, to my surprise, tucked away in a corner, was a London address of a centre belonging to Baba devotees. How strange, I thought to myself – all these years of summer visits to London and it hadn't even occurred to me to check for a Baba Centre, even though I knew that He had made personal visits to the West in the 1930s.

Some days later, I impulsively looked into the telephone directory and dialled the number of the centre. An answering service gave me a forwarding number to a lady called Susan. As the conversation progressed, Susan offered to drive me to one of their Thursday meetings, always held at No. 228, Hammersmith Grove. A date was set for the next week.

Being on holiday and having a lot of leisure time to spare, I was invited by some friends to go apartment hunting. Their agent led us around two or three different places until we reached an old building that had a lovely feel to it. I fell in love with its ambience and knew at once that if I ever needed to reside in an apartment in London, it would be this one – but it was only a thought!

As we drove out of Susan's house the next Thursday, we wound our way up a hill towards Hammersmith Grove and, after a point, the area became increasingly familiar. Then I remembered, "Oh, I had come here yesterday to look at this property which is for sale." Susan looked at me in surprise, for the house that I had fallen in love with was none other than the one that Baba had selected to hold His *darshan* programme, when He had come to London some fifty years ago!

Of all the innumerable apartments and buildings in London, how had Baba directed my steps to the place where He had given His blessings to His first group in the UK? "Baba and Karl, are you up to something?" I asked myself.

The evening at the centre passed pleasantly enough. After the seven o'clock *aarti,* stories were shared over biscuits and coffee. I knew that Susan's curiosity would no longer hold out and that sooner or later she would get around to asking me to share mine with everyone. Not having any place to hide, I sat below a large picture of Baba with His Universal Message beside Him and nervously narrated a little of Karl's story.

On our way home, Susan told me that a very old Baba lover, Delia Delon, was still alive. As she was considered to be part of Baba's *mandali* in the west, I was very happy to be invited to meet her. With chocolate eclairs and flowers, we drove to Richmond to meet Delia, ninety-two years of age. What an experience it was! Love for Baba exuded from all sides of her room. Baba's face was everywhere. Graciously, she sat listening to my story when I so wanted to hear hers.

I don't know how long we spent with her, but it seemed timeless and just as we were ready to depart, she brought out a little box and asked me to pick out one of the many pieces of paper that lay in it. The one that I drew out is the one I treasure to this day for it has the following to say:

> "When God is found, you can have no idea what Infinite Bliss and Peace is gained. I give you all My love so that you can love God as He ought to be loved."

A few days later, I received another call from Susan. She informed me that they had organised a *sahavas* at the end of June. Baba lovers from all over the UK, Europe and the US, were converging to commemorate Meher Baba's visit in the early years.

They had reserved a beautiful place where they were planning a programme of songs and talks. This would be followed by a lunch cruise down the river to see some of the places that Baba had visited. She invited me to the *sahavas* and insisted that I be one of the speakers and share my story.

My heart hammered out a fast retreat, and a cold sweat broke out on my brow. "How many people?" I asked fearfully.

"Oh, over a hundred," she casually replied. The ensuing silence gave Susan a clear indication that I needed time to consider. "Don't answer now, please ask Karl tomorrow," she said, "for Delia would like everyone to hear this story of Baba's love and compassion."

"I knew it – I knew it," I said angrily, as I put down the phone – "I have been conned!"

I thought back to the sequence of events and ultimately had to smile at Karl's deviousness and the manner in which everything had been so beautifully stage managed. So, expecting the inevitable, I faced Karl with the question next morning – "What shall I do Karl?"

"Mummy, I am so happy to hear this, for the more people that know about Meher Baba, His love and His life, the more will profit by the knowledge. So who are we to say yes or no – Baba wills it, and so be it."

I sat there numb as the realisation hit me. I had been snookered by the Master Himself!

I tried to make a hundred excuses. How shall I get there, for I do not know the way? Promptly, someone organised a car and chauffeur. How can I go alone? My husband Jimmy happily agreed to accompany me. It seemed as if all my defences were crumbling and that I could not fight Baba's almighty hand of gentle persuasion.

On the day of reckoning, we walked into a beautiful chapel, the Violet Needham Chapel, which stood amidst a cluster of trees and manicured lawns. A silent and gentle calm pervaded the atmosphere, but that did not deter me from taking note of all the chairs facing a small stage. We took our seats in the fifth row and watched the hall fill up.

My heart began to race as Susan began her introductory speech and it wasn't long before I heard my name being called out. I walked, trembling, onto the stage and looked out at what seemed to be a sea of faces. My eyes felt very strange as I began to speak, but not a word could be heard except for some unintelligible squeak. "Can't hear, can't hear," said voices from the back of the hall. And then, to my horror, a mike was brought and fixed to my shirt! Desperate, I looked around for help, and found my eyes focusing on a friend – a big picture of Meher Baba, that stared at me saying, "True love is no game of the faint-hearted and the weak." He was there – right there, goading me into speaking, knowing full well that I would accept His challenge. Faint-hearted? Indeed!

I began slowly and hesitantly, till finally the floodgates of my heart opened and I shared my experiences with the audience. As I progressed, I saw tears pouring down faces and I thought to myself, what need had I to be afraid? These were Baba people, being touched by HIS STORY, HIS LOVE. We were all one.

"Be assured," Karl had said, *"that you will be received with love. Baba wants people to know that He is still there and you must make that known to them, for He wishes them to know that He will always be there. He wants all of humanity to know and be aware that He can and will be with them and it is not just speaking that makes it so. He is the Silent Master. Baba is the One who can give whatever He is asked for."*

Thereafter, we assembled on a launch and drifted down the river. We sang beautiful songs in unison and shared a rare quality of love. The world had no haven such as this one and although each day has to come to an end, I knew that this day would live in my heart forever.

CHAPTER 25

To Look Within

On this very same trip to London, I could not resist going back to the Spiritual Centre to get some more knowledge of psychic phenomena. I was determined, this time, not to let myself get emotionally involved, but to look at everything from an objective point of view. I collected more books, attended a few more demonstrations and spoke with informed and articulate persons.

I discovered that besides the medium of the occult, there is also another way of communication, the meditative term of "going within." This is a term that means, literally, to establish contact with the guardians of your evolutionary pathway. I have come to believe and am convinced of the fact that each soul has spirit guardians who are always waiting in the wings to guide you, if you so wish.

I would never have understood the meaning of going within, were it not for the positive experience of Karl and his role as my *farohar*. The meeting with Coral Polge, the psychic artist who had drawn three beautiful pictures of my family guides, further validated the existence of my spirit guardians, other than my son Karl.

Every bit of information that I have received to date has not been for my personal gratification, but is there to teach me the true meaning of growth and a love that is a constant flow of energy from those that are our guides in the spirit realm.

The power to communicate with the spirit world is a dormant ability that everyone possesses, but cannot be successfully put into practice by every person through the occult medium. "Going within" is not limited to any particular group or groups of people, but is a wonderful opportunity available to everyone. Inspirational guidance can be established by anyone through meditation.

You need to spend some time alone, be with yourself and link within with your spirit guides. All spirit guides will eventually lead to the one divine source within.

This is how I have come to understand Baba's love and His compassionate way of reaching each and every soul. If I did not believe this, I would not have been able to share my experience with everyone.

I know that there will be many who will question the validity of an experience such as mine. Realists will dismiss it altogether as being imaginative and far-fetched. There will be some whose hearts will be touched enough to believe in its authenticity and there will be others who will question its propriety from the spiritual point of view. These will surely include Meher Baba's followers, for it is known that Baba never encouraged the use of the occult.

In His book *'God to Man and Man to God'*, Meher Baba has discussed the role of occult experiences as well as their special precautions. Reading through the relevant pages, I can understand Baba's reservations in allowing for the widespread use of the occult; He felt "...that egoism can flourish...," that men "...must be left to their own limitations, resources and possibilities for working out the law of Karma." Most important of all, "the use of occult power, therefore, has to be restricted to the furtherance of spiritual purposes."

Reading further, I discovered that He also said, "The unity of the inner plane makes it possible for the Master to use His disciple as a medium for His work even when the disciple is unconscious of serving the purpose of the Master." This is possibly what had happened to me. There I was, ignorant and unaware till along came Baba who used my love for Karl as an instrument for His work.

When the communication first began, much "work" had to be done by Karl to help me overcome all the feelings of delusion that arose in me – I was always nervous and apprehensive about the reactions of the many who heard of Karl's efforts to prove his existence in the spirit world. It was difficult for them to understand or have any conviction about the messages and "appearances" that came through. But Baba knew exactly how to touch each person's heart. This was just one of the Master's inexplicable ways. Of course, there were times when the appearances were not what we expected them to be – more often than not they were never apparent. Taking people to Meherabad for Baba's *darshan* has always been a fulfilling experience for me and something I look forward to, for I have seen many blossom under His care. All I do is to take them to Baba and leave them in His hands. He awakens Himself in their hearts whichever way He chooses, for only He knows how, and He knows best.

Now, all the earlier doubts and reservations that I had experienced regarding the mystic writings have slowly disappeared over the years. Karl's words have taught me to trust my innermost self, and I have realised that personal messages from those that we love are not an end in themselves, they are just steps along a pathway to spiritual knowledge.

I know that all those who have come to my doorstep to seek Karl's help, have not come because of a sign of weakness, but because they have somehow reached within, and are not consciously aware of the fact. Their sincere cry for help is heard by their own guides and as all thought processes are linked together, the call is heard and the appropriate source of help is reached.

For example, "*Help, help*!" said the writing as I sat with Sabita one morning in London. "*Help, Sanjeev Jail*!" Oh, my goodness, someone is going to jail, I thought to myself – what can I do?

"*Help him,*" repeated Karl.

"How will I know him?" I asked.

"*Through Rutty and George Chapman,*" he replied.

I was bewildered. There was no connection between my husband's sister, Rutty, and George Chapman – the spiritual healer in whom I have great faith and confidence.

The next morning, I received a phone call. "I am calling from Bombay," said a soft cultured voice, "and I need help for my husband who is very ill and has gone into a coma. I need the telephone number of George Chapman in Wales."

I gave her the required details and promised to do my best to help her. As an after thought I asked how she had got my reference and phone number.

"Through Rutty," she replied.

Sabita was going up the stairs when she heard me repeat the word "Rutty," and she came hurtling down again.

"Ask the husband's name, Mummy!" she prompted urgently.

"His name is Ranjeev Jain," replied the lady, and thanking me, she put the phone down.

In my experience of writing, names have often been misspelt and this was also one such case. "Ranjeev" had come through as "*Sanjeev*" and "Jain" as "*Jail*." Mrs. Jain's call for help had been answered and the pieces of the puzzle fell into place.

* * *

Pretty, vivacious, doe-eyed Michelle Mody had not bargained for the fact that after the initial glow of romance had worn off, life would turn into one of denuding self-confidence, suspicion and fear.

Having been in the same profession as her husband, a flight attendant with an international airline, she missed the glamour of flying to other countries, the excitement of meeting people of various cultures, the shopping and the heady exhilaration and abandonment of dancing the night away. Her marriage placed restrictions on her natural exuberance and tied her down to a routine of waking up every morning, making meals for her family, doing the housework, and single-handedly bearing the responsibility of raising her two children. She began to feel excluded and resented the fact that her husband was still able to continue an enviable life style, while she was left with the drudgery of everyday life.

The discontent festered and soon turned into an illness of major proportions, for suddenly, there loomed in her already fragile psyche, suspicions of her husband's fidelity. There were days of depression when she continued to feel sorry for herself and did nothing but cry.

Finally, there came a day when she could not bear the pain any more – she decided that she did not want to live. She cried out to God in anguish, "Why am I here? What is the purpose of my existence?"

The answer came in the form of her friend Amie, who simply told her the story of Nicol and Meher Baba and the beautiful messages of love that came through Karl. This was a critical time in Michelle's life, where her own self worth was in denial. Therefore, she came to me hoping to get some kind of message that would turn her life around.

Karl said to her, "*Life will now begin to be rosy, and the lilac tinge of happiness is going to blaze with lots of pinks, and finally the golden glow of love will make itself felt and you will be very happy. You will never be alone any more.*

"You may not know it now, but all of you who come here have a special place in Baba's heart. He feels your pain and your fears; your laughter gladdens His heart so much and you will never know how hard He tries to help those who call to Him. I know sometimes some of you will be disappointed and sometimes you will think Baba is a great man, but that has no meaning at all. There is no such thing – it is all in your own mind. Baba is what He is – someone to make a Bridge of Life for you to cross when you have the inclination to do so; to cross to the other side and see what it is like. When you find out what it is, then you will not like to go back to what you were before you set foot on that bridge. Baba is Baba and He will remain Baba for you to call and say, 'Help me over this pathway and I will walk by your side forever'. Baba responds to every call and takes your hand to make a pathway of stars for you, and you will find the light shining for you to show how beautiful it is to go there and not to remain in the darkness of where you were.

"Please call me sometimes, anytime and all times – I am there for you all. Karl."

So Michelle decided to hold Baba's hand and put her foot on that "*bridge of life.*" She made her way to Meherabad, sat in the *Samadhi*, broke down and wept. She was overwhelmed by Baba's love, which she felt everywhere, and knew instinctively that her salvation lay in her love for God and not in her tortured mind.

On that very first trip, an impulse guided Michelle to walk towards Nana Kher, an old and trusted Baba lover, who held the keys to the library on the hill. She requested him to open the little room so that she could browse through some of Baba's books. As she picked her way through the stacks, she suddenly felt a peculiar light-headedness – a sense of joy that she had no way of accurately describing.

In the meantime, quite oblivious of Michelle's experience, Nana Kher began talking about Baba. He plunged straight into a story about a lady who had contemplated taking her own life. A close friend and Baba lover, knowing of her distraught state of mind, begged her to accompany him to Baba. As she entered the doorway of the *darshan* room, Baba's gaze turned to her and He gestured,

"You have something in your possession – give it to me." She looked at Him blankly, not knowing what He was referring to. But on second thoughts, she realised that it was actually the gun that He wanted. How did He know? She broke down and wept. She ran to Him and felt His loving grace as the fact of His knowing overwhelmed her. She knew that she was in the presence of her saviour, someone who had miraculously turned her away from the disastrous act of taking her own life.

Michelle heard Nana Kher's words as if in a dream. Was it the voice of her companion, or was it the gentle but loving voice of Baba who was telling her that He knew of her pain.

A few days later, Karl added to Michelle's experience by making it clearer still. He explained why it is necessary to complete the experiences that you have chosen to undergo in any given lifetime, no matter what the cost. To cut short your life is to cut short your learning experiences, the happy times as well as the suffering you are meant to endure. In actual fact, the wilful termination of life does not give you the freedom from pain that you so wish to escape. Freedom only comes when you are able to conquer the challenges and rise above them. Till you are able to do so, you have to wait for another opportunity, another rebirth, to complete what you have left undone.

Michelle was stunned by all the attention that was being suddenly given to what was her moment of weakness. Deep down in her heart, she knew that she would never contemplate the act of self-destruction again.

Now, although the circumstances of her life remain the same, Michelle has been able to give up her fears and resentments to Baba. She is aware of the dangers of sliding back to an old pattern of being, but her love for Baba makes her look within and she is able to see more of what others are going through and less of the self-pity that once had so consumed her. She finds herself able to live happily with her family, go on holidays with them and answer their calls with understanding. The burdens of everyday living have been "made lighter and her life brighter." "Why am I here?" she had asked. God had answered her.

* * *

What happens to those who cross over? Do they retain a physical body, a mind, a will of their own? Where do they roam, what do they do? These are questions that normally come to mind. We guess – but is there anyway of definitely knowing?

The instance of Amie and Nicol provides some kind of explanation as to how some spirit souls choose to work. Although you have read about the progress of the mother in the earthly realm, you may well wonder about Nicol in the spirit world.

After Karl had made contact with Nicol, he came through with anecdotes that described her as a little minx, who loved to follow Baba around, laughing, singing and teasing Him. When it was time to return to her place of abode, she would hide from view, hoping to avoid being caught by both Baba and Karl. When reprimanded, Nicol would *"toss her curls and run into the woods to have a good cry."*

There was a short period of time when the communication between Amie and Nicol was discontinued. Amie was given to understand that Nicol was "off" for special training – she was going to study further to enhance her understanding of Baba's truths and teachings concerning life.

In the meantime, Amie continued with her vast amount of reading, following Baba's instructions to the letter and was not perturbed by Nicol's absence. She trusted in Baba's orders. It wasn't long before Nicol "returned" and renewed the channelling with her mother. At the first stage, Amie was disciplined by Nicol into understanding Baba's truths; at the second, Nicol began to slowly train Amie to "go within" and allow for the freedom to express herself with words that are always inspired from her guides within. Together, they have forged an inseparable link that continues to date.

However, there were times when Nicol continued to be headstrong and sometimes appeared to give Baba quite a headache. The anecdotes via Karl would warm Amie's heart and lighten the serious nature of her work with Nicol. On November 25, 1994, Karl said, *"You will see her face with smiles, now that she has got her way, for she is going to handle the lives of her family not in the way Baba wants, but in the way she wishes. Baba has allowed her to have her way, because He wishes to see the result of how she is going to handle the problems and she will be successful for her love will do it for her. She will prove herself to Baba. He is looking on with pleasure and anticipation for her success. Baba is really quite sure that she will do it His way and is smiling at the possibility."*

By the middle of January 1995, I received another message which said, *"Mum, you have to tell Amie that Nicol is going to get the first prize for change. She has made a quick change from prankster to jobster. She has taken on the most difficult job of making the world a better place for people to live in. She has chosen it with her own heart for she now wants to go public and not keep herself only for family. Her horizons have widened considerably. She is going places!"*

I consider these to be two of the most delightful and enlightening messages that I have ever received. It made me realise that apart from the fact that there is continued life after death, a soul can progress even after it has crossed over. There is so much to do and learn, and the possibilities are limitless with the help of a loving Master.

CHAPTER 26

Some Lessons to Learn

I have been on many trips before, but each pilgrimage to Meherabad has been unusual and special. Beginning with the "message," and then the "Hamma Macklane" experience, many more have followed. I used to leave Bombay with knots in my stomach, worrying whether Karl would come through for me and the many others with me, but experience has taught me that Baba has always orchestrated each trip and that my worry was baseless. I had to learn the hard way though, that nothing was ever in my hands and that my apprehension was just characteristic of an earlier conditioning, and the fact that my ego would not allow me to fail.

Baba became a wily but beautiful teacher, presenting situations that turned into opportunities.

Karl once said, *"Meher Baba says you haven't got a chance in heaven if you do not make your way to Baba on earth. Your way to Him comes in your lifetime in the world, and not when you come here. You can find your way to Him in the only way possible by doing what He asks of you. This will bring the best opportunities to go to Him. He has made this possible by giving you these situations and He makes it possible for you to make these opportunities into successes and that is how you get closer to Him. You don't know all these things and so you call them sufferings. I call them opportunities – that is how you must look at them and then you will find that the difficult ones are the most rewarding. You will ask yourself that question when you are no more in the world, that why did I not realise this earlier? Well now you do, and so treat life as such and do what you can to turn these opportunities into successes."*

Any imagined loss strikes terror within me. What I did not see earlier was that here existed a great opportunity for me to give up this attachment to fear of any loss – imaginary or otherwise. Is this what is meant as surrender? I have often sat in on discussions about the topic of surrender, but, for the life of me, I have not been able to understand its real meaning. So, I decided to ignore what was being discussed until a trip to Meherabad made me sit up and take notice.

Zeenia Mehta, Rhea Pillai, Priya Dutt and a girl called Kitty were along for the ride. An interesting fact was that Kitty's father-in-law had been a sincere Baba lover. His total dedication and love for Baba had filled his nine-year-old son with much resentment. He always remembered one fact – that his father gave away much of his wealth to Baba. He could not understand why.

Kitty's story instantly rang a bell in Zeenia's mind. Her parents had been against *gurus*, saints and *babas*. She had spent her childhood being told to be extremely wary of getting involved with them. The general belief was that they took away everything from you. Even though Zeenia believes in Meher Baba and has been on many trips to Meherabad before, she still gave me a knowing look as if to say, "See, maybe my parents were not wrong after all."

On reaching the centre, we checked in and retired to our rooms to rest after the long journey. However, Zeenia had different ideas. She had heard that the most delicious strawberries were available a few kilometres down the road. So, off she went in search of the farm. She returned with two crates of the succulent red fruit which spent the night between our beds. The aroma was too heady for my liking, and by morning, I had decided never to look at another strawberry again. But Zeenia looked as if she had spent the night blissfully in Baba's gentle care, dreaming of serving the strawberries to her family in crystal glasses, sprinkled with crunchy sugar and topped with dollops of rich fresh cream.

At the morning *aarti*, we were especially moved by the singing of a Baba devotee who I instantly recognised as Hilla Talwar. She had just come in from London and was spending a few days in her beloved Meherabad. I was so happy to meet her again that, after breakfast, I invited her to travel with us in the car to Meherazad. I was hoping to share experiences and get to know her better.

As we rattled down the bumpy road to Meherazad, we were soon engrossed in the story that she had to tell us.

"My family lived here with Baba for many years. We lived in the small room up on the hill, which now serves as a library. This is where I grew up and was blissfully happy."

Zeenia could not contain her natural curiosity. She wanted to know why, of all things, they wanted to live here in the back of beyond with Baba? Hilla smiled to herself as she recalled the days.

"My father was searching for a *guru,* a spiritual teacher. He went from place to place, from one master to another, till at last he found Meher Baba and knew that Baba's home was where he belonged. He bowed before his Lord and told Him that he wished to surrender himself and everything he owned to Him.

Baba shook His head. 'No', He said. 'You have a wife and family – you owe them. You have to fulfil your duty towards them first'. Baba sent him away.

"My father was heartbroken, for he could not see beyond Meher Baba. He spent many hours in solitude, and in his wanderings, began to give away money and possessions to whoever came his way. In desperation, my mother went to Meher Baba and begged Him to take all of us into His care.

"'Do you really wish to give up everything'? asked Baba pointedly, 'for that is what you will have to do if you come to Me'.

"'Yes Baba', answered my mother without hesitation.

"And so we sold everything, including the little gold *karees* (earrings) we wore in our ears, and came to Baba."

Hilla seemed to have concluded her story, but we were full of questions, particularly since we had already heard Kitty's similar tale. "As a child, did you not resent your father for giving away everything in order to be with Baba? Did you not hold it against him?"

"Oh no," she replied, "we understood perfectly. There was nothing to resent; in fact I put my head on my father's feet for giving me the opportunity of getting to know of Meher Baba's divinity and the chance to love Him. You see, in all those years, we never lacked for anything. When our clothes tore, He gave us more; our stomachs were always full and we looked forward to the times when Baba would play with us and make us sing for Him. He sent us to the best of schools and even had each of us learn a profession when we grew up. Now, we are all well settled and contented."

We were so engrossed in her story that we did not realise that we had overshot the turning to Meherazad and were well on our way to Aurangabad. I happened to remark that the terrain looked unfamiliar. "Oh, no no," insisted Zeenia, "I have excellent road sense and I am sure that we are on the right track." So, on we sped, blissfully listening to Hilla's tales of her love for Baba.

I learnt a lot that day from all that Hilla had to say about the term "surrender." Her family loved Baba and unreservedly surrendered to Him from their hearts. Their contentment lay in the fact that they trusted Baba implicitly. Through the act of selling all material things, they gave up their attachment to them. With empty hands, they surrendered themselves to Baba, thereby declaring their willingness to experience their true selves as God.

I tried to think back and put myself in Hilla's place – fear clutched at my heart as I imagined losing everything. So much for my surrender! What opportunity was Baba trying to give me with Hilla's story? An opportunity to learn something more perhaps? But what?

The car sped on – I forced myself to think.

By this time, thanks to Zeenia's "road sense," we were far from where we should have been. It took us quite a while to retrace our steps, and finally we arrived at Meherazad when lunch was nearly over. Zeenia was so deep in thought, trying to figure out her own reactions to Hilla's story, that she had almost forgotten her precious strawberries; she was more than relieved to see them still safely packed with the luggage.

Time passed swiftly with Mani and the *mandali,* who were always so happy to be with Baba lovers, both old and new. But we could not stay long. We rushed through our goodbyes for we were already running behind schedule for our return journey to Pune, from where we had to catch the 6.45 p.m. train back to Bombay.

The movement of the car and the strong afternoon sun must have lulled us all to sleep, for we suddenly awoke to discover that we were still on the outskirts of the city and it was already 6.15 p.m. Always in control, Zeenia instructed the driver to branch off the main road. "Don't worry," she said, noticing our worried looks, "I will get you to the station in no time at all." With little choice in the matter, we watched helplessly as her flash of inspiration seemed to get us deeper and deeper into the heart of the city. Caught in the middle of scooters, hooting rickshaws and clanging bicycles, we came to a sudden standstill. What now? It was 6.30 p.m. Ten minutes to go and we had no idea where we were.

This time Zeenia panicked – her "road sense" had somehow failed her! "Call Karl," she yelled. "Ask him to use his influence with Baba to get us out of this mess." Poor Rhea and her friend, Priya, were most perturbed and looked at me appealingly as if I had the solution to our problems.

Something must have worked, for suddenly, the crowd dramatically thinned out in front of us. Seizing the opportunity, the driver swerved into the only opening in front of him. Bouncing off pavements and careening round corners, we eventually found ourselves on a somewhat familiar road. The station loomed in front of us. Zeenia's hands flew up in jubilation as we screeched to a halt. "I know where I am!" she shouted. Her "road sense" had returned.

Two minutes to go!

There was a mad rush as we grabbed duffel bags, thermos flasks, suitcases and Baba books and jumped out of the car. Zeenia lunged for her strawberries, terrified that they would get left behind. Somehow, some of the trays flew open and out they tumbled, rolling in all directions. For a split second, she was stunned – and then ran frantically hither and thither, not knowing which ones to save. Now it was a question of the train or the strawberries. Unfortunately, in the mad scramble of moving porters and commuters, most of the little fruits were being crushed underfoot. None of us had the patience any more, so we yanked her towards the train.

"Which way to the first class?" we shouted, as we dashed onto the platform. The whistle blew and we were still running. Finally we threw ourselves into the compartment just as the train began to slide out of the station. I plonked myself into my seat, my heart beating like a sledge hammer. I had not run so fast in a long, long time. With eyes gratefully closed, I waited till my breathing returned to normal and then glanced over at Zeenia to see whether she had recovered from the marathon. She was already biting into a sandwich. "Would you like a nibble?" she asked calmly.

My face registered the shock that I felt, for I thought her heart must have been squashed along with the strawberries! "Oh, so what if they are gone," she said, "it's nothing to be upset about. Baba has said that if you are attached to something, it hurts dreadfully if you lose it. But if you are not, it is alright. See, I am okay." With these words, she popped the last of the sandwich into her mouth and dusted the crumbs off her fingers.

My eyes narrowed into slits – I could have cheerfully throttled her. But a vision of Karl, sniggering behind the clouds, had me laughing instead.

Baba had used a simple strawberry to drive home a much bigger lesson – one I was not likely to forget.

We all go through life accumulating attachments – attachments to children, family and loved ones. We are tied to our identities, wealth, achievements, righteous beliefs and everything that gives us a false sense of happiness and a false experience of love. Why? Because all these attachments are transient. Therefore, it has to follow that though we may accumulate our needs and desires in life, it is the attachment to having them that has to be given up.

Very few are born brave enough to go through life without a care in the world and fear is a dominant emotion that makes us cling to what we possess. I am also a victim of this, for my attachment to the family has been the ruling factor in my life. I have lived in terror of losing what I hold most dear. Having lived with this for so long, and also the fact that one of these fears became a reality, made me accept that life has to go on this way. What I did not realise is that Baba was trying to show me that there was something I could do about it. I needed to give up my attachment to this fear. How? By surrendering it to Baba. This is one of the lessons I had to learn.

CHAPTER 27

Meher Baba's Cricket Team

"Baba works hard to put you on a good wicket and then He throws the balls. You have to hit them in the right direction. You must pick up the bat and strike those that you feel can go to the boundary but look to the bouncer for that can be dangerous and so you must try to avoid it. I am the wicket-keeper for I keep guard over everything and catch whatever is the extra. I catch the balls that Baba throws and you are unable to hit. That is Baba's game of cricket and He is enjoying it so much."

I sat back and laughed at my son's clever play on words. The game of life has to be played with all its experiences and lessons. Instead of being bowled out by a bouncer or "knock" in life, Karl's advice is to take up the challenge and go for the runs. No matter what your destiny or *karma,* and in spite of the failure to hit the ball to the boundary, Meher Baba will always be waiting for you, finally taking care of the bruises you have received along the way.

To participate in a game of cricket with the Master Himself, is an ever-rewarding experience. He is invited to bowl His overs, interrupted sometimes with the overs of another bowler, *karma.* But, a game with the Master makes for freedom, security and happiness that comes from the love that is thrown at you, ball after loving ball.

I look back at the years that have gone by and think of the many people who have come for the help and guidance of my son Karl, and through him, have met up with the Divine bowler, Meher Baba. They have all taken up the game, for Baba reaches out to everyone equally, the timid as well as the brave. There are some who have run the singles, others the twos and threes, and there are those who have hit the boundaries and the sixers. To mention each one by name would be a meaningless exercise, but their names and scores lie forever in the hearts of Meher Baba and His wicket-keeper, Karl.

Freny Peddar discovered Baba by a chance call to Amie, that was to turn her lonely days into ones fun-filled with chatter and laughter. Her acquaintance with Amie changed into a close friendship that is held together by the love they share for Meher Baba. Many a game has been played by the two, running frantically between the wickets, totally supportive and loving of each other. Despite bruises and knocks, this pair never tires, and can truly be called the opening batsmen in Baba's game of cricket.

Another person who decided to walk out onto the pitch and take a crack at the ball was Suraya Masters. I did not really know what her problems were but I did sense that at this time of her life, she was emotionally at her lowest ebb.

Suraya was the owner of a few racehorses and though Karl had jockeyed some of her stable horses to victory, he had never been available to ride any of her own. A sensitive person, she had felt his passing with great sadness. She was deeply moved by the story I narrated to her, but even more fascinated by Meher Baba's part in it and all the "happenings" that followed. We soon became good friends.

"Let's go and have a drink at the bar," she insisted on my last day in London. I could not stop talking and she could not stop listening until we discovered that we had lost count of the strawberry daiquiris that we had consumed. Looking around in amazement, we found ourselves all alone in the entire bar!

One glance at my watch had me flying back in panic, for I had a flight to catch that night and much to do.

On reaching the door to my apartment, I fished into my purse for the keys. To my horror, I realised that they were not there. "Oh, please Meher Baba – this is no time to play games," I scolded. "Please help me to find the keys." Suraya looked at me quizzically. How could she know that I had conversations with my *"guru"* all the time?

I rang the doorbell – Jimmy opened it, his face like thunder. "Do you know what time it is?" he bellowed as I raced past him to begin my search for the elusive keys. I looked in every nook and corner of the flat, terrifying thoughts flashing through my head. What if the landlady did not let us leave without the keys being returned to her? What if she made us pay an exorbitant fine for losing them? "Oh Lord, please Meher Baba – do something," I begged, as I proceeded to throw stockings, combs, make-up, soap, toothbrush etc., out of my toilet case in a mad hunt for the missing keys.

"Why don't you look in the pocket of the jacket you wore this morning," suggested Suraya, looking on with consternation. Unlocking my suitcase, I feverishly dug into the middle and found the jacket. From within the folds, a face peeped out at me. It was a framed picture of Meher Baba that always travels with me. Next to it was Karl's picture and there, nestling in between them, were the keys!

"Do you think Karl will somehow make his presence felt for me?" Suraya asked hesitantly, on her first visit to Meherabad. "I do hope so," I replied, as we sat on the parapet, drinking in the quiet tranquillity and looking up at a sultry sky filled with rain clouds.

A Swiss lady joined us and began sharing her thoughts and experiences with us. "Did you know that Baba had come to Switzerland? Did you know that He went into seclusion, and whilst in that state, He had a meeting with High Spirits on the Fallenfluh to work towards peace during World War II?" Having said that, she ran back to her room and returned with a pamphlet. She handed it to Suraya. I heard her gasp and saw her turn pale.

"I don't believe it – Nan just listen to this," she cried, her voice cracking with emotion. "This pamphlet tells us how to get to the Fallenfluh. You can reach the spot from Schwyz by car upto the stop, Grundel. Now leave the street to Ibergeregg and walk or continue with private car – DIRECTION ST. KARL."

There it was underlined strongly in ink!

With tearful eyes, Suraya looked up and smilingly acknowledged Karl's ingenuity for putting her in the right direction, closer to Meher Baba and therefore closer to God.

I write in her own words. "The first time I went to Meherabad, I think it was more a sense of curiosity and, I suppose, I went to please Nanny. But the peace, serenity and joy that I felt at being there has definitely made me go back every year; now no longer out of curiosity or for anyone else, but just for me. What I love best is that there are no rituals and nobody asks anything of you. Yet everyone at Meherabad is so generous with their love, concern and care and never ask for anything in return except that you remember Baba and learn in time to love Him."

* * *

In life, many persons have had the misfortune to have splintered beginnings and childhoods that leave many wounds to heal. Left alone in the world to fend for herself, Rhea Pillai discovered Baba. Nobody provided her with a source of constant love and protection the way that Meher Baba did. He became her whole world.

How do I describe the bouncers that almost destroyed a dream of happiness and, in a matter of seconds, turned life into one of much pain and torment. As much as I would like to say that I understand life much more now than I ever did, I am still astounded by the fact that I know so little. I do not know which is worse, to go through grief due to the death of a beloved child, or to go through uncertainty and agony over the fate of a loved one. The tale that follows tears at my insides every time I think of a courageous and beautiful girl who brought sunshine and comfort into all the lives that she touched.

Although quiet and introspective to the outside world, Rhea presented a different picture to us when she fell in love with the man of her dreams. It happened in this way. Rhea was staying with us during an interim period of her life and career as a successful model. She soon began to look upon Karl as a friend and companion and loved talking to him. So we called on him for a chat one day, just before she was due to leave on an assignment to Mexico.

"I hope my trip will go well and that you will look after me," she requested.

Karl came straight to the point. *"Rhea, stop hoping – you will not meet the person you want to continue relations with, but you are destined to make contact with another who will fall in love with you – his name is Moon."* Taken aback by his unusual directness, we burst out laughing. Good gracious, who on earth could be Moon in Mexico? The young lady was off and away and, before we knew it, she was back with the disappointing news of not having met Mr. Moon, or even Mr. Right.

It wasn't long after that, that Rhea was introduced to an actor, whose life in the tinsel and glamour world was similar to hers. The first time she looked at Sanjay Dutt with interest, apart from admiring him on the Hindi film screen, was at a coincidental meeting in a lawyer's office. He was there because he had been arrested for the illegal possession of lethal arms, the charges being his alleged involvement in the Bombay bomb blast cases. As she gazed at him sitting there, hunched and desolate, she was struck by his apparent vulnerability and instinctively felt the need to reach out to him in some way.

She came home in tears and spoke to Karl. "Please Meher Baba and Karl, help him, help to get him released – he looks so sad." A few days later, much to our delight, the court granted him interim bail and he was free to go, pending a further trial.

They were soon dating. Sanjay wined and dined Rhea till we became witness to a starry-eyed girl who knew her heart was captured. One night, after a particularly romantic dinner, Sanjay reminisced about his late mother Nargis, a lovely actress of her times. As they drove slowly homeward, he said wistfully, "You know Rhea, my mother was really a very special person – I think about her all the time." He looked out of the car window with his dreamy eyes, let out a long sigh and said, "I remember, she always used to call me her moon, her moon-child."

Rhea's heart stopped beating. She could have willingly died at that moment, such was her ecstasy. She dragged a bewildered Sanjay to our home and knocked at Sabita's door, insisting he repeat what he had just said. Sabita sat through the remainder of the night, giving him an explanation about *"Moon,"* the communication, and about Karl and Meher Baba. Sanjay was overwhelmed by the story and confirmed that he had indeed cancelled a scheduled trip to Mexico, the very same trip that Rhea had taken. He had little choice – he had been arrested.

Needless to say, everything was going well for Rhea and her "Moon." Bridges were still to be crossed, but the future looked bright and hopeful for the young lovers.

On July 4, 1994, the unexpected happened. Sanjay's bail was cancelled by the High Court and Rhea's life went up in smoke in a matter of seconds.

Sanjay was incarcerated behind bars for what was to be fifteen months, while his lawyers, family, and friends ran from pillar to post, trying to appeal for some kind of clemency. There were times when hopes ran high and times when they felt despondent, for the wheels of justice turn slowly in our country.

"He will get a reprieve," said Karl. *"Those responsible for putting him in will lessen the charges. He will get a reprieve."* I argued with Karl, telling him that he was mistaken, for judging from newspaper reports, things didn't look good for Sanjay at all.

"Take a bet," said Karl.

Rhea herself never gave up hope. She said, "In spite of terrifying reports in the newspapers and the threat of a sentence that may put Sanjay away for years, I never give up hope. It is natural for me to be still afraid and react to the vision of Sanjay's suffering and yet I never give up hope, for I believe totally in his innocence. Anyone so beautiful, kind and loving can never be guilty of what he is charged with.

"I open my book and read Karl's messages over and over, and they give me strength to face a new day. One of them said *'Life has to be faced and if you face it with your head upright you have crossed one big hurdle... and less pain is there for you later on'*. I look to Baba and I get a renewed strength, a feeling of peace, a belief, a trust. There is so much I don't understand, so many questions that go unanswered, but I know Meher Baba is with me as He is with Sanjay. I believe strongly that Baba lives in each one of us and if you look within yourself, in the stillness, in meditative thought, you will find Him – you will find YOU. The days become easier, for you know that you are not alone, Baba is with you. He is always with you."

On October 16, 1995, the Supreme Court granted bail to Sanjay. He was free to go home. There was much jubilation all around and Rhea's happy face reflected the joy she felt.

"The faith I have in Meher Baba," Rhea said, "has brought Sanjay safely home and it is His love that will one day set Sanjay completely free. I await the day of his total release. Till then, by God's grace, I have the support of my few close friends, my family, and Meher Baba."

* * *

And then, there is the night watchman, the cricketer who has not a care in the world, but has the courage to defy circumstances and survive the closing overs of the day. One such person I must tell you about is Mahinder Jani.

A lovable rascal, full of life, full of fun, ready to drink, dance and outsmart anyone he came across, Mahinder was so often without a thought for the morrow. His aim in life was to make hurdles for himself and then jump over them!

It was indeed a surprise to find a very quiet and lonely Mahinder at a party in London, where he had now made his home. I noticed him in deep conversation with Jimmy but it wasn't long before he marched over to me and insisted that I give him some time the next day. He wanted to know more about Meher Baba and Karl. With little chance to refuse, I must say that I smiled to myself and wondered at Baba's ways. I knew that Meher Baba made no exceptions. He barred no one, no matter his caste or creed, whether sinner or a saint. I had a happy vision of a Mahinder whose roguish energies were to be dissipated by Baba along a pathway to paradise!

He arrived the next day, suited and smiling. He spent the whole day with us, and over a lovely meal, I told him all about Meher Baba.

On my return to Bombay, as per my promise, I packed off books about Meher Baba to Mahinder. I sent him "Much Silence" and "Avatar," together with many pictures of Baba and His different quotes, praying that all these would help him lead a calmer and richer spritual life.

When we returned to London the following summer, Mahinder was the first to greet us with some wonderful experiences that he had through Baba.

On entering the USA for his son's graduation, he realised that his British visa had expired and that he had only the morning available to obtain a new one. Ordinarily, the immigration department insists on the visitor obtaining a new visa from his place of domicile, particularly when the passport is close to the expiry date. In his case, since his passport was only valid for a couple of months, there was no way that he could obtain a visa for longer than the validity of his passport. Although he worried about making an unnecessary trip to India, he plucked up courage, stuffed Baba pictures in all his various pockets, slipped one into his passport and entered the embassy with his head held high. He strolled past the various immigration officers and characteristically chose to join the line that led to an attractive lady. Though inwardly nervous, he put on his most charming smile and boldly submitted the visa application forms to her. He stood pretending to be nonchalant, but his eyes were riveted on the two stamps she had before her – one that said, "Rejected," and the other, "Granted." He held his breath, shut his eyes and turned away as he heard the dull thud.

Something had been stamped – what was it going to be?

He picked up the passport and walked away, hardly daring to look. But when he opened it, there smiling impishly was Meher Baba's picture, and on the same page, a stamp which said FIVE YEARS, instead of the customary THREE!

His story did not end there, for back in England, in spite of being accompanied by his butler and chauffeur, he drove back home from a party where, naturally, he had had more than one round of drinks. As luck would have it, a siren blared behind him and he pulled up to the side of the road. One of the officers politely pointed out that he had been driving with his headlights on and no dipper, while the other asked him for his licence. His heart sank, for he knew his licence had expired. As his hand stretched for his wallet, a voice reached him, "Have you had a drink sir?"

"Just one to keep out the cold, officer," he replied, with his most charming smile.

Not swayed by Mahinder's suave response, the officer opened the door and requested him to step out of the car to take a breathalyser test.

With shoulders drooping, Mahinder resigned himself to the inevitable, a hefty fine, a jail sentence and the confiscation of his licence for two years. He inwardly groaned with regret as he thought about the number of highballs or B-52s that he had consumed at the party.

He took a deep breath, shut his eyes, and blew into the breathalyser with a desperate call to Baba for help. The arrow stopped short of the danger level mark! "Once more sir," said the officer. Mahinder used Meher Baba's name repeatedly as he took another deep breath and blew again. The arrow inched up to the red mark and slowly descended. "The last time sir," said the officer, as Mahinder pictured the blade of a guillotine descending swiftly over his head.

The arrow never went over the red-level marker! It just would not go beyond. Somebody was holding it back and not letting it rise!

Mahinder could not believe his good fortune as the officers wished him a polite good night and waved him on to go home, forgetting to even look at his licence!

In the safety and warmth of his home, he poured himself a drink. For some unknown reason, he opened his wallet to check on his licence, and there, nestled in the plastic jacket was a picture of Meher Baba! He lifted his glass and grinned. "Cheers!" he said.

* * *

Thinking with deep fondness of how the team had grown, I spoke to Karl one day, thanking him, and telling him how happy I was to be so confident with the game. I reminded him about the length of time that had lapsed since he had last done anything spectacular to prove his presence to us. I think the remark annoyed him, for the next day, a really fast ball came along the pitch.

"Mum, there is a leakage in your house, a leakage in the house where you live." I was taken aback. A leakage, what kind of leakage and where? I walked all over my house looking for signs of a leak. Could it be a gas leak, an oil leak or a leak in the electricity? I could not find a thing.

That evening, the doorbell rang. I opened the door to find myself confronted by a neighbour who lived on the floor below. He complained loudly about a leakage in his flat which, he was sure, came from mine. He requested me to accompany him downstairs, where three plumbers were waiting to convince me of the fact.

"Don't go," hissed Jimmy. "Remember what Karl said this morning." But I did not listen.

We trooped downstairs to his flat and into his bedroom, where he pointed to a large pool of water on the floor. Tracing the fault, I was taken aback to discover that the leaking pipes which were responsible for his dilemma, were none other than the pipes that belonged to the bathroom in my flat.

Baba's game of cricket was over for the day, for I was stumped and my bales went flying!!

"HOW'S THAT!" shouted Karl.

CHAPTER 28

The Bouncers

By 1991, I had reached a stage where I looked upon Meher Baba as All Compassionate, All Powerful and All Divine. Through His grace, I am a first-hand witness to the help that Karl has given to so many. I have seen Him giving a young girl the confidence to struggle through her last and final examinations. I have seen Him give a bereft husband the strength to pursue the killers responsible for the brutal murder of his wife. I have seen Him bring a teenager safely home to her parents after her plane was grounded with a threatened hijack. He has helped untangle household problems and settle lovers' quarrels. He protects the lonely and gives courage to those who are afraid – in fact there is no limit to His reach and to the love He is capable of giving.

In the span of the last ten years, I have indeed travelled a long road from being an absolute non-believer to being able to accept and really love Meher Baba. I had come to understand that all we had to do was love Him and hold Him in trust and He would surely protect us. Therefore, on that chilly winter evening, February 25, 1991, I was totally unprepared for the first terrible "bouncer" that came my way. Suddenly, the spiritual umbrella that He had spread over me, was whipped away and my world was no longer a safe place to be in.

My husband and I were returning home after an enjoyable evening with friends. Chatting amicably, we drove into the parking lot, when the car suddenly swerved, shuddered and came to a halt inches away from the garage wall. I turned to Jimmy expecting an explanation, but instead, I saw an ashen face and hands that shook uncontrollably as the keys fell with a clatter to the floor. Not wasting a moment, I opened the door and ran around to Jimmy's side of the car, crying, "Oh, my God – what has happened?"

Somehow, we struggled to the lift and made our way to our apartment. The children and I tried to make him as comfortable as possible but, on realising that the colour had not returned to his face, we decided quickly to take him to the hospital. Driving through the gates, I was filled with a strangely familiar fear. The doors of the ICU shut and I was left alone to relive a painful memory, a memory I had hoped I would never have to confront again.

The minutes seemed like hours and I cried out to Baba and Karl for help as we waited for the doctors to give us their final diagnosis. Jimmy had suffered a stroke and that too on Baba's birthday!

My mind began to race as the gathering forces of doubt began to crowd me from all sides. What bothered me most was the realisation, that even though Baba was with me, something terrible was about to take place. My worst fear was being played out – the possibility of losing Jimmy.

The nightmare stayed with me for the next forty-eight hours, till I was absolutely sure that Jimmy was going to recover from his tryst with destiny.

It was only after Jimmy returned home that I was able to take a better look at reality. Philosophically, I concluded that sickness has to be faced by everyone in the normal course of life – so why had I overreacted? Why had I panicked? Where were all the lessons that I had learnt? Why had they been so easily scattered to the winds? Why had I found it so hard to conquer my fears, let go of attachments, control my emotions and bow to the will of God?

But soon, something again happened that was to further shake my confidence in Baba, and make me think twice about the protection that Karl so often promised to offer.

I had a maid, Stella, who looked after my grandchildren with much love and care. She came from a poor family and worked hard for a living. Unfortunately, she got carried away by the promises and attention of a married man and soon found herself carrying his child. Eventually, after much heartache, he bought her a small hut on top of a hill; she furnished this sparsely from her small savings and this is where she proudly took her baby home from the hospital. She was a devoted mother, loving and caring for her child to the best of her ability, making do with the little help we could give her.

The monsoons were soon upon us. Although the rains beat down on the hill and flooded her little home, she stubbornly refused to move out. She continued to come and go, till one day tragedy struck. On a particularly stormy evening, she was struggling up the muddy slope with her precious baby in her arms. She lost her foothold and fell. As fate would have it, she fell on her baby and the impact killed him!

When eventually Stella came to see us, the pain in her enormous black eyes made my heart bleed. Why, oh why, did God have to do this to a poor young girl? What a terrible cross to bear for the rest of her life!

All this time, following Karl's advice, I had not allowed sad stories and problems to have an effect on my own life and feelings; I just put them to Baba, confident that He would look after all those who came to Him. Stella's story and every subsequent tragedy that now came my way, seemed to have a crushing effect on me and I became depressed by everyone and everything.

To add to all this, my own life took another turn. Why, and what exactly happened, involves too many people and, therefore cannot be explained simply. Suffice it to say that suddenly my life changed from being one of love, laughter and harmony, to one of uncertainty, problems and a search for solutions. All the confidence I had built up over the years went down like a pack of cards and each day continued to be more difficult than the last.

"Karl, why do all these things have to happen – why can't you do something to help?" I cried.

"Baba says you will find out in the course of your life why things are meant to be and why you have to wait for your answers," he replied. *"We can only make few helpful changes for you but cannot alter the course of your life's pathway. That is ordained and you have to follow that pathway. Baba will give you help along the way, but to send you from left to right is not possible. I do not have the power to do that. All I can do is to clear the pathway of sticks and stones and little pieces of glass that may cut your feet and stop the bleeding, but I cannot send you along another road. You have to travel your own road, but the road will be made smoother by Baba for you. You will be helped as much as possible but you have to go along the same way and BE YOURSELF, but I can tell you this much – you will get stronger and better and be able to see to your life and do your own things and surprise yourself that you are able to do so, for these things come to make you a better person."*

Amidst all the chaos, I tried hard to digest Baba's words, to understand the fact that a chartered course cannot be changed. Messages of kindness and thoughts on spirituality began to hold no place in my memory and were not going to get me out of my present predicament. I needed reinforcements, I needed solutions, but all I kept receiving from Karl were placatory words and promised hope in a distant future. I was disillusioned and angry and was sorely tempted to give up my game of cricket with Meher Baba. I did not want to walk out onto the pitch or take up the bat. I did not want to face the bowler or strike any ball at all. I wanted to declare my innings and retire from the game!

I became unapproachable to many who called for help. I needed the space to gather my thoughts – too many of them were being squandered on anger and doubt. All the efforts made to understand God seemed to have vanished overnight as, once again, I questioned His existence. What was the use of being with Baba, if He could not come forward in times of need? Where was He? Where was Meher Baba? Did Baba the Compassionate Father really exist, or did He exist in my mind that wanted so desperately to hang on to Karl?

I am very aware of the fact that the general impression in today's world is that those who depend on the spirit world do so because of despair. Having started this way, I admit that sometimes there is a tendency to rely too much on answers. Therein lies the danger, for this reliance can allow for foolish imagination to flourish and the possibility of deceiving ourselves into believing just about anything. Therefore, I have to agree with people who insist that every answer can and should be found within the parameters of day to day living.

Ever since I began the communication with Karl, I had resolved never to allow the writings to take the place of good solid thinking on my part. I have made it clear to all who come for help, that my writings are not for the purpose of personal or material gains, and are not there to reveal what the future holds or to play the game of lost and found. Although help and guidance is available to all who are searching for respite from life's problems, the main thrust of Karl's guidance has been and is highly spiritual in nature. He encourages a bewildered soul to ultimately search for answers from the right source – God.

It has been all the more heartbreaking to watch and comfort the many who have suffered the loss of a child or a loved one and those whose relationships have soured into separation or divorce. It is at this time that a void is created and the heart cries out for fulfilment. It is at this time that you need help outside of yourself, you need to be comforted and loved. This human need to transcend pain and reach out for love, goes far beyond the understanding of ordinary minds – it is the cry of the soul! This inner search is what leads you to Baba.

Even though it was difficult at a time such as this, I tried hard not to deviate from the line of my original purpose – that of just holding on to Baba and Karl and asking them for their protection and support during these difficult days. But being human, I could not help hoping that Baba would use some of His grace to help lighten the load and that His love would somehow "stop the bleeding."

But all I kept receiving from Karl, were just words of hope, like, *"Hold on, everything will pass – it will be alright in the end – Baba will not let you down."* And yet, everything seemed to get worse, or just remain much the same. So much so, that I began to wonder if I was fooling myself into believing that He had the wherewithal to make things better.

In desperation and anger I shouted, "Baba, You have failed. You have failed to keep Your promises. You made me believe in You, You made me love You and now when I need You the most, all I receive are platitudes – words! Where is Your love?"

Prompt was Karl's reply, *"Mum, I am not able to find the answers to many of your questions. You have to find the answers from life, not from the spirit world. Your life cannot change by being with me, it can only be lightened. Heavy-duty things like changing the timings of events in your life is not possible. We can only make it easier for you to set out on your path and find the distance getting shorter to Baba.*

"I am aware that you need much more than that and you feel, why should I believe in Baba if He can do nothing for me, so you fall out with Him – but that is what you should not do, for benefits have to be seen with eyes that are not earthly, eyes that see beyond ordinary things – eyes that can look at blue skies and see the faces of other things and not only the fleecy clouds. Those eyes can look into the grey waters of the ocean and see not only the waters, but the smiling face of Baba who awaits you from inside the dark and murky depths – so if you get into the ocean by chance, He is there awaiting you with open arms. He will gather you up and push you forward with a force greater than you have experienced before."

I argued with Karl every morning, but he would not give in. He resolutely held up my spirits, reassuring me of Baba's help and love. He understood very well the turmoil in my heart. Again and again, he would tell me that nothing mattered except love – the love we had for each other and for Baba, would not let us down. And then he said,

"DESTINY IS UNAVOIDABLE. KARMA IS YOURS TO RULE OR TO LET IT RULE YOU. Baba can turn your love and direct it towards Him, so that He can help you, but as I've said, besides this, He does not change that which is going to be. We cannot change Time. But – God is kindness, love and understanding and if you also acquire these qualities, you have more wealth than any other.

"Baba says nothing is so bad that you cannot surmount the difficulty. You must wait patiently for life's problems to pass, for even the worst passes away and peace comes after the storm everywhere. So, hold on to Baba till the storm passes away, for He is there for you to hold on to. The storm ravages the countryside and all things get swept away by the tides that flow over you, so if you can stay with Baba through the storm, it will rage all around you and you will still be standing at the end of it, ready to take a step forward just as soon as it has gone past you. So I feel you must stay calm and strong, with your hand outstretched for Baba to hold, so that you will still be where you had to be before the winds, rain, clouds and snow descended on you. We do have the power to help you stay calm and strong, but we cannot stop the rain from falling, nor the clouds from rolling over you, nor the snow from covering you. So you must be in the way you are till everything passes away – for pass it will. The rain will dry up, the clouds will roll by and the snows will melt away. I will help you whenever you need me, and I assure you Baba will get you through everything successfully – I just know He will. I have complete faith in Him to do what is best for you always. I love you all – Karl."

CHAPTER 29

Faith

I tried my best to understand and come to terms with what was repeatedly explained by Karl. Too many years had gone by and too many unbelievable events had taken place for me ever to doubt his existence or his intentions of helping us all – but now, I felt a certain kind of despair, not so much for what had happened, but because I thought Baba had let me down. Although I understood that He was not at my beck and call to solve life's everyday problems, I did hope that He could and would come forward in a crisis and lend a helping hand. How could anyone believe in Him if He didn't?

By now I had told so many about Meher Baba, for I felt His closeness deeply, but somewhere along the way, the tables had turned and I became more and more doubtful about what I had trusted the most. What I was most afraid of was the thought that maybe I had put too much meaning into being with Baba. I had worked so hard over the years to learn to trust Him, and I had got so used to having Him around and calling out to Him, that I could not resign myself to the fact that perhaps my faith had little basis and that I had deluded myself all along.

My questions and doubts seemed endless. What was I to do? Should I turn away from Baba or should I accept him permanently and forever as being a part of my life, as a part of my very existence. Should I put out my hand and say, "Stop – I have had enough!" Or should I still look upon Him as friend, companion, spiritual guide and loving Father in heaven?

It was at this time of agony and doubt that I had a dream. I saw a strange blue glow; it took on a pinkish hue and out of that ethereal light came Meher Baba. He walked towards me and put His right hand on my head. His face was old, His eyes infinitely kind, for they were the mirrors of a profound sympathy that flowed from Him as He enfolded me in a loving embrace.

I had hardly recovered from the euphoria of my dream when, that evening, a letter arrived by post. It was from a lady by the name of Naju Kotwal whom I had met a few times in Meherabad. I slit open the flap to find enclosed, an article written by her sister, Hilla Talwar. It was entitled, "OUR FAITH MUST NEVER WANE." I stared at it in astonishment, knowing instinctively that Karl was about to prove something. What was he trying to show me? Why had this letter arrived and at this moment? I recalled my meeting with Hilla in Meherabad, when she had told me how her family had literally been educated, fed, nurtured and brought up by Baba. I had seen the love for Baba written all over her face and was so glad to have made her acquaintance.

Imagine my horror when I read that her brother and his wife had perished in a major automobile accident while on their way to Meherabad to bow down to their Beloved Father, Meher Baba. Incomprehensible was the fact that although their little son Meherwan, aged ten, had survived the accident, he was left with the burden of having to face life alone.

I can do no better than to reproduce her beautiful article that arrived at my doorstep just when I needed it the most.

OUR FAITH MUST NEVER WANE

I am writing this article in the hope that no matter what suffering we have to endure, our faith in beloved Baba must never wane. He too suffered pain when He was in our midst for the sake of mankind.

Always remember that love is the reward of pain and you will become much stronger and come out of the darkness into the sunshine with "His" hand firmly clasped in yours. Last year was one of the worst years of my life and for a lot of people I know. It began with a great deal of stress and continued thus, getting worse each month.

Since July, my husband Dev was literally crippled with severe sciatica and backache. We tried all the alternative medicines to avoid surgery, but in the end when all the other treatments failed, he had to undergo surgery in October. It was major surgery especially for a man with a triple bypass of the heart. But with Baba's infinite grace and mercy, the operation was successful and I brought him home on November 1, glad that the ordeal was over. But the very next day, I had the most horrible news from India, that my beloved only brother and his wife and son were involved in a road accident between Pune and Ahmednagar on their way to their annual pilgrimage to Meherabad.

My brother Adi and his wife Freny had both died and their son Meherwan, who is only ten years old, was unconscious and in a hospital in Pune. I was totally shattered by the news and wanted to fly to my dear mother, Nergis Kotwal, and my sister to help them nurse little Meherwan, but did not want to leave my husband either, since he needed care following his spinal operation. I was in such a dilemma. But beloved Baba is all merciful and at that very time my son's mother and father-in-law, who is a doctor, were on holiday in London and offered to take care of Dev so I could fly home to India on November 4.

I cannot remember my flight back to Bombay. I was in such a state of shock and wept all the way. I kept hoping that it was just a nightmare that I would wake up from, but alas it was all too true! I reached Bombay at last, and ran up the stairs to my dear mother's flat and broke into uncontrollable sobs. My mother held me in her arms and gently said to me "Hilla, do you know that by crying this way you are insulting beloved Baba! For whatever has happened was all His Divine Will and you must accept it as such." I was really taken aback by my mother's words and felt rather ashamed of my tears, but I could not stop them from flowing then, and I can't stop them now, even though nine months have passed since the fatal accident.

Believe me, my faith in beloved Baba has not wavered in the least, but I have always been a very emotional person and was extremely close to my brother and sister-in-law. I am not implying that my mother loved them less, for I know she adored her only son who is the youngest in our family, and brought him up with great difficulty, for he was always very delicate as a child. My brother was only two years when my father, Savak Kotwal, renounced the world and we all came to live with beloved Baba in the *ashram*, according to His divine wish. Once my mother told me that Baba had carried my little brother Adi in His arms from the top of Meherabad hill to the railway line below, which we always thought was so fortunate for him. He was indeed a special Baba child. I was totally devastated and numb to know that the two people whom I cared for so very much had gone away forever.

My faith in our Beloved continued steadfast but I was so angry at what had happened and told my mother so. My mother said to me, "Hilla, dear daughter, please calm down and be grateful to beloved Baba that you had your darling brother for fifty-four years, because if it was not for His divine mercy, Adi would have died as a child. Baba has saved his life several times; now how many more times did you want Him to go on saving Adi. Adi and Freny are with the Beloved, and far happier than they have ever been. So, for their sake try not to be so unhappy; instead, be grateful to Him for those lovely years with them. Also, it would not please Baba to see you crying your heart out."

Everyone who heard the news of the accident was shocked and numb. I was so upset that several friends and relatives whom I was trying hard to bring to our Beloved, were now turning away and saying, "How can Baba have allowed them to die when they were on their way to His shrine, we just cannot understand this." Even some Baba lovers were wavering and thinking how could this have happened. When my mother heard of this she said, "It is Baba's way of sifting the strong and devoted ones from the weak, who fall by the wayside."

Some people who came to give their condolences to my mother, said to her mockingly, "You are constantly taking Meher Baba's name and your husband was part of His *mandali*, now see what your Meher Baba has done!" My mother told them gently, "Have you never heard of hundreds of Muslims going on their Haj and dying on the way, or thousands of Hindus drowning during the holy festival of the Kumbh Mela. Similar things have happened to people of various religions. Besides, we are alive and are constantly struggling and striving to make our pilgrimages to our Lord's abode, whereas my son and daughter-in-law have gone straight to His loving arms, so they are far more lucky than we are. They have gone from this world of turmoil and trauma to greater peace and abounding joy."

I have never been more proud of my mother than when I heard this. People who came to the funeral to condole, were really amazed at the dignity and brave face she put before them in spite of her aching heart. They all admired her unswerving faith in beloved Baba. My mother is a very frail eighty-three-year-old, but at that time she emanated strength and others looked frail beside her. They left with deep respect for her, some with renewed faith and some deeply puzzled. I am truly blessed with a remarkable woman for my mother.

After a week, she insisted on my going to Pune to help my sister Najoo look after little Meherwan in the hospital. I did not want to leave her alone, but she would not hear of it and said her wonderful neighbours would be there if she needed them. Meherwan had a fracture in his forehead, and both bones of one lower leg were broken. He was in a Pune hospital for three weeks, and the Baba lovers there were splendid. There were some Baba lovers there from Bombay and they all rallied around and gave us every kind of help. They were like members of our family. Some of my brother's friends and my friends did whatever they could for us. It was all possible because of beloved Baba's divine mercy and grace.

After three weeks in Pune, we had to move Meherwan to a hospital in Bombay, for his leg had not set properly. He was operated on in Bombay, and the operation was, by Baba's grace, successful and we were grateful. Meherwan was not aware that he had lost his parents in the crash. We had told him that they were in a serious condition in another hospital in Bombay. For a whole month, this weighed like a heavy stone around our chests, worrying about how to break the news of this tragedy to a ten-year-old.

We were afraid of his reaction as he was so close to his parents. Najoo and I were dreading the day when we had to pluck up courage to gently break the news to him. For four weeks, we had to laugh and joke with him, pretending that all was well, when we were both so shattered inside and the pain of our loss so excruciating. We used to take it in turns to go out of the room for a little while and give vent to our grief and then return dry eyed and cheerful. It was a great strain on Najoo and myself. A most difficult time for us. We kept praying to Baba for strength and He was there for us all the way.

Just before Meherwan left the hospital, with palpitating hearts, we gently broke the news to him after praying to our Beloved for help and guidance and strength. We will never forget the expression on his dear little face when we broke the horrific news of the double tragedy. He took it like a true Baba baby, and did not scream or faint. He just took the bedsheet in between his teeth and buried his little head in the pillow and sobbed his heart out. We both suffered intense pain for we adored him so. It was one of the worst moments of our lives, believe me. We all gave vent to our grief and were relieved to do so after holding back for four weeks. It was all the more difficult for my dear sister, for she had been with Meherwan, day and night, for a full month. I used to help her during the day but she would not let me stay at night. She is a wonderful and remarkable woman with the utmost faith, devotion and love for beloved Baba.

My husband joined us after a month. My son's in-laws brought him back with them to Bombay. How grateful I am to them for their help and sacrifice on their holiday. Dev was a pillar of strength to our family and Meherwan cheered up a great deal after his arrival, for he loves his Uncle Dev very much. My sister and I would take turns in sleeping with Meherwan for a while, just so he had some security and comfort. At times, he would wake up at any hour of the night and ask me to hold him close and his little body would give out great sighs, which would break my heart. For a long time, he was not able to sleep and kept awake until 2 a.m. and kept tossing and turning and sighing and crying. Those days and nights were unbearable for all of us. Christmas night was the worst of all, for he missed his parents and kept seeing them everywhere and cried until late into the night and we all grieved with him and for him. We did our best to make Christmas day enjoyable with loads of presents and love.

Most of all, we had tremendous support from Baba's sister Mani, who wrote to us and telephoned several times with words of love, comfort and encouragement. Her telephone conversations meant a great deal to my mother, to Meherwan and to us all. Arnavaz also phoned and spoke so lovingly. We had letters from all the Baba family and Meherwan was inundated with gifts and get well cards from all the Baba family at Meherazad and Meherabad, and from Bombay Baba lovers as well as his teachers and friends. Also, my brother's bosses and colleagues were wonderful and we are eternally grateful to each and every one. Dear Mani's phone calls gave us strength, hope and courage, especially to me who needed it most. When she spoke to us, I felt as if our Beloved was speaking to us. I really longed for the day when we could all go to Meherabad and Meherazad after Meherwan fully recovered, for only there would I feel better again and at peace.

After that uncontrollable bout of tears on Christmas eve, Meherwan woke up the next morning and said he was going to be very brave and cry this way no longer, and he kept his word. There were times when the tears would well up in his eyes, but he would not allow them to fall and would compose himself and show his strength. He has a lot of my mother in him and his love and devotion to our Beloved is wonderful to behold.

We took Meherwan to Meherabad for Beloved Baba's birthday and there was not a dry eye at the *Samadhi,* for those who knew about the tragedy, when Meherwan sang "Count Your Blessings." On Baba's birthday he sang a lovely song, which Najoo had taught him. He sang before Mani and all the Baba lovers, and received resounding applause. We all felt a great deal stronger after laying down our tormented heads at our Beloved's *Samadhi,* it was like crying on one's mother's shoulder with loving arms enfolding and healing us. We all felt the same way, a beautiful experience of warmth, love, comfort, healing and an inner strength to help us through our sorrow. We know now that there is a reason for our pain and suffering, that we had to resign ourselves to His Divine Will and keep on holding steadfastly to His *daaman,* no matter what suffering we have to go through or how troubled and steep the path we tread.

My father, who was the night watchman for Beloved Baba for many years when he lived in the *ashram,* once said to us that the first thing he would say to the Beloved when he bowed down to Him at the start of his night duty was, "You are the Ocean of Mercy." And I know that He is the Ocean of Mercy for the tragedy could have been worse if my brother and his wife and child were all paralysed or brain-damaged for life. In his Infinite Mercy, Baba saved us from that ordeal. In that accident, there were several people involved, all either paralysed or unconscious, whereas Meherwan has recovered and is back at school and very cheerful once more, which is amazing. Our Beloved Baba has given him peace, courage and strength. He is truly blessed. In fact, once when I burst into tears, Meherwan lovingly embraced me and said, "Whatever was to have happened, has happened. We must be brave about it. Look at my eyes that are dry, but if you cry this way, then I too will cry and that would make Beloved Baba very sad." His love, faith and courage are admirable for a ten-year-old and we are truly proud of him.

This poem was found on my brother Adi's desk after the accident. It was written in his own handwriting. We don't know whether he wrote it himself or he copied it from somewhere.

"My time in life is yet to come
When I can rid my mind of worldly call
Breath, the pure sweet air of paradise
My time in life is yet to come.
When I will see the truth and not be blind
Crystal streams will wind through paradise
Paradise is peace, paradise is love
Paradise is having time to do the things you like best
Paradise is having those you love around you when
you are alone
Paradise is feeling warm when the world is feeling cold
My time in life is yet to come
When I can live in peace with all mankind
And with truth find my way in paradise."

Jai Baba

– Hilla Talwar

I sat in silence as tears streamed down my face. My lesson came from a ten-year-old, a little boy who had his parents snatched away by the hands of destiny. Could I learn from Meherwan's intense but natural love for Meher Baba – a love that seems to defy all logic – or was I still going to expect Baba to do everything that was only good for me and mine. Should I not have faith in Him even if everything goes wrong and sorrow comes my way? I sat ashamed, for I realised that I did not deserve to have so much and still demand more from Baba whose love and patience had nurtured me for so long. I looked within myself again.

How deep was my faith, how strong my trust?

I knew I was slowly going to get my answers, for Karl's faith and love were reflected in the strength of this little boy who had lost so much and yet loved Baba with all the intensity of his soul.

CHAPTER 30

Baba's Gift

Meherwan's story touched my heart and provided me with the strength and determination to get on with my life. This lesson was the shot in the arm I so sorely needed – it gave me the reason to reflect on Baba, to have faith in Karl's judgement, and to trust that whatever happens is for a good enough reason. I knew that even if I sank any deeper, I would somehow find my way up again. Although old resentments still surfaced at times, I tried not to let the worrying get the better of me. Instead, I began to hold onto a tiny glimmer of hope that the worst could be over – but just in case, I resolved to leave the pendulum to Baba as to which way it was to swing.

No sooner had I come to terms with this, Karl came through with something that promised to be most exciting. *"Baba is going to make a declaration on the TV tonight. You will hear it on your TV set at 9 p.m. Switch it on, you must listen to it tonight. Baba is going to tell the world what He wishes them to be."*

I flew to the phone and called as many Baba friends as I could. Most excited, we all stayed glued to the various channels, for I had forgotten to ask Karl for the specific one.

The clock struck nine.

Jimmy and I took our chance with channel two. We hitched onto a programme that documented discoveries under the ocean. After about twenty minutes, we were feeling a little let down, for nothing seemed to present itself as being spiritual or remotely like a profound message. Could Baba be trying to show me some new way of life, I wondered somewhat stupidly?

Just then, my thoughts were rudely interrupted by the

simultaneous ringing of both my telephones. Breathless, excited voices flew across the wires – "Did you hear it, did you understand what was said?"

"Where? Which channel?" I cried.

"Oh it was so clear and wonderful... it was on channel one," came the reply.

I groaned loudly. The most astonishing proof of communication from another world, the world of Baba and Karl, and I had to be the one to miss it. However, my disappointment was short-lived, for my dear nephew and Karl's dearest friend, Phiroz, had had the foresight to tape the whole programme from start to finish.

The nine o'clock slot that night had an ongoing serial called "*Udhan*." It involved a policewoman whose special achievements along the line of duty did not give her the satisfaction that she was looking for.

The scene opens as she enters a party in full swing with music blaring, women gossiping and men gambling around a card table. Being from the civil service, we sense her discomfort as she creeps silently through the room with her head lowered, looking from under half-closed lids for a friendly face – but alas, all she can see are the disdainful glances from women who belong to the upper crust of society and who make no effort to disguise their feelings of superiority from her.

Saddened and embarrassed, she fidgets self-consciously with her simple *sari*, till suddenly, finding an open doorway, she escapes the stifling atmosphere and heavy tinkle of glasses, and finds herself on an open terrace. Away from wagging tongues and disparaging glances, she breathes a deep sigh of relief and gazes into the distance.

Jimmy and I looked at one another – nothing so far had struck us as having any meaning. Where and what was Baba's message – what did all this mean?

A gentleman enters the scene. He is well dressed like the others, but there is something in his manner of greeting that gives her confidence. We hear him gently drawing her into conversation and soon he asks why she prefers to be so alone. She looks at him shyly and confides, "I have achieved so much success and reached the top in my line of duty, but somehow the fruit seems tasteless instead of sweet and I am not happy within myself and am searching for something more."

"And what is that?" he asks.

She turns and looks straight out at us as the camera focuses on her face. Her words that follow tell us all we need to know. "*Mera Baba bola*" (my father says), she says, sounding exactly like *MEHER BABA BOLA*, "to reach the heights does not mean you have to achieve success in everything. It means you have to grow from within – you have to become a better person and that is the only success worth winning."

Her eyes reflect her deep thoughts as if she wants us to really understand what she is about to explain. "I am at the crossroads," she declares, "and I have to decide which way I want to go. Do I wish to be lured by the blazing false lights of this party, or traverse the path of truth to the little light twinkling in the simple hut below this terrace?" Her eyes lower as she turns her head away and the music turns low. The picture fades away...

Our heartbeats slow down – Baba's amazing message has come through!

I sat still, drinking in the importance of this wonderful message. Another feather in Karl's cap, I thought, proud of my son's efforts to continue to teach me in spite of my reservations and stubborn stance. But suddenly, another thought took over and became of prime importance. What did the message mean and where was I going to discover this little light and where would it lead me?

A small voice inside my head seemed to answer, "Don't struggle, leave it to Baba. You are not the only one, for most people are at the crossroads and do not know what to make of the path of Truth and the little light below." I tried to relax and wait for my answers, but the fact is that too much was still happening in my life and I did not have the strength or energy to look too deeply into my own feelings.

Besides, I was rather annoyed with Baba.

There was still a crisis in my life, problems to be solved and decisions to be made – that was my first priority and I did not have time for much else.

But the pressure mounted, for suddenly, I was faced with another heart-wrenching problem, mostly of my own making.

There comes a time in life when all parents are faced with the fact that their children have grown up and need to find a life of their own. It is always difficult to part, but more so, when you have come to depend on their love and moral support and have lived together in harmony for so many years. It so happened that everything took place for me at this particular time of my life. Neville was offered a business opportunity abroad and decided to leave with his family to make a new life for himself. Pesi shifted his base to South India. This meant that Tina and her little son Yohann, were not going to be with us too often. It seemed that even Baba had taken a long holiday!

I moped around the empty house for days. Seeing me so depressed and unhappy, my husband decided it would be better if we also made a new beginning and put the past away. In spite of my resistance, he insisted we temporarily move out of Bombay. Nothing that I said would sway his decision or change his mind. It took some time for me to accept the fact that I was leaving the house we had lived in for twenty years. It was a home we had made for ourselves and a place where we had spent many happy days with the children. Even though the move was just for a while, my mind began to blow it out of proportion.

The last day approached.

The early morning sun shone brightly, the sea was a shimmering blue as the city began to stir. The first sound I heard, was the familiar call for prayers from the Haji Ali Mosque. With a heavy heart, I walked slowly through the rooms and for the last time, looked on the bare walls of my beautiful home.

Jimmy left to move into a hotel, for he needed to be in Bombay to complete some final details, and I left with my small bag for the station to catch the morning train to Pune, which was where we had eventually decided to make our new residence. The tears welled up as I looked over my shoulder to see my bedroom balcony fade away – and there was nobody there to say goodbye.

For the first time in my life, I was all alone. The taxi sped along the road.

By the time I reached the station, I was in a state of deep depression. I made my way to the train, oblivious of the jostling passengers and red-turbaned *coolies* carrying heavy luggage. I crossed the familiar platform with its carts full of the morning

Meher Baba

newspapers and ignored the appeals of the *boot-polishwallas*, the *coffeewallas* and little *chokra boys* vying with each other to sell packets of biscuits, cashewnuts and crisps. With leaden legs and wooden heart, I heard and saw nothing.

Just as I reached up to climb aboard the train, I felt a gentle touch on my shoulder. "Jai Baba," said a voice. I turned in astonishment to see a familiar face. It was Baba's – Meher Baba's! It shone through a medallion worn by Hughie, a Baba lover, who was on his way to Meherabad along with a group of friends from the USA. Looking around, Baba's face danced before my eyes from the many lockets, brooches and badges that soon began to settle all around me in the train.

I felt a sudden joy. My spirits lifted like a bird on the wing and flew with me all the way to Pune. Suddenly, I knew with a certainty that surpasses understanding, that there was no need for me to be sad any more, for I was not alone at all!

CHAPTER 31

Baba's Love

Pune was not as bad as I thought it would be. The tiresome events of the past were locked away as I began to busy myself decorating my new home. There was so much to do as basic amenities had to be taken care of; a telephone connection, a gas cylinder application, electricity and, last but not the least, a ration card, which is second in importance to an identity card or a passport. As each day went by, things began to take shape and my house began to look like a home. Finally, the curtains and paintings went up and I nailed the last picture to the wall, just outside my bedroom – that of Meher Baba, with His amber eyes and golden locks. I stood back proudly, looked at Baba, and resolved to build up my relationship with Him in spite of the pain of the past.

One morning, a few months later, I awoke to the urgent strident tone of Jimmy's voice. "Nan, wake up! Come quickly, look what's happened."

I jumped out of bed, followed Jimmy into the guest bedroom and confronted a scene of chaos. Clothes, shoes, bags, documents, books, sprays, kitchen and household articles lay strewn all over the floor. The cupboards had been wrenched open and the drawers broken into by what looked like a menacing crowbar; a hammer and other tools lay scattered around. I walked warily through the rest of the rooms, amazed at the dexterity and daring with which the thieves had entered and left without disturbing the sleeping occupants. When we questioned the ground security guards, they too had seen and heard nothing.

Jimmy stormed back and, with arms akimbo, stood glowering at Baba's picture on the wall. It further infuriated him, for Baba continued looking serenely down at us. The police arrived shortly after with sniffer dogs and fingerprint experts to investigate the break-in. There was little that we could do, except make an inventory of what had been stolen and wait for the officers to come to their own conclusions.

Jimmy sat around throwing accusing glances at Baba and demanded, "What were You doing Baba, when everything was being taken from right under Your very nose? Didn't You see anything, couldn't You do anything?"

Just then, the inspector joined us, and in a grave tone, gave us his conclusions. "You are very lucky sir, lucky that you didn't hear anything – for if you had, you would have come out of your bedroom and been confronted, we suspect, by more than three armed men. Who knows what might have happened!" And with these ominous words, he departed.

I glanced at Jimmy as he lowered his eyes and sneaked an ashamed look at Baba. I imagined that I definitely saw a twinkle in Baba's eye as He continued looking serenely down at us.

We had to reluctantly acknowledge that though we had lost out materially, our lives were intact and Baba had indeed protected us after all.

In the meantime, people from Pune had begun calling with questions about Baba and asking for His help. The trips to Meherabad resumed and this provided me with an opportunity to spend many hours at the *Samadhi*. The strong spiritual vibrations never failed to lift my flagging spirits and always provided me with the time to ask many questions.

I also felt the need to bridge the gap that I had created, beginning with Jimmy's illness, right through to the time of changing homes. I had been filled with misgivings and doubts. But the dream, Meherwan's story, the deeply meaningful TV message, the brush with the burglars and, most of all, the dancing medallions at the station, helped to bring me to a point of asking the one question that had plagued me for so long. "Baba, You are God, so how is it that You are not able to help? What manner of man are You ... why do You love us and also let us suffer so?"

The walls of Baba's tomb echoed my cries – "Karl, when will I rest knowing that my deepest fears and worries are being taken care of by Baba? When? In what possible way can Baba assure me that everything is going to be alright from now on?"

"Baba is... Baba is... Baba is..." came the answer from the deep silence within me.

"Baba is what?" I cried, frustrated.

"BABA IS LOVE," answered my son.

"Meher Baba loves all of you dearly. You do not know what His Love means – IT IS NOT YOUR KIND OF LOVE, His is a love that glows all the time. You will not know, till you can do the same for someone else, what happiness it gives Him to give you that love. He will not make it more or less – it remains constant throughout your lives in the world and beyond – to Him. HE IS LOVE PERSONIFIED. He loves you all and all you have to do is love Him in return – and everything will fall into place. Baba wishes for nothing from you except Love – but that love must come from within – for inward love is the most wonderful gift that you can give Him."

I was taken aback by the simplicity of Karl's answer. There was little left for me to understand, there was nothing more to be fathomed – no deep mystery to Baba – Baba is LOVE.

"His love is beautiful," continued Karl, *"for it has the light of happiness glowing within. Marigolds have that love and flowers of the earth blossom with that love. People of the world should be like the marigolds who do not know who and what they are – they only stand and accept the light that is given to them – but a human being keeps asking and wondering and thinking and making problems for himself, so the light that can shine directly gets diffused with thoughts and that is why you all go through tears and painful experiences, because the whole of you does not get into that light of love – so Mum, please learn to accept the beauty of His Love for it will always be there for you.*

"The only real way to solve the problems of life is love – a great love takes you onto greater heights and you attain a certain status in Baba's eyes. The light of His Love will never diminish, for it has been LIT BY THE HAND OF GOD for you and you will be forever united with Him."

From the moment that Baba had entered my life, my thinking began to undergo a radical change. Although new thoughts, ideas and concepts caused a whirlpool of confusion in my mind, there seemed to be an inner awakening that opened up a new dimension in my way of being.

It had started off by my being so happy just to be with Karl and, if I had my way, that was all that I really wanted. Spiritual? No, not me! I never had any aspirations or desires to go along a spiritual pathway, nor did I wish to be convinced of God's Love. In fact, my resistance to laying myself open to anything spiritual was made abundantly clear to many who discussed Baba and His teachings all the time. My sense of reality always lay in life's experiences and not in any great spiritual search.

But now, somehow, it began to go beyond that, for I had spiralled into a way of thinking very alien to my nature, influenced not only by Karl, but by many others who came to Meher Baba through me. In retrospect, I suspect that, like Karl, they too had been intentionally sent by Him to show me that life held much more than I had bargained for.

Afraid to change and mindful of what others might say, I clung tightly to an old image of myself and refused to get carried away by the new spiritual horizon that suddenly presented itself. Therefore, I found myself at the crossroads. The confusion lay in the fact that Karl was somehow using every available opportunity to slowly but surely awaken me to some truths on life.

Like me, there are many who do not really know or understand who God is. I always liked to believe that He was this Super-Conscious Being who had all the power to alleviate the pain and suffering in the world of today. But, I could not understand how He could just sit back and look down upon a world filled with chaos, destruction, war and natural calamities. How could He be a passive witness not only to all of the above, but also to the senseless taking of another person's life? Why could He not do something about it?

First, I learnt of the exacting law of *karma* – that which you sow, so shall you reap. The pathway chosen has to be the pathway marched, with its preordained lessons, *karma* and destiny. This will always be an inevitable truth in our lives. God's passive role was thus explained by Karl who said to me one day, *"Mum, sometimes I feel so sorry for you that I feel like doing what I should not do to make you happy, but Baba is here to show me that I love you too much to break the way for you, and I have to sit here to see that you make your own problems go away. I do not love to see that really, but you do have to make them go away yourself."*

Secondly, it is Baba's Compassion that tells me another truth – that He loves each soul unconditionally and if you allow Him to,

He will carry you over the "... *sticks and stones and little pieces of glass that may cut your feet. He stops the bleeding and helps you to smile through the storm.*" Why? Because He loves us and knows that it is our ignorance that causes the struggle to understand Him.

Last, but by no means the least, Meher Baba awakens you to another indisputable truth – that the goal of life is to be ONE WITH GOD. Whilst on your way, you have to live your life in the world, and deal with time. You have to deal with its brutal atrocities, its tragedies and its pain and make the best of the happiness that you can find and the lessons that you can learn in-between. More often than not, life gets you so down that you cry out, "Why was I born?" And then you wonder – of what use is life if time or death takes away those you love?

Of what use is life if time has its natural disasters, wars, and holocausts that descend upon mankind in the name of religion, race, or the gain of financial power?

Of what use is life if time has death that mows you down, and everything that you have worked hard for and achieved eventually comes to naught?

I have wrestled with these questions, struggled and doubted, but eventually begun to understand that there is a link between life, *karma* and reincarnation. I have come to the conclusion that the answer to all the unanswerable questions of life lies in the collective incarnations of the soul. Each life experience is a piece of a puzzle and all the pieces have to fall into place before it is finally complete. In the process of this journey, we have to go through every emotion, every experience, every way of life, overcome all adversity and enjoy every happy moment. We have to be king, beggar, thief, rich or poor, have a large family or none at all. Every hurdle has to be overcome, every heartache borne and every success enjoyed. In all of this, there are debts to be paid and dues to recover.

Though you seek happiness, love and success in many different ways – none of these states of being is permanent, for finally, there is death! Oh yes, life will give you many exciting experiences, for the world is a playground where you can choose at will to do as you please. But does your time in the world provide you with what your heart is yearning for? Everlasting peace, bliss, happiness and love? NO!

Then who or what does?

I have stood at the crossroads for a long, long while, thinking of everything that has happened and everything that Karl has subsequently told me. I have stood there, wondering who I was, where I came from and which way to go. But of late, even though circumstances are the same, the complications and confusions seem to have suddenly cleared and the crossroads have lost their significance. I used to worry about making the correct choice. Now, I have decided simply that, whilst the choice of road is still important to the way I would like to live my life, what truly matters is that there is no need to seek God outside of myself – seeking God within is all that matters. I have to keep Meher Baba as my eternal companion and guide on any road I take.

I have to allow myself to experience a new concept of life – the Love of a Divine Being with a face and a form that I know – Meher Baba. For, I cannot but admit that through all that has happened, Baba has been there, is still there and will always be there silently and unobtrusively giving me His Love, no matter how hard I try to deny the fact to myself.

In other words, the acceptance of His presence, the surrender to His guidance and the willingness to use His strength to overcome every adversity that comes my way, are factors that have to be kept in my mind all the time. I also have to keep reminding myself that all the ups and downs in my life are just hiccups – hiccups that will not keep me from moving towards my goal.

I remember my first step into Baba's *Samadhi* and the words emblazoned in gold letters across His white marble tombstone – "I HAVE COME NOT TO TEACH BUT TO AWAKEN." Yes, that was all that was really meant to happen. I still have a lot to learn, but I certainly have been awakened to a new beginning with solid foundations and roots that go deep, and more so, because I have come to experience for myself what God is all about – LOVE.

The Tomb-Shrine of Meher Baba at Meherabad

CHAPTER 32

Karl

Karl's story can never end, for he lives on and will live on in my heart forever. He also lives on in the hearts of his beloved family and in the hearts of many who have since come to know about his proud and indomitable spirit that shines through from another world.

The year 1996 is drawing to a close. Almost seventeen years have gone by since the unforgettable day when Karl's physical body was carried into the Towers of Silence. My son has come a long way from being the little jockey boy who fell from his horse one April afternoon. He has "risen" to win the most glorious race of his life, that of winning me over to the acceptance of God and showing me what His Love is all about. He has helped me to achieve the victory of all victories – to win over myself. In the process of this, he has helped many others onto the road leading to Meher Baba.

The experience of Karl and all his representations, with or without his spirit friends, has always seemed to fascinate those who have heard Karl's story. It is his faith in Meher Baba that enables Karl to give messages of hope to all that come to him. At times, his messages have been astounding in their truth and clarity and sometimes there have been doubts; at other times they have made no immediate sense, but proved themselves at a later date. Although Karl has always persisted in producing indisputable proof in order to validate the communication, the ultimate contact with Meher Baba has given each person a bond of love and above all, a trust in His non-physical presence.

Little did I know that distances are never a barrier to the energy that belongs to pure selfless love. It is this spirit of love that is my son Karl, and is that which made me write this book.

This book may seem to belong to the category of life after death, of communicating with those who have passed on and of proving the existence of the spirit world. It may also appear to be about who or what I am and what I have become. But, it is much, much, more.

This book is about love.

It is a story of the love of a son for his mother, father and family and, above all, his love for his God.

I thought at one time that I had lost Karl forever, but he "came back" to prove that there is something far, far beyond the life that we live. His love for us made him struggle hard to prove to us the existence of the spirit world and of another beyond that – the world of Meher Baba. It was as if he had set out on a quest, a mission – and he was determined never to give up until he made us accept that there is a God above, a kind and compassionate God, whose only role is to help through Love.

From the first words of Karl's communication, *"MUM... HOME, WHEREVER MUM HOME,"* I knew that his last words to me, "Mum, I want to go home," had remained uppermost in his consciousness. Subsequently, through the writings, he cleared our doubts about the reality of the spirit world and spoke about his thoughts and feelings which still reflected the intense love he always had for us.

"I am not able to separate myself from you Mum. Baba feels that to separate me from you is not possible. So, He lets it be and I feel glad that it is so, for I could not make any further progress if I was away from you Mum – I have had too many lives with you and too much love to be able to go anywhere except with all of you. That is why I am here.

"Now, because of love, I have come to a stage of being happy, free and completely having the way open to do as I please with whoever I want – and that is how it should be. And so it is also with those others who have since come to be with their parents and loved ones.

"The way is difficult for us, but we do our work with high hopes that people become aware of spirit life, so that it will merge with ordinary life and unhappiness and partings like ours do not take place – we wish to eventually come to this.

"The relationship that happens between your world and mine has to have no strings attached that bind you – they should be like a spider's web – transparent and beautiful, yet still strong enough to build your life on.

My home here is strong and beautiful for all those who wish to enter it and I will keep them with me so that they feel protected, but not bound; and we can all look forward to a glorious life that comes with being with Baba."

At this point in time, I can truly say that we have developed a very beautiful relationship together. In this way, our love continues and Karl still continues to be a part of our lives, sharing, laughing, arguing and sometimes even sulking with one another. Often, he delivers stern lectures, sometimes just says *"hi"* and *"bye"* and, at other times, he describes briefly, life in the other world. But most of all, he talks about his beloved Meher Baba, his *"Father in Heaven."*

Without the untiring efforts of Karl, I would have lived on at war with God, looking upon Him as an enemy for the rest of my life. Now I have learnt to accept what happened without bitterness and have decided not to heap the blame of everything at God's door. In fact, I understand the importance of maintaining a relationship with God. I call Him Meher Baba because that is how He has chosen to make Himself known to me. However, you are free to call Him by any name that you choose – Jesus, Buddha, Ram, Krishna, Zarathustra, Mohammed or Meher Baba – call Him friend, companion, shining spirit or God. Whoever He may be or whatever form He takes, you can be sure it is only through His Grace that you will reach your goal, for God the Creator is where we originated from and He is where we ultimately go.

As Karl explains, *"There comes a time in everyone's life when Baba must come. If they miss out on loving Him, they are the losers. So when the time comes, Baba comes. If they cannot realise Him, they continue an existence devoid of love and understanding. If you have been lucky enough to receive Baba, then you must continue to be with Him, for as you know, it helps in every way possible. The way you take will be easy and the path swift and broad, and you will travel the distance to Baba in no time at all if you continue to love Him and to cherish His dear love. I wish you to realise this."*

I have always seen the words, "MASTERY IN SERVITUDE" written on top of the *Samadhi* and have never stopped to think of its in-depth meaning. But now I know, that Meher Baba's role is in serving us to find our way back to Him. It is Meher Baba who listens, waiting to respond to the one prayer that gives Him the greatest joy and satisfaction to hear. He waits patiently for us to step out of ourselves and ask to be one with Him. Baba comes to silently touch the heart of each soul, to awaken it to His Love. He comes to awaken you so that you can find yourself and be eternally happy.

Meher Baba has watched silently and has remained unflinchingly close in spite of all my outbursts, protests, arguments and withdrawals. He has helped me through my darkest moments and shown me the light. Meher Baba has never pushed me beyond my limited understanding, never expected me to do more than I am capable of. He is always available to me as my guide, companion and friend. He is my inner voice, my conscience. He is my Higher and Real Self.

I have been through the gamut of a hundred emotions but, eventually, life has begun to make more sense to me. Now, I am happy loving and serving Him and being with Karl. If decisions and choices have to be made in life, be they right or wrong, I will go on making them myself to the best of my ability. But, from this point onward, I will never again doubt Meher Baba's Love and its meaning.

As I come to the end of my story, I find myself more at peace and the inner struggle seems to be over.

I can hear Karl heaving a sigh of relief as he says, *"At last, she's got it!"*

Meher Baba

APPENDIX A

The Master's Prayer

This Prayer was given by Baba, and during the twenty-one days of Baba's special work (from the 13th of August to the 2nd of September, 1953), and on several subsequent occasions too. It was recited every evening by one of the mandali in Baba's presence.

O Parvardigar, the Preserver and Protector of All,

You are without beginning and without end;

Non-dual, beyond comparison; and none can measure You.

You are without colour, without expression, without form, and without attributes.

You are unlimited and unfathomable, beyond imagination and conception; eternal and imperishable.

You are indivisible; and none can see You, but with eyes divine.

You always were, You always are, and You always will be;

You are everywhere, You are in everything; and You are also beyond everywhere and beyond everything.

You are in the firmament and in the depths, You are manifest and unmanifest; on all planes, and beyond all planes.

You are in the three worlds, and also beyond the three worlds.

You are imperceptible and independent.

You are the Creator, the Lord of lords, the Knower of all minds and hearts; You are Omnipotent and Omnipresent.

You are Knowledge Infinite, Power Infinite and Bliss Infinite.

You are the Ocean of Knowledge, All-Knowing, Infinitely-

Knowing; the Knower of the past, the present and the future, and You are Knowledge Itself.

You are all-merciful and eternally benevolent;

You are the Soul of souls, the One with Infinite Attributes;

You are the Trinity of Truth, Knowledge, and Bliss;

You are the Source of Truth, the Ocean of Love;

You are the Ancient One, the Highest of the High;

You are Prabhu and Parameshwar;

You are the Beyond God, and the Beyond-Beyond God also;

You are Parabrahma; Allah; Elahi;

Yezdan; Ahuramazda; and God the Beloved.

You are named Ezad: the only One worthy of worship.

* * *

The Prayer of Repentance

Dictated by Meher Baba on 8.11.1952

We repent, O God, most merciful, for all our sins, for every thought that was false or unjust or unclean, for every word spoken that ought not to have been spoken, and for every deed done that ought not to have been done.

We repent for every deed and word and thought inspired by selfishness, and for every deed and word and thought inspired by hatred.

We repent most specially for every lustful thought and every lustful action, for every lie, for all hypocrisy, for every promise given but not fulfilled, and for all slander and back-biting.

Most specially also, we repent for every action that has brought ruin to others, for every word and deed that has given others pain, and for every wish that pain should befall others.

In Your Unbounded Mercy, we ask You to forgive us, O God for all these sins committed by us, and to forgive us for our constant failures to think and speak and act according to Your Will.

A Prayer for Baba Lovers

This Prayer was dictated by Meher Baba in 1959

Beloved God, help us all to love You more and more, and more and more, and still yet more, till we become worthy of Union with You; and help us all to hold fast to Beloved Baba's *daaman* till the very end.

APPENDIX B

Meher Baba's Universal Message

I have come not to teach but to awaken. Understand therefore that I lay down no precepts.

Throughout eternity I have laid down principles and precepts, but mankind has ignored them. Man's inability to live God's words makes the *Avatar's* teaching a mockery. Instead of practicing the compassion He taught, man has waged crusades in His name. Instead of living the humility, purity and truth of His words, man has given way to hatred, greed and violence.

Because man has been deaf to the principles and precepts laid down by God in the past, in this present *Avataric* Form, I observe Silence. You have asked for and been given enough words – it is now time to live them. To get nearer and nearer to God, you have to get further and further away from "I," "my," "me" and "mine." You have not to renounce anything but your own self. It is as simple as that, though found to be almost impossible. It is possible for you to renounce your limited self by my Grace. I have come to release that Grace.

I repeat, I lay down no precepts. When I release the tide of Truth which I have come to give, men's daily lives will be the living precept. The words I have not spoken will come to life in them.

I veil myself from man by his own curtain of ignorance, and manifest my Glory to a few. My present *Avataric* Form is the last Incarnation of this cycle of time, hence My Manifestation will be the greatest. When I break My Silence, the impact of My Love will be universal and all life in creation will know, feel and receive of it. It will help every individual to break himself free from his own bondage in his own way. I am the Divine Beloved who loves you more than you can ever love yourself. The breaking of My Silence will help you to help yourself in knowing your real Self.

All this world confusion and chaos was inevitable and no one is to blame. What had to happen has happened; and what has to happen will happen. There was and is no way out except through My coming in your midst. I had to come, and I have come. I am the Ancient One.

– Meher Baba

APPENDIX C

The Perfect Masters

In order to understand the significance of Merwan's (Meher Baba) passage through the most important period in His life, and the role of a Perfect Master, it is necessary for me to give you an explanation as to who and what they are. Therefore, in Baba's words:

"The five greatest thieves in the world
are the five living Perfect Masters
of their time.
They often steal the hearts of people,
and periodically they also steal Me and
bring Me down amongst you.

Again and again, I must become what I am,
and each time it is due to
the five Perfect Masters.
Wherever I may incarnate,
(Persia, India, Israel or Arabia,)
at whatever time,
it will always be due to those five.

I never come of My own wish.
It is always the five Perfect Masters
who bring Me down (into human form)
in each Avataric period.
Those five hold the key to all of creation –
which contains an infinite number of universes.

Man can become God –
and men who become God,
can become Perfect Masters.

It is because of the five Perfect Masters
that I appear on earth as man.
They fetch Me down,
and I experience Myself as everything
and so I tell you that I am God –
I am everything.

The state of God-Realisation –
Infinite Knowledge, Power and Bliss –
cannot be described.
It can only be known to those
who achieve that supreme experience
of the conscious state of God.
God-Realisation is beyond the domain of the mind.

The five Perfect Masters are
the five persons of their age
who not only become God, but,
after achieving God-Realisation, also come down
to the ordinary normal consciousness of man.

Thus they possess simultaneously, God-Consciousness
plus mental, subtle and gross consciousness.
The world is never without the five Persons
who are God-Conscious, who are Perfect Masters.

Inspite of appearing as five different Persons,
they are and always remain one God,
as each one has exactly the same supreme experience
of God-Consciousness.
Nevertheless, in external relations with the world,
each shows a different personality,
with his or her own characteristic traits,
tastes, nature, habits and ways of dealing with people.

All the five Perfect Masters -
BABAJAN,
NARAYAN MAHARAJ,
TAJUDDIN BABA,
SAI BABA,
UPASNI MAHARAJ,
put together mean Me – THE *AVATAR*.

All five of these Perfect Masters
have brought Me down,
and all that I have become
is due to these five.
I am made of all the attributes
of all five of these Masters,
and My *Avataric* state comprises the five states
of these five Perfect Masters.
Therefore, the qualities of all five
are in Me."

– Meher Baba, 1954

Babajan

Narayan Maharaj

Tajuddin Baba

Sai Baba

Upasni Maharaj

APPENDIX D

Messages from Karl

BABA AND HIS LOVE

You must think of Baba in whatever way you feel, for that is the only way for you to really love Him.

Baba has powers, there is no doubt, for He has the way to make you happy, but the word happiness has another meaning for Him. You think happiness is comfort, easy life, money and no internal illness or material worries. To Baba, happiness is your way to the goal of life and that is why He is here for you – to make you finish your worldly journey taking your karma in your stride, knowing He is near you and then, finding your way to Him with ease at the end of it all.

Nothing can change this. Once He takes over your journey, He guides you step by step – and that is why, sometimes, He makes the sufferings more than normal so that you get to your goal faster than normal and then for you everything will come to pass with ease.

No, it is not a false sense of security. I am assuring you that this will be proven to you in time, that Baba really and truly cares. Baba has come to be your friend – He loves you all and understands you all. Baba has faith in God – He has faith in the thought of God. He has powers that make Him do for you what could not have been possible otherwise. He can do things for you. Baba travels on the path with you and carries you on His shoulders to avoid the pitfalls you would have gone into along the way, for Baba has to make you reach your goal.

He has gone through suffering Himself and knows how it feels – He has gone through the pain of having someone taken from

Him, the pain of losing love and family, the pain of existence He knows only too well, so, don't mistake the feeling, for His love will never change for you, no matter how you feel or how long it takes for you to know Him as He should be known and understood. He loves you and this is the only way He knows.

Baba is near all of us and Meher Baba's love is very important in our lives. Believe me you have to know how much He loves everyone of you individually and collectively. He asks me everything in detail about everyone of you to know how to help each one separately. So, all of you must know this is true and have love and courage to finish your earthly life with the utmost love for all your fellow beings and to help everyone that needs you.

ASK AND YOU SHALL RECEIVE

You have no reason to ask for something He has the power to grant, so He cannot ask you for your love when you ask for His help. You must give of yourself to Him and He will automatically give of Himself to you, but if you do not have the feelings towards Him, He cannot help you without your co-operation. So if you do not feel like loving Him, then it is your loss, of course. But you have to find your level in His heart and then He will make Himself in your life what you allow Him to be.

THE KINGDOM OF HEAVEN

Baba loves to have you make waves and with these waves comes the understanding that there is more to life than living it, so when people read or hear of untoward happenings, they begin to think, and when their thoughts are activated, they start to go one step towards something other than normalcy and this is how it all begins. Baba is the Awakener and finds His own instruments to help.

The Kingdom of Heaven will come to you in the shape of Baba in human form. When you come here to meet Him, His shape will come as Baba that you know, so that coming here will be a pleasure for you.

Love has that quality which is translucent, yet very powerful, and you must look upon this love to take you through painful days and nights that make you feel afraid. You must consider that Baba rules the days and the nights – He makes the sun shine, so when the night comes, be sure you will soon see the day and look forward to a glorious life – a life that comes with being with Baba.

HAPPINESS

Baba says that happiness is of small value if you cannot appreciate it. When you have it, you must understand what it is actually weighing with the outside chance of you not ever experiencing it again. But of course, the moment of happiness has tremendous value in itself, for it never gets repeated in the same way. Other moments will come and go, but that same one is over, and you have to look back on it with love and not regret that it is gone.

Happiness is an elusive feeling and the happiness that we wish to give you is sometimes cloaked with lots of unnecessary things. When you remove that cloak, you find the happiness inside of you.

We here do not have a cloak to hide our feelings and so we have a happiness that shines forth without anything to cover it. I want to show you that nothing should be allowed to cover happiness – it is what comes from inside.

Baba works wonders with the inner mind and He gives bliss to the inner soul and remember that the outward doesn't count.

MERCY

Meher Baba says that you must have people told about His mercy. He has plenty of this, so when the one that has done a grave mistake appeals to Him for His mercy, He sends His love to them in a big cup, so that they can drink it and remain filled with this love forever, so that they love and forgive others with the same loving fullness. So you must also try to do the same, for it is not our work to think of people in terms of right and wrong. If they have done wrong, they will do right to right the wrong and go to Baba for the one thing that will help them – HIS MERCY.

I have no wish to be a teacher, but I do wish to help people to be happy, to feel strength and happiness and go towards a life of love and most of all to a life of fulfilment.

Baba never punishes anyone. They punish themselves by their crimes and help themselves by their deeds of goodness – so you only are responsible for what you do and what you are. But till such time that you can fathom the ultimate love of God, you have to feel that He is the one that does things for you and against you. So that you can understand, I am saying all this to you time and time again – Baba loves you and cares that you should be happy and He works hard to help make you happy. Baba is everything to you and me.

OPTIONS

Meher Baba says your life is your own to go where and whichever way that you choose. He will go with you just in case you need Him, but if you wish to go alone, that option is also available to you. Your life can be lived Meher Baba's way when the will is there to do so and if your will says you should go to another for guidance, that option is also open to you. So, to make a mistake or to go along to love and spiritual peace is up to you – just do not worry, do what your heart dictates and you will find your peace.

Baba says that you should not feel upset if your mind wavers sometimes to wonder just how much He is capable of doing for you. He thinks of you all in terms of yourselves and not as how much you love Him or can do for Him. Do not ever worry that you are not doing enough for Him – a little is a lot – remember that.

BABA'S DISCRETION

I have powers that exceed those of ordinary people. Because I am with Baba, I can see you and be with you more than ordinary, but I haven't got powers to change things for you. Baba can but does not do it unless it is necessary. His discretion is His power.

I am sure that you will come to understand at some stage in your life His true heart. Yes, my darling Mummy, He has a true heart.

Yes Mum, I know sometimes that you do hurt and so really things do feel wrong, but that is what life is all about and what is granted is what you have to take with two hands and be thankful for it. Life has more pain than pleasure, but with Baba, it becomes more pleasure than pain – that is the difference.

ANSWERS

Mum, I am not able to find the answers to many of your questions and you have to find the answers from life, not from the spirit world. Your life cannot change by being with me, it can only be lightened. Heavy-duty things like changing the times of events in your life is not possible, only they can be taken with a pinch of salt to make it easier for you to set out on your path and find the distance getting shorter to Baba.

I am aware that you need much more than that and you feel, why should I believe in Baba if He cannot do anything for me, so you fall out with Him – but that is what you should not do, for benefits have to be seen with eyes that are not earthy, eyes that see beyond ordinary things – eyes that can look at blue skies and see the faces of other things and not only the fleecy clouds. Those eyes can look into the grey waters of the ocean and see not only the waters, but the smiling face of Baba who awaits you from inside the dark and murky waters – so if you get into the ocean by chance, He is there awaiting you with open arms. He will gather you up and push you forward with a force greater than you have experienced before.

PRAYERS

I am sure your prayers can be as effective as any offerings to God. Feeding the poor or good deeds will help in some way, but your sincerity is necessary. To find peace, you have to get peace and you will get peace when you give peace. Mummy, I will say to you what I have told you many times – do good to others and others will be good to you.

TROUBLE

What I mean by trouble.

Trouble is something you have with your own self because you have to face something that you do not like. But by facing it, the trouble goes away and you have a way to overcome this particular thing that you thought was trouble and then it doesn't become trouble any more. So find it, look at it, and do what you have to do to overcome it and then it is over and finished with.

Why have you made it your trouble? Because of fear of it, it has turned into trouble, and when you overcome it, then it is not something you fear any longer – so, face the lion in his den and he becomes a lamb for you. I love that saying Mum.

When trouble comes, you have to face it and then forget it – do not blame Baba for it, for it is your own fate that makes it so. You have your fate in your own hands. He does not hold it for you – He makes you hold it and drop it and go on to another existence.

THE TIDE

Baba says, "Life is not all rosy. You must go with the tide, and that is the most important lesson that you must learn. Don't oppose anything – run with the tide and all will be well. So that you may understand, I will give you an example -

I was in the worldly substance in some place you would not know about. At that time, I went against everything that I was told to do – I suffered – but that suffering made me strong that now I can stand any amount of suffering because of that experience. What I mean is that – experience makes you grow higher. You can fly if the experience is strong, then you get rid of things you could not have done so easily.

Be not disturbed, I am there for you always – BABA."

NEED

Baba says, "Never fear the weak, never fear the coward and never fear the most unhappy, for they need you more than those who have the courage to come to you with their troubles and ask for help. Those that cannot come are those that need you most and haven't the courage to say, I need the One Being who can help me."

LOVE THY NEIGHBOUR

Loving people for their own happiness is good, but loving them when things go wrong is much better. Baba teaches this to all his friends. He says, "Love many or love few, but those you love must have all your good and sincere wishes without reservations and they will come out of all their problems."

Teach all that come to you that Meher Baba sprays all these beautiful thoughts on everything and everyone – the lovely fragrance and vibrant colours of His bounty will descend on each one. Day and Night will blend together and make life into one long and lovely journey. All of them, in their turn, will pass this love on to others.

I believe in this.

YOU ARE ALWAYS ADVANCING

Baba says "All things that advance you are good for you and you should use your thinking; to do good to anyone is one step forward in your lifetime. It is when people do nothing, that is upsetting. Never sit back to do nothing. You are your own judge, so never doubt your thinking when it is for the good of others. Baba's lessons tend to teach you this and the teachings of all Saints and Gurus are the same, only, all have their different ways of teaching – that's all. Meher Baba is the most kind and the most gentle of them all, and in my eyes, the most knowledgeable One. He will be happy you are learning and thinking for the good of others. Look up, not down – the sun is high in Heaven.

Baba says that you all must make a forward move towards a particular goal. You must always move forwards. Those who remain in one place can never do well. Pick up your thoughts and move forwards, not in space, but in the mind. That is why those that are dull and soft remain where they are put, but those that speed forward, reach their goal much faster. Those are in Baba's thoughts for they will see God.

So try to think the way Baba does and your mind will get illuminated with thoughts that you never had before and these light your pathway for you and lead you to the knowledge of truth and love.

To be successful in life needs work, hard work. You must do your best in everything that you do and when you become unhappy, you tend to let things go by, without the effort to pull out of it. Get moving – you must get moving to be able to lift the burdens that life throws on you.

JUDGEMENT

Meher Baba says He is not there to punish, only to help. He will never pass judgement on anyone else. All people judge themselves and know what they are. Baba is not there to say, "You are wrong." He only makes a move to help you when he knows you have called Him and He comes. Those who have done wrong have to find their own mistakes in Heaven, that is how it is.

You cannot expect to say, Baba will do this for me, and think that all you have done wrong will be taken away. No, that is there for you to realise it for yourself. Then He comes to make you a better person. By His love, He will make you a better person, so that you will find your way on your own.

FORGIVENESS

Forgiveness is a matter of values and degrees. In your world you have things like sorrow, happiness, forgiveness and hatred. Nothing counts really, except your path towards heaven and I will show you the way – so you must direct your thoughts towards this way. You must keep good thoughts that have to be translated into good deeds and then everything will be good for you. So it is relative, and goodness in any form is happiness. Divine knowledge has its own form of happiness.

Many things will come out of it and you will come to have this divine knowledge because of Baba and this in itself will make you happy. Baba says that you must have the strength to give this divine knowledge and love and you will find forgiveness everywhere.

THOUGHTS

There are many times when we think certain things and believe that our thoughts are better than yours – that means our thoughts are more powerful than yours for they have greater foresight and more hope for the future. They are positive and definite. Baba's thoughts, therefore, transcend everything that they touch and make it into being, so that it becomes a definite thing. Baba thinks powerful, He thinks definite and positive and feels the same as He thinks. You may think one thing and feel another, that is not good. Thought and feeling have to be together and only then does it become a positive thought. That is what I wish to explain to you today. I am not God, and although I can see a bit into the future, I cannot make a thought into a positive being like Baba. I am not the end of all, I am a spiritual being helping you, not an Oracle of Truth.

I am trying to make you all some kind of perfect thoughts. Transference of that perfect thought is necessary for a life of perfect happiness. You must always think in terms of happiness and when these thoughts are transferred from one to another, Baba is very happy when that occurs, for you may think, but to make another think is good and you know then that Baba is awake for work.

GURUJIS

There are many Gurujis in this world who have a variety of powers to make things happen. They are men of understanding and knowledge. They have travelled widely and know a great deal. They are well informed by spiritual knowledge in many ways. But Meher Baba does not follow the same pathway as they do. They may be two of a flower but of different colours. You may love one colour, someone else may love another, but the path, the spiritual path can be traversed in many ways. Baba is the straight way and the gurujis are the winding ways. Baba does not think in the same way but all thoughts that lead you to God are good, those that lead you away from Him are not. So follow any thoughts that you feel you would like to, and as long as they lead you to the correct goal, that is fine.

A CALL FOR HELP

There will be many people that will call on you for help, so you have to keep an open mind. You can judge them by their attitude to Baba. Of course, some take a while to get to know Him and love Him the way He should be loved, so you must always allow for this. Some may love Him and not be able to show it and some may not feel so much towards Him, but all are welcome to His help and so you must tell them all that you know about Baba.

I can only bring Him to you and hope that you will follow the life that He makes you lead, so whoever comes to you for help, you must take them all to Baba and once they come to Him, He takes care of them and looks after them and never lets them down.

All you have to do is bring them to Him.

Meher Baba says that anyone who asks Him for help always gets help no matter who, when or where. Many may not know much about Him but this does not stop Him from helping them.

So, please do not think that you will be left to work out your destiny by yourself. From now on, you are one of the family, Baba's family, and He has you in His heart. He will do whatever He can to help and guide you along the way.

You will find peace.

If you help others, that will reward you in after life. You have no idea how much this will help you. First of all, there will be a swift transition to where it takes long to travel; that is the period of loneliness, after leaving the world, that is the most lonely period and your period of travel will be swift and quick – so that is the first thing. Secondly, you will find that all your deeds of goodness help you to get to those waiting to help you, and more than anything, you will find them making an effort to make you comfortable. Thirdly, I am here for all of you. You have to work out your own destiny so that in the next one nothing can be so bad for you or yours and you can have peace and happiness.

BABA MEANS LOVE

Baba says that when you love someone, you should do all you can to help this someone. When you are on a spiritual pathway you must leave your human emotions behind you. Learn more about Baba and then do what your heart tells you, then you will become good and strong emotionally to help those that are weak. So don't ever look back, for high up sits the Almighty and He and only He can fulfil you and help you to love your fellow beings and then make you into an evolved soul. High up sits the Almighty. The stars shine from above, the moon rises in the sky.

That will be because of Baba.

Be assured that all those who work for Baba will be received with love, for Baba will make sure of this. He wants to make people believe that He is there – still there – and you must make the world believe this. He wishes it to be known that He will always be there.

He wants all humanity to be aware that He can be with them and it's not just speaking that makes it so.

He is the Silent Master who works for everyone's happiness.

Meher Baba lives on.

A CLOSED ROAD

We never tell you, 'don't do this' or 'don't do that' – you must travel your own pathway. Somewhere, you may take a left turn and you may come across the sign of the road closed, and then you must retrace your steps and take the right turn. In short, you must find your signs and take your own turns. You must discover yourself.

BABA THE ORDINARY BEING

Many people look upon Him as a Being, not of your world. But you know, He longs to be known as an ordinary person, not an Infinite Being. He longs to be called a man who has powers to help ordinary souls to gain knowledge of God and of our world. He has been made into a being that has more thought, more power and more knowledge than you or me, but although He has all this, He does not wish to be thought of as something extraordinary – He is ordinary and wishes to remain as such.

That is what He has told me to tell you today.

GOD NEVER CHANGES

In life, there are times when you have failed and times when you have done well. These are things you have to work out for yourself and not think that Baba is letting you down.

Times change, people change, lives change, but God never changes. Many times, we think that things have gone wrong, but we must never doubt the subject of Baba.

He remains constant, kind, strong and powerful forever.

So, remain constant to Him and your life will remain happy and you will see how, when the world suffers, you, who are in Baba's dear love, will be secure and happy.

WHO IS BABA?

The more you see Baba, the more you feel Baba, the more you know Baba, the better you hear Baba. The more you know, see and feel Baba, the safer you are. Meher Baba is your OWN TRUE SELF.

He is that which is within you at all times and all you have to do is to bring Him out and share Him around – then your whole life is illumined and you sparkle silver and gold. Let Him pass around from one to another and be a lover of all those who need Him, lighting up their lives and seeing to their light.

He is all that is in everyone,
He is Nothing and Everything,
He is the Sun, Moon and Stars,
He has love and laughter to give everyone,
Let him give it – that's all I ask of you.

– KARL

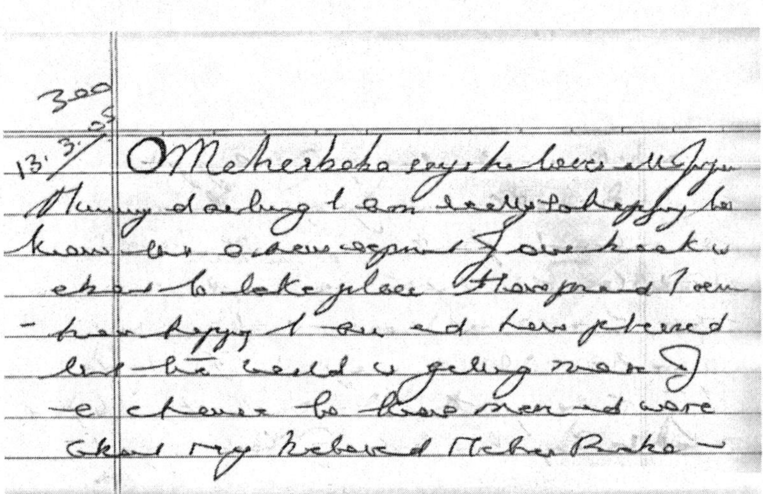

"Meher Baba says He loves all of you.
Mummy darling I am really so happy to know that
a new reprint of our book is about to take place.
How proud I am — how happy I am and
how pleased that the world is getting
more of a chance to know more and more
about my beloved Meher Baba."

– Karl
March 13, 2005

APPENDIX E

Information for Pilgrims to Meherabad

MEHERABAD

Meher Baba's Tomb-Shrine (*Samadhi*) situated in Upper Meherabad is open for darshan throughout the year from 6.30 am to 8.00 pm. Prayer and aarti are performed every day at 7.00 am and 7.00 pm.

Accommodations for the pilgrims, separate for men and women, are given at the Meher Pilgrim Centre, the Dharamshala and the Hostels at Lower Meherabad. Prior reservation is necessary. With the scheduled opening of the new Meher Pilgrim Retreat at Upper Meherabad in June 2006, the existing Meher Pilgrim Centre will function as a Pilgrim Registration Centre.

MEHERAZAD

Home of Meher Baba where He lived with some of His *mandali*. It continues to be the private residence of the existing *mandali* members. It is open for pilgrims on Tuesdays, Thursdays and Sundays, during the posted timings.

REGISTRATION AND CHECK-IN

It is suggested that pilgrims get detailed rules and regulations current on the date of their proposed visit from the Avatar Meher Baba Trust Office in Ahmednagar. Request for reservation should contain full name of each person, date of birth, mailing/email address and phone numbers, to:

Pilgrim Reservation, Avatar Meher Baba Trust, P.O. Bag 31, King's Road, Ahmednagar 414 001, Maharashtra, India.

Meher Pilgrim Retreat
Reservations – Tel: 95241 2548733 / 95241 2548736
Office: 95241 2548211
Reservations – email: pimco@ambppct.org
pimco@mail.ambppct.org

Reservations can be confirmed maximum 6 weeks in advance. However, to allow the Reservations Office time to respond, it is helpful if requests are made as close as possible to this 6 week's limit.

HOW TO GET TO MEHERABAD

From anywhere in India: Meherabad is in Ahmednagar Dist., Maharashtra State, and is accessible by rail and road from various parts of the country. Once you reach Ahmednagar Railway Station or the Bus Depot, you could cover the 6 kms distance to Meherabad by auto rickshaw or by local transport going towards Arangaon village.

From Mumbai (Bombay): By train, state transport buses or private coaches or taxis. By road, Mumbai-Meherabad distance is around 300 kms and can be covered in about 5 hours using the express highway and the Chalkan bypass, without entering Pune.

From Pune (Poona): By train, state transport buses, private coaches or taxis. Pune-Meherabad distance is around 100 kms and can be covered in 2 hours.

The Pilgrim Reservation Office provides information and help regarding travelling, and may also arrange for private pick-up from airports at Mumbai and Pune.

APPENDIX F

Centres of Information about Meher Baba

INDIA

Avatar Meher Baba Perpetual Public Charitable Trust,
P.O. Bag 31, King's Road,
Ahmednagar, Maharashtra, 414 001.

Avatar Meher Baba Bombay Centre,
Navyug Nivas, 'A' Block, 3rd fl.,
Dr. D. Bhadkamkar Marg, Opp.
Minerva Theatre, Mumbai 400 007.

Avatar Meher Baba Poona Centre,
441/1 Somwar Peth, Near K.E.M.
Hospital, Pune 411 011.

Avatar Meher Baba Centre Delhi,
50A Tughlakhabad Industrial Area,
M.B. Road, Near Batra Hospital,
New Delhi 110 062.

Avatar Meher Baba Hyderabad
Centre, Essamia Bazar, Koti,
Hyderabad 500 027,
Andhra Pradesh.

Avatar Meher Baba PPC Trust,
Meher Dham Nauranga,
Taluka Rath, District Hamirpur,
Uttar Pradesh.

Avatar Meher Baba
Tamil Nadu Centre,
22, Moorthy Nagar, Villivakkam,
Chennai 600 049.

OVERSEAS

Meher Spiritual Centre On The Lake,
10200 Highway 17, North Myrtle
Beach, South Carolina 29577, USA.

Sufism Reoriented Inc.,
1300 Boulevard Way, Walnut Creek,
California 94595, USA.

Avatar Meher Baba Centre of
Southern California,
1214 South Van Ness Avenue,
Los Angeles CA 90019-3520, USA

Meher Baba Association,
1/228 Hammersmith Grove,
London W6 7HG, England, UK.

Meher Baba Foundation Australia,
P.O.B. 22, Woomby, Queensland
4559, Australia.

Meher Baba Information,
Anthony Thorpe, 3 Flowers Track,
Christchurch 8, New Zealand.

SOME WEBSITES

avatarmeherbabatrust.org
avatarmeherbaba.org
meherbaba.com
meherabode.org
jaibaba.com
lovestreetbookstore.com

APPENDIX G

Glossary

Aarti: A devotional song or prayer with a refrain or theme which expresses the yearning for the offering of oneself to the One worshipped.

Afurganyu: See Parsi fire temple.

Ahuramazda: The only God of the Zoroastrians, the Lord of Wisdom, helped by the seven attendant deities or the *Amesha Spentas*.

Allowance: An apprentice jockey starts his career with an allowance of 'X' kg., which means he has to carry that much less than the desired weight allotted to the horse by the handicap.

Ashram: The simple abode of a spiritual teacher; a place of retirement from the ordinary business of life.

Automatic writing: An occult term, writing that is inspired by a spirit source other than the self.

Avatar: God who comes down as man; The God-man, Messiah, the Christ. Literally, "descent of God;" the term refers to the appearance of God in human form, which constitutes The Advent.

Avataric period: An age during which the *Avatar*, as the supreme God-realised One, takes His place at the head of the spiritual body of the Five Perfect Masters and of the spiritual hierarchy as a whole. During His tenure as the *Avatar*, He brings about a new release of power, a new awakening of consciousness, not merely for a few, but for all.

Daaman: The hem of a garment. When Baba says, "Hold on to My *daaman*," it connotes love, obedience and surrender to Him.

Darshan: Audience. The appearance of the Master on some occasion, to bestow blessings on devotees. The spiritual presence of the Master at the *Samadhi*. It also refers to the act of folding of hands in adoration of or bowing at the feet of one's Master to express devotion.

Diyas: Oil lamps.

Dropped His body: The *Avatar* is Eternal and therefore drops His body at the time of death, until such time as He incarnates Himself in another body.

Ghazal: A poetic composition, especially in Persian or Urdu.

God-realisation: The goal of every spiritual seeker is to realise his own Divine Self, which is One within all and which is completely manifested in the Perfect Master.

Gulab jamun: A popular Indian sweet made out of burnt milk and sugar.

Guru: A spiritual teacher.

ITP: Idiopathic Thrombocytopenic Purpura.

Jai Baba: Victory to. Used in the sense of "Hail to." "Jai" in a greeting is used in the sense of calling upon the name of the *Avatar*, or in remembrance of the *Avatar*.

Karma: The law of action and reaction. Fate. The natural and necessary happenings of one's lifetime, preconditioned by one's past lives.

Kurta pajama: A traditional Indian male garment; draw-string trousers over which a long-sleeved, knee-length shirt is worn.

Loban: Incense that comes in blocks, normally powdered when used.

Mandali: The members of the Master's Circle. The intimate disciples of an *Avatar* or Perfect Master. The *Avatar* has ten concentric circles for a total of one hundred and twenty-two *mandali*. The innermost circle consists of twelve men and two women.

Meher Baba Ki Jai!: see Jai Baba.

Occult: Beyond the range of ordinary knowledge; mysterious. Not apparent on mere inspection, but discoverable by experimentation; the supernatural or supernatural agencies and affairs.

Occultism: Belief in the existence of certain mysterious or supernatural agencies that can be known and communicated with by human beings.

Ouija board: Board lettered with alphabets and other signs, used with movable pointer to obtain messages in spiritualistic séances.

Parsis: Ethnically of Persian origin, with an ancestry that can be traced to the province of Khorasan known in ancient times as Parthia. Forced to leave Persia (Iran) because of persecution, the Parsis arrived on mainland India in 936 A.D. Followers of the Zoroastrian religion.

Parsi fire temple: A temple in which *Parsis* revere fire which is kept in a vessel called the *afurganyu*. The original ash, *alat* (implements for religious rituals), were brought from Iran in the 10th century to maintain the ritual continuity.

Parvardigar: Vishnu. The Preserver (as in the Hindu Trinity – Creator – Preserver – Destroyer.) The Sustainer.

Perfect Master: A God-realised soul who retains God-consciousness and creation-consciousness simultaneously, and who works in creation to help other souls toward the Realisation of God. See Appendix C.

Prasad: A small gift, usually edible, given by the Master as a concrete expression of His Love and Blessings. When swallowed, it acts as a seed which will eventually grow into full-blown love. A gracious gift of the Master.

Racing pictures: At each furlong, frame by frame photographs are taken, showing the position of individual runners in a horse race until they pass the winning post.

Sahavas: A gathering of devotees where the physical or spiritual presence of the Master is celebrated.

Salwar: Loose trouser worn by Indian men and women.

Samadhi: The tomb-shrine of a spiritual Master.

Sanskaras: Impressions. Also impressions which are left on the soul as memories from former lives and which determine one's desires and actions in the present lifetime.

Shairie: A tale that unfolds itself in rhyming couplets.

Sherwani: A long knee-length coat with a Chinese collar.

Silver Birch: The Red Indian "spirit" guide of a medium called Maurice Barbanell.

Sitters: A small circle of men and women who sit around a medium during a séance meeting with departed spirits; either with a trans-medium or an ouija-board medium.

Spirit world: A realm of imagination, where departed souls reside as spirits without gross bodies.

Surrender: The self-surrender of a disciple whose wholehearted devotion to the Master opens himself for receiving the Divine Love which the Master pours on him. The disciple offers his life to the Master without reservation; his weaknesses as well as his strengths, his virtues as well as his vices, his merits as well as his sins. Until God-realisation, the faith that the disciple places in the Master is his guide.

Tikka: Traditionally, a red dot worn by Indian women on the centre of the forehead; depicting the third eye or the sixth *chakra* (internal wheel of energy).

Towers of Silence: Circular structures, about 20 ft. high surrounding a stone courtyard where Zoroastrians expose their dead to the elements.

Trance-medium: One of the more difficult forms of mediumship in which a medium goes into a trance and is taken over by a guide or guides.

Work: Morning exercises or trial work-outs.

Zarathustra: The ancient Prophet who lived in Iran, and who founded the Zoroastrian religion.

Zoroastrian religion: A system of thought, feeling and action which is shared by the followers of *Zarathustra* the Prophet.

APPENDIX H

Source Notes

CHAPTER 16

How to Love God – "Path of Love" by Meher Baba. Published by the Awakener Press, 938, 18th St., Hermosa Beach, California 90254.

CHAPTER 18

Story of Gordon Higginson – "Mediums and their Work" by Linda Williamson. Published by Robert Hale Ltd., Clerkenwell House, Clerkenwell Green, London ECIROHT. Printed by St. Edmundsbury Press, Bury St. Edmonds, Suffolk, Great Britain.

CHAPTER 19

Umer Tree – Pamphlet of "The Umer Tree," Society of Avatar Meher Baba, New York.

Background Information on Zoroastrianism – Copyright Khojeste P. Mistree 1982, "Zoroastrianism an Ethnic Perspective."

Meher Baba's life – The account of Meher Baba's life in chapter 19, has been based on notes collected from Bhau Kalchuri's book "Lord Meher" Vol. 1. Copyright Lawrence Reiter. Originally written in Hindi by the author, 1971-1973. Translated into English by Feram Workingboxwala. Published and distributed in the USA by Manifestation Inc., P.O. Box 991, North Myrtle Beach, South Carolina 29597.

CHAPTER 20

Mehera's Life – "Mehera," Compiled and edited by Janet Judson with the assistance of Shelley Marrich. Published by Naosherwan Anzar, Beloved Books, 599 Edison Drive, East Windsor, New Jersey 08520, USA Copyright 1989, Avatar Meher Baba Perpetual Public Charitable Trust, Ahmednagar, India.

Stories of Mani – "God-Brother," by Mani S. Irani. Copyright 1993, Avatar Meher Baba Perpetual Public Charitable Trust, Ahmednagar, India. Printed and published in the USA by The Sheriar Foundation, 3005 Highway 17, North Bypass, Myrtle Beach, South Carolina, 29577, USA.

CHAPTER 21

Farohar – Permission granted by Rubina Patel to print extracts from the book "Reveal Thy Grace" by Meher Jamshed Patel.

CHAPTER 25

Role of the occult as explained by Meher Baba – "God to Man and Man to God," by Meher Baba. Edited by C. B. Purdom. Copyright 1975 Adi K. Irani. Printed in the USA by The Sheriar Press Inc., 1st Printing 1975, 2nd 1984.

APPENDIX A

The Master's Prayer, The Prayer of Repentance and *A Prayer for Baba Lovers* – Published by Adi K. Irani, Meher Publications, King's Road, Ahmednagar.

APPENDIX B

Meher Baba's Universal Message – "Path of Love" by Meher Baba. Published by the Awakener Press, 938 18th St., Hermosa Beach, California 90254.

APPENDIX C

The Perfect Masters – "Lord Meher" Vol. 1, by Bhau Kalchuri, Copyright Lawrence Reiter.

APPENDIX I

Recommended Reading

The following books on Meher Baba are available at Avatar Meher Baba Perpetual Public Charitable Trust, Ahmednagar, and the Bombay Centre, Navyug Nivas, Bhadkamkar Marg, Opposite Minerva Talkies, Bombay 400 007. Also available are brooches, lockets, audio/video cassettes, VCDs/DVDs.

God Speaks, *Meher Baba*
Discourses, *Meher Baba*
Listen, Humanity, *Meher Baba*
In God's Hand, *Meher Baba*
Life At Its Best, *Meher Baba*
Beams From The Spiritual Panorama, *Meher Baba*
The Everything And The Nothing, *Meher Baba*
Silent Teachings Of Meher Baba, *Meher Baba*
Infinite Intelligence, *Meher Baba*
Lord Meher (XX Volumes), *Bhau Kalchuri*
The Nothing And The Everything, *Bhau Kalchuri*
Glimpses Of The God-Man, (Vol. I to VI), *Bal Natu*
Conversations With The Awakener (4 Series), *Bal Natu*
That's How It Was, *Eruch Jessawala*
The Ancient One, *Eruch Jessawala*
The Beloved, *Naosherwan Anzar*
How A Master Works, *Ivy O. Duce*
Much Silence, *Tom and Dorothy Hopkinson*
Meher Baba: "The Awakener Of The Age," *Don E. Stevens*
The Wayfarers, *William Donkin*
Treasures From Meher Baba Journals, *Jane B. Hanes*
The Mastery Of Consciousness, edited by *Allan Y. Cohen*
from the works of Meher Baba
God Brother, *Mani S. Irani*
Stay With God, *Francis Brabazon*
Mehera-Meher, (Vol. I to III), *David Fenster*

For further details, contact:
Yogi Impressions LLP
1711, Centre 1, World Trade Centre,
Cuffe Parade, Mumbai 400 005, India.

Fill in the Mailing List form on our website and receive, via email, information on books, authors, events and more.
Visit: www.yogiimpressions.com

Telephone: (022) 40115981, 22155036
E-mail: yogi@yogiimpressions.com

Join us on Facebook:
www.facebook.com/yogiimpressions

Join us on Instagram:
www.instagram.com/yogi_impressions